Creating a New
Teaching Profession

Also of interest from the Urban Institute Press:

Saving America's High Schools, edited by Becky A. Smerdon and Kathryn M. Borman

Good Schools in Poor Neighborhoods: Defying Demographics, Achieving Success, by Beatriz Chu Clewell and Patricia B. Campbell with Lesley Perlman

Examining Comprehensive School Reform, edited by Daniel K. Aladjem and Kathryn M. Borman

THE URBAN INSTITUTE PRESS
WASHINGTON, DC

Creating a New Teaching Profession

EDITED BY

DAN GOLDHABER

AND JANE HANNAWAY

THE URBAN INSTITUTE PRESS
2100 M Street, N.W.
Washington, D.C. 20037

Library of Congress Cataloging-in-Publication Data

Creating a new teaching profession / edited by Dan Goldhaber and Jane Hannaway.
    p. cm.
  ISBN 978-0-87766-762-9 (alk. paper)
  1. Academic achievement—United States. 2. Effective teaching—United States.
3. Educational productivity—United States. 4. School improvement programs—
United States. I. Goldhaber, Daniel D. II. Hannaway, Jane.
  LB1062.6.C74 2010
  371.1020973—dc22

                                                                    2009041263

Printed in the United States of America

13 12 11 10 09   1 2 3 4 5

THE URBAN INSTITUTE is a nonprofit, nonpartisan policy research and educational organization established in Washington, D.C., in 1968. Its staff investigates the social, economic, and governance problems confronting the nation and evaluates the public and private means to alleviate them. The Institute disseminates its research findings through publications, its web site, the media, seminars, and forums.

Through work that ranges from broad conceptual studies to administrative and technical assistance, Institute researchers contribute to the stock of knowledge available to guide decisionmaking in the public interest.

Conclusions or opinions expressed in Institute publications are those of the authors and do not necessarily reflect the views of officers or trustees of the Institute, advisory groups, or any organizations that provide financial support to the Institute.

Contents

vii

PART III. Politics of Education Reform/Prospects for the Teaching Profession

Acknowledgments

The authors gratefully acknowledge the generous support from the Bill and Melinda Gates Foundation to the Urban Institute and the National Center for Analysis of Longitudinal Data in Education Research (CALDER) that made this volume possible. They also wish to thank Miriam Okine for her help in coordinating this overall effort.

PART I
Why Focus on Human Capital Systems in K–12 and What We Might Learn from Other Countries and the Private Sector

1

Overview

Dan Goldhaber and Jane Hannaway

Education is fundamentally a human capital enterprise. At the most basic level, the nation's public schools are given the crucial task of helping provide students with the human capital—the knowledge and skills—required for their success in college or the workplace. And the human capital of the nation's teachers largely determines whether schools are successful at this endeavor. Unfortunately, there are troubling signs about the quality and distribution of the teachers staffing many of the nation's classrooms. These signs have far-reaching implications for student learning, economic and social equality, and the growth rate of the U.S. economy as a whole.

Although many skilled professionals are staffing the nation's classrooms, growing consensus exists among policymakers and researchers that, on the whole, schools are not attracting or retaining the most able teachers, or training them effectively, and that the most needy students are most likely to be hurt as a consequence.

Teachers are the most valuable investment schools make. Not only do teacher salaries represent the largest share of school expenditure, but in many places, where teachers have extensive job protections afforded by tenure, up-front investments in teachers (e.g., recruitment, professional development, and so on) might be better thought of as permanent commitments to pay a teacher's salary for his or her life in a school district. More important, research clearly shows that teacher quality is the most important schooling factor influencing student achievement. Having one very effective versus one very ineffective teacher can make a difference of more than a year's growth in a student's achievement. Having multiple effective teachers versus multiple ineffective teachers can make or break a student's entire schooling experience. And having a very effective versus a very ineffective teacher workforce can profoundly influence a country's economic growth trajectory.

This edited volume is about the human capital systems that help determine the quality of the teaching workforce in the nation's K–12 schools and about how to improve them. The myriad systems that determine the quality of teachers today are too often disconnected, incoherent, and out of step with the market mechanisms that govern the broader labor market. As Sean P. Corcoran notes in chapter 3, "A defining feature of the teaching profession is that its structure, compensation, and entry requirements are a product of another era, in many ways incompatible with the modern labor market for skilled professionals."

This volume is part of a larger project designed to critically examine what researchers know about the systems that govern human capital in U.S. public schools. The goals are to generate new notions and angles on issues associated with human capital in schools and to stimulate thought about innovative ways to improve these systems. To facilitate these goals, we invited a diverse set of noted scholars to contribute essays on various topics related to human capital. Some of these experts are well-known education policy analysts. Others may be less familiar to those who focus on the U.S. school system, but they offer insights from their areas of expertise, other countries, or other sectors of the U.S. economy. Scholars often back their views with empirical research, but we asked them to go beyond what could be shown empirically and speculate what human capital policy changes might improve the teacher workforce.

The volume is intended to be accessible to a broad audience of policymakers and those who are interested in or concerned about teacher quality. Authors were asked to provide independent input, but the issues they describe and ideas they put forward fit well together. We believe a number of important themes emerge when one looks across the contributions.

The 16 chapters in the volume are organized into three parts. The first focuses on the importance of rethinking our K–12 human capital systems in light of the skill sets that students are likely to need in the future, what we know about the trends in the quality of teachers over time, and what we might learn from looking at other countries or other sectors of the economy.

In chapter 2, Alan S. Blinder discusses the provocative notion that schools should focus far more attention on two very different skill sets that are both likely to be in demand in the labor market of the future. The first is an emphasis on "the development of skills that a computer cannot replicate and that an educated worker in a low-wage country will have a hard time doing nearly as well as an American." To Blinder, that suggests "emphasizing things like creativity, inventiveness, spontaneity, flexibility, interpersonal relations, and so on—not rote memorization." The second is vocational education, often encompassing high-end personal services. We agree with Blinder that schools should be structured, as much as is possible, to prepare for the needs of tomorrow's workforce, and this may require different types of assessments than those typically in place in schools today. At the same time, we would argue that we must not lose sight of the fact that many students today are not even learning the basic skills that would allow them to be successful in college or the labor market. Thus, if anything, Blinder's analysis suggests that tomorrow's teachers will need to be even more talented than today's.

In chapter 3, Sean P. Corcoran provides an overview of the characteristics of recent entrants into the teacher labor market compared with those who entered teaching as far back as the 1960s. He notes that, "For decades, a small and declining fraction of the most cognitively skilled college graduates have chosen to become teachers, while rigorous national standards and school accountability for student performance have pushed demand for teaching talent to an all-time high." While cognitive skills do not necessarily predict that an individual will make an effective teacher, the broad trends that Corcoran describes are indeed troubling given the likelihood that these individuals would tend to be productive in most walks of life, teaching or otherwise.

Corcoran hypothesizes that the decline in teacher quality, as he is measuring it, may be traced largely to changes in the relative salary that women could earn in and outside the teaching profession. As readers will note, the theme that compensation—and incentives more generally—is a key tool in explaining occupational choices arises throughout the volume, in comparing teacher quality both over time and across nations. Not surprisingly, change in teacher compensation emerges as a key educational reform option. But, compensation reform is potentially far more complex than simply debating whether to increase teacher salaries. The *structure* (the reward system for teacher attributes and different teaching jobs) and the quality of school system selection from the pool of potential teachers are also fundamentally important in determining the quality of the workforce.

Having laid some of the groundwork on teacher quality, chapter 4, by Michael M. DeArmond, Kathryn L. Shaw, and Patrick M. Wright, moves away from a narrow focus on human capital in education to a broader look at human capital in the labor market. These authors describe changes in human resources management in the private sector and what lessons these may hold for education. In particular, they focus on two critical human resource issues: recruitment and selection. DeArmond and colleagues argue that these functions are particularly critical in the case of teachers, where a large body of empirical research suggests that readily quantifiable teacher attributes (e.g., degree level and certification status) appear to poorly predict teacher quality in the classroom.

To understand how good human resource management can improve teacher quality, the authors advocate approaching the issue from two perspectives. First, they "zoom in" to confront what is now largely a "conspiracy of dysfunction" in most school systems and advocate searching, both within and outside public education, for new management practices given that "public education is about twenty years behind the noneducation world when it comes to thinking about human resource management . . . impact on organizations." Second, they "zoom out" to think about how *systems* of human resource practices work jointly to affect school and district performance.

One important lesson from the private sector appears to be that the adoption of *specific* innovative practices often does not lead to productivity benefits. Instead, the research suggests that packages of *complementary* reforms often make a difference. For example, DeArmond and colleagues cite some of the virtues of local flexibility—for instance, giving schools greater discretion over teacher hiring. But they also caution that this flexibility is only likely to lead to systemic improvements if school systems adopt stronger feedback systems, which at a minimum would typically require greater data collection and analysis, to identify the human capital practices that lead to better teacher quality.

The idea that human resource system reforms often work only when they are implemented as a package or in an environment in which the reform can be supported emerges as a major theme in this volume. In fact, we argue that many reforms that might be efficacious are actually implemented in ways or in environments that do not support their success and thus come to be seen as failures. DeArmond and colleagues' contribution suggests that, as is the case in the private sector, there are unlikely to be single, silver-bullet human capital reform policies. Yet, packages of reform should be particularly useful in a K–12 environment because the value of innovative human resources is greater in environments that produce more complex products. It's difficult to imagine a more complex product than the academic and social development of children.

In chapter 5, Dan Goldhaber looks to what lessons might be learned from examining cross-nation differences in the array of human capital systems and policies (what he calls "teacher development systems") that ultimately influence the quality and qualifications of those who enter the teacher workforce. One should be cautious about drawing strong conclusions from cross-nation comparisons, given different institutional and cultural arrangements. That said, Goldhaber's review suggests a number of reasons that the teaching profession in the United States is not as desirable as it is in many other industrialized countries. Specifically, Goldhaber's review suggests that the U.S. system is among the more decentralized among industrialized countries, leading to a narrowing of the teacher pipeline *only after* prospective teachers have completed their training. As a consequence of these features, the U.S. system as a whole looks to be incoherent and creates "significant political and structural hurdles to crafting cost-effective teacher development policy reforms along the lines of making the U.S. system look more like, for instance, systems in high-achieving Asian countries." He suggests several divergent strategies to make teaching in the United States more attractive to a broader segment of the workforce, but he notes that these strategies would make the U.S. system even less like most other countries'. Thus, drawing more talented people into teaching in the United States probably requires uniquely American reforms.

Part II of the volume focuses on specific reform ideas that authors believe would lead to improvements in the human capital of the teacher workforce. Many of the reform notions put forth in this volume are not terribly novel if one steps back from K–12 education. In fact, as several authors in the volume describe in their chapters, many of the reforms suggested represent changes that have occurred in the private-sector labor force. That said, the ideas are still likely to be seen within education circles as fairly radical, representing fundamental shifts in the way that individuals enter into the occupation, how many are counseled out of it, and the career paths and workforce and compensation structures for those who remain. Frederick M. Hess leads off in chapter 6 with the following observation:

> The existing human capital pipeline in education is the result of more than a century of compromises, incremental adjustments, and calculated moves designed in response to the exigencies of another era. During the late 19th and early 20th centuries, the teaching profession was designed to match the rapid expansion of schooling. It relied on a captive pool of female labor, treated workers as largely interchangeable, and counted on mostly male principals and superintendents to micromanage the predominantly female teaching workforce. Later, in the mid-20th century, collective bargaining agreements, more-expansive licensure systems, and local and state statutes and regulations were layered atop these arrangements. Today, would-be reformers must recognize that machinery and assumptions that may have been sensible in the past are ill-suited given existing opportunities and challenges— and that merely tweaking familiar models is unlikely to deliver satisfying results.

With that as his backdrop, he pushes us to examine new ways to think about teacher careers, from recruitment and training to staffing and reward structures in teaching. Additionally, he suggests a number of school system workforce structure reforms that would allow teachers to focus greater time on their teaching and specialize far more than they do today. Consistent with these ideas, he makes the implicit case that the current flat hierarchy in teaching be replaced with "finely graded, new hierarchies . . . The aim should be to create a profession with various roles and specializations" and a professional compensation structure that recognizes the systemic contributions teachers make. Finally, he notes that technology could play a crucial role in helping restructure personnel in ways that allow greater specialization.

Paul T. Hill, in chapter 7, delves more deeply into the use of technology by schools and explores some specific examples of innovative use of technology to deliver instruction. We do not know how effective they are, but Hill's study of "cyber schools" illustrates the potential for technology to revolutionize the teaching profession, changing not only the skill set of teachers but also potentially the size and composition of the teacher workforce. For example, just as technology breaks down barriers to enable doctors to work across geographic boundaries, one could imagine it being used by multiple remote school systems to share a teacher they could not each employ full time.

Clearly, there are educational limits to the cyber school model; many parents would likely want their children, particularly young children, to be in a more traditional classroom. But Hill suggests that parental preferences are unlikely to limit the use of technology. Rather, the use of technology may threaten school employment or imply differentiated compensation for those with particular skill sets. Those resisting change are well equipped, by state laws and funding formulas that favor the status quo in teacher employment, to resist some of the changes that technology could bring. Again, we see the theme emerge that it could require multiple systemic changes to make a particular type of reform successful, so it makes sense to consider packages of complementary reforms.

In chapter 8, by Eric A. Hanushek, the focus changes from how to rethink the roles and structure of the teacher workforce to an examination of which teachers ought to remain in the workforce. Hanushek makes the case for school systems to be far more serious when it comes to evaluating the productivity of teachers and using that information. Specifically, he says they ought to identify poorly performing teachers and systematically "deselect" them from the workforce. He makes the empirically based argument that students would greatly benefit if even a relatively small share of ineffective teachers were removed.[1] For example, removal of the least effective 6 to 10 percent of teachers would be predicted over time to increase the performance of U.S. students to a level comparable to that of Canadian students (who score about a half a standard deviation better on international tests).

Clearly, a policy built around teacher deselection would be a radical change to the existing system and would not happen without considerable political will. Thus, it is instructive to consider the potential gains from such a reform. In fact, as Hanushek describes, the economic consequences associated with student achievement improvements are staggering. For example, his calculations suggest that, had teacher deselection policies been put in place in 1989 (when the nation's governors met and set the goal of having the U.S. education system be first in the world in math and science), the gross domestic product of the United States in 2009 would have been about 1.6 percent larger. Hanushek describes how striking this seemingly small number really is:

> In the U.S. economy in 2005, 1.6 percent amounted to $200 billion. That year, total spending on instructional salaries and benefits was just $233 billion. In other words, the increased GDP through improved student achievement would almost

immediately cover current teacher salaries and benefits fully—suggesting considerable room to pay for better teachers and to compensate for the higher risk of entering teaching.

Underlying the idea of teacher deselection put forth by Hanushek is the notion that we can make at least some judgments about the quality of teachers based on their students' test scores. This idea also arises in the context of teacher pay. As authors throughout this volume note, teacher compensation is fundamental to determining the quality of the workforce. So it is no surprise that policymakers debate using pay as a tool to shape the teacher workforce and encourage greater levels of teacher effort. In fact, the idea of shifting traditional teacher salary structures toward a system more reliant on performance measures related to student achievement is very much in vogue. In chapter 9, Steven G. Rivkin describes the idea of using statistical methods to tease out the contribution that teachers make toward student gains on standardized tests and of connecting this teacher "value added" to their pay.

Rivkin carefully lays out the way data can be used to assess teacher effectiveness and the potential statistical complications associated with doing so. He makes it clear that it is not easy to cleanly separate the contribution of teachers from other influences on student achievement growth—for example, families, peers, and the way schools tend to match students and teachers. Although Rivkin concludes that, "despite potential shortcomings, value-added analysis can provide valuable information for evaluating and compensating teachers," he does not take a strong policy position on whether policymakers should use value added. Instead, he digs into some of the key questions of pay for performance: What is the appropriate comparison group for teachers? Should incentives be targeted toward individuals or groups? Should one use multiple years of data when considering performance? There are, of course, no "right" answers to these questions, but Rivkin's chapter describes the trade-offs inherent in using one option over another.

In chapter 10, Robert M. Costrell, Richard W. Johnson, and Michael J. Podgursky discuss another important area of teacher compensation: deferred compensation in the form of pensions and retiree health insurance, which fall under the general heading of "retiree benefits." As they note, only recently have researchers and policymakers begun to focus on teacher retirement benefits. One reason for this may be that many state retirement systems are greatly underfunded, meaning that serious structural adjustments will need to be made. Regardless, the prior omission of retirement benefits from the policy discussion is problematic, given that retirement benefits constitute a relatively large share of teacher compensation and likely influence teacher behavior. For example, the authors note that the structure of pension systems create powerful incentives for teachers to formally retire when their pension wealth peaks, often in their mid- to late 50s, but that the need for qualified teachers has led many states to allow "double-dipping," a phenomenon whereby retired teachers can be rehired by school systems while still collecting benefits.

Perhaps more important, this chapter describes the structural changes in pension benefits that have occurred in the private sector and speculates about how these changes influence the attractiveness of teaching as a profession for potential new entrants into the labor market. In particular, the shift from defined-benefit toward defined-contribution retirement plans in the private sector diverges from the continued reliance on defined-benefit plans in teaching. As a consequence, the compensation associated with retirement is likely to be seen by prospective employees as far less flexible, and perhaps less tangible, in teaching than in other sectors of the economy. For example, "many young teachers, who are paying off student loans, starting families, and buying homes, might prefer to receive more of their compensation up front rather than have it diverted into a system that may never benefit them." Not surprisingly, like Corcoran (chapter 3) and Hess (chapter 6), Costrell, Johnson, and Podgursky advocate changes in teacher retirement benefits to make them more flexible, portable, and more in line with the private sector to be more attractive to potential new teachers.

Part II of the volume closes with a contribution by Jennifer King Rice, who explores the potential to use teacher professional development as a vehicle for improving the human capital of teachers in the workforce. As Rice notes in chapter 11, "public school systems are making substantial investments in these various forms of teacher professional development," but their investment decisions (i.e., what is purchased with these resources) "are often based on thin, if any, evidence," and the return on these investments (i.e., what we're getting back in improved teaching practices and student learning) appear to be "uneven and, in many cases, disappointing." As she goes on to explain, this finding is not terribly surprising when one considers the incentive structure that governs the professional development offerings that teachers receive. Specifically, she notes that the current system rewards "seat time" rather than improvements in performance, and that the intrinsic rewards of becoming a more effective teacher may not be sufficient to get a large enough number of teachers to choose in-service training that is appropriately rigorous. Although the chapter does not go into great detail on changes to the reward structure, it does suggest that pay for performance could be a more powerful motivator to improve the efficacy of professional development.

In part III, a diverse group of scholars and policymakers react to the ideas put forward in this volume. These authors were asked to read parts I and II and provide feedback not only on the substantive educational merits of the ideas, but also on their political feasibility. Four distinct perspectives are represented. David H. Monk, a noted scholar and dean of the school of education at Penn State University, offers well-grounded commentary on the development of teaching professionals. Joel I. Klein, chancellor of New York City Public Schools since 2002, provides the view of a reformer who instituted major human capital reforms in the nation's largest school district. Randi Weingarten, president of the American Federation of Teachers, offers the vantage point of the organization responsible for protecting the interests of teachers, the object of much reform. Andrew J. Rotherham, one of the most insightful political analysts of education, puts parts I and II within the broader frame of education reform.

Like Rotherham, we believe that "American public education faces a human capital crisis." It is a crisis for the many students who are not receiving an education that will allow them to realize their potential in college or the labor market. Education is potentially the greatest social equalizer in society in the sense that it can and should provide students from disadvantaged backgrounds a means of escaping poverty. As far as inequities in society help drive other problems, which they undoubtedly do, the crisis extends beyond individuals directly affected by poor schooling. In addition, the K–12 education crisis affects all of us by diminishing the growth potential of the economy.

We hope that this volume helps make the case that teacher quality is key to improving our nation's schools—and, as such, concrete steps are essential to address the human capital shortcomings that influence it. We believe that all the ideas put forth in this volume merit careful consideration. Despite a long history of rhetoric of concern about teacher quality, the nation appears to have made relatively little progress. Although many of the ideas expressed in this volume are untested, we think it unlikely that schools will show anything more than marginal improvements without radical changes in the nation's human capital policies.

NOTE

1. Hanushek's metric of effectiveness is a teacher's value-added contribution toward student learning (typically measured by performance on standardized tests). The idea of value-added analyses is discussed in greater detail in chapter 8.

2

Education for the Third Industrial Revolution

Alan S. Blinder

At the risk of sounding like a crass economist, I want to assert at the outset that one major purpose of the K–12 educational system is "vocational" in the broad sense. Specifically, the K–12 system is a mechanism for preparing cadres of 18-year-olds (many of whom will go on to higher education before entering the workforce) to perform (or be trained to perform) the tasks needed and remunerated by the U.S. job market. To be sure, this narrowly economic purpose of mass public education is not the *only* reason to educate America's youth; an educated citizenry clearly has other benefits. But I believe it is an important purpose and is the perspective that guides this chapter. Thus, any reader who does not accept this initial premise might wish to stop reading at this juncture.

My second, and much more controversial, premise is that the needs of the U.S. economy are changing in ways that are at least somewhat predictable. I am not foolish enough to believe that we can predict in detail the mix of jobs that will be available in the United States in, for example, 2029 or 2039 and then fine-tune the educational system to meet those demands. But I think at least two broad trends are clearly foreseeable.

First, machines will continue to take over more and more of the work that was previously done by humans, a process that has been going on since the dawn of the first Industrial Revolution. Today, "machines" generally means computers of some sort, as some well-known research by Frank Levy and Richard Murnane (2004), among others, has emphasized.

Loosely speaking, employment in jobs that can be routinized sufficiently that a computer can perform them do not have a great future. This will hardly be news to most thinking people.

But the second major trend—sending jobs offshore—is less obvious and far less well understood or commented upon. Its implications for the educational system are the focus of this chapter. Specifically, sending formerly American jobs to lower-wage countries—where they are done by humans, not by computers—is changing and will continue to change the menu of jobs available to American workers. In its more-recent variants, in which service jobs as well as manufacturing jobs are migrating abroad, offshoring is enabled by the remarkable advances in information and communications technology. So, in a sense, the computer is driving both phenomena. Nonetheless, the two are different.

Note that, just as in the case of automation, the claim is *not* that we are heading for a world of massive unemployment as cheap foreign labor takes over the tasks Americans now perform. Rather, the claim is that sending jobs offshore will change substantially and systematically the *mix* of jobs available to American workers, just as automation has been doing for centuries.[1] To be more specific, I believe that 20 to 30 years from now the U.S. labor market will have (relatively) more jobs in what I call the "personally delivered services" and (relatively) fewer jobs in manufacturing and what I call the "impersonally delivered services." (These terms are defined more precisely below.)

If these first two premises are accepted, it follows that the United States should reform its K–12 education system, and perhaps higher education as well, in ways that make the schools prepare (relatively) fewer young people for jobs in manufacturing and impersonal service occupations and (relatively) more young people for personal service occupations. Further, because there is a 13-year gestation period between the 5-year-old inputs of the K–12 system and the 18-year-old outputs, the time to start initiating these changes is now. The kindergarteners who enroll in fall 2009 will be the high school graduates of 2022, and they will graduate into a job market quite different from our current one. We do not want to equip these students with skills that will, by then, be in demand mainly in India and China (or skills that will be supplied by computers).

But what changes in the educational system are appropriate to that end? I am an economist, not an education specialist. And for this and other reasons, I can give only partial and incomplete answers to this important question. With all due modesty, and much is due, I share my preliminary thoughts and speculations on the indicated directions for K–12 education.

Offshoring and the Next Industrial Revolution

There have been two great industrial revolutions to date.[2] The first was the biggest. As labor in the industrializing countries migrated from farm to factory, beginning in the late 18th century, societies were transformed beyond recognition. How and where people lived, the organization of business, the laws and practices of government, and—most germane to this chapter—how societies educated their children all changed dramatically to accommodate an important new economic reality: Fewer people were earning their livings on farms, and more were earning their livings in factories. The shift off the farm was massive. It has been estimated that in 1810 some 84 percent of the U.S. workforce was engaged in agriculture and 3 percent in manufacturing. By 1960, the manufacturing share had risen to almost 25 percent and the agricultural share had dwindled to just 8 percent (U.S. Census Bureau 1975, Part I, 139). (Today it is less than 2 percent.)

The United States reacted intelligently to the skill demands of the first Industrial Revolution by building what may have been the world's best system of mass public education. Although the country adopted an agrarian-based school calendar (with a long summer "vacation" to raise and harvest crops), the K–12 system was aptly designed to turn out great numbers of literate and numerate workers for the nation's factories. It was highly successful. Indeed, mass public education was a key ingredient in the recipe by which the upstart United States of America thrust itself into the forefront of industrialization.

But that was then and this is now. The prototypical American school still resembles too much a factory built on Tayloristic principles, even though factory work now employs less than 10 percent of the U.S. workforce.[3] Students enter the building when the bell rings in the morning. Much like factory workers, they sit (mainly quietly) at their desks (which resemble workbenches) except for prescribed breaks; do well-defined assigned work, much of which is highly standardized; and leave when the bell rings in the afternoon. This design builds in a not-too-subtle behavioral message. As Alan Lesgold, dean of the University of Pittsburgh's School of Education, put it, "For the industrial age, the hidden curriculum had components like following directions, showing up on time, respecting authority, and sticking to the standard modes of learning and doing."[4] The problem is, the industrial age is over, and too few schools seem to have noticed its passing.

The second Industrial Revolution, which is still in progress, is the massive shift of employment away from manufacturing and toward services. Oddly, the shift to services is still viewed with alarm in the United States and many other rich countries, where people bemoan rather than welcome the resulting losses of manufacturing jobs, even though more new service-sector jobs have sprouted up than old manufacturing jobs have disappeared. In round numbers, in 1960, about 35 percent of American nonagricultural workers produced goods (principally, manufacturing and construction) and 65 percent produced services. By 2007, only about 16 percent of America's nonagricultural jobs were still in the goods-producing industries, with 84 percent producing services.

This trend is worldwide and continuing. Between 1967 and 2005, the service sector's share of total jobs increased by about 20 percentage points in the United States, but by about 23 percentage points in Japan, about 26 points in the United Kingdom and Italy, and about 29 points in France.[5] The shift toward services has also led to numerous major changes in our lives—from television to the Internet and the decline of physical labor, to name a few.

At the risk of some (but not much) exaggeration, the nation's K–12 education system never adapted to the second Industrial Revolution. Yet we are now, I believe, in the early stages of a *third* Industrial Revolution, often called the Information Age. The cheap and easy flow of packets of information around the globe has vastly expanded both the volume and variety of services that can be traded across national borders, and there is much more to come. Like the previous industrial revolutions, the Information Age will require vast and unsettling adjustments in the way we work and the way we live. To cite one trivial but illustrative example, there is already a huge generation gap between those who "text" (a verb, if you're young; a noun, if you're not) and those who don't. I want to focus on one adjustment we will need to make: how we will educate our children for the jobs available in the United States.

Although the main labor-market story of the past 25 to 30 years was the growing schism between those who have college degrees and those who do not, I argued in a recent article in *Foreign Affairs* that the greatest problem facing the next generation of American workers may not be lack of education, but rather offshoring—the movement of certain jobs overseas, especially to countries with much lower wages, such as India and China (Blinder 2006).[6] Of course, manufacturing jobs have been migrating overseas for decades. But the recent wave of offshoring, that affecting *service* jobs, is something new—and different.

Traditionally, we have thought of service jobs as largely immune to foreign competition. After all, you can't get your hair cut or your broken arm set by a barber or a doctor in a distant land.[7] But stunning advances in communications technology, and the emergence of a vast new pool of educated labor in Asia and Eastern Europe, are changing that picture radically. In the process, these forces are subjecting millions of presumed-safe domestic service jobs to foreign competition. And it is not necessary to actually move jobs to low-wage countries in order to restrain wage increases in the United States; the mere threat of offshoring can accomplish this.

Service offshoring is a minor phenomenon so far, but it appears to be growing rapidly. I believe it will eventually equal or exceed manufacturing offshoring for three main reasons, two of which I have already mentioned.[8] The first is just arithmetic: there are vastly more service jobs than manufacturing jobs in the United States (and in other rich countries). Second, the technological advances that have made service-sector offshoring possible will continue to enlarge the range of services that can be moved offshore and will enhance their quality. Third, the number of workers capable of performing service jobs offshore—for example, in India and China—is certain to grow, perhaps exponentially.

For a while, it seemed that only American manufacturing workers and a few low-end service workers (e.g., call center operators) had to compete with hundreds of millions of people in faraway lands who were eager to work for wages that are a pittance by U.S. standards. But offshoring is no longer limited to low-end service jobs. Computer code is routinely written overseas and e-mailed back to the United States. So are tax returns and lots of legal work, though not the sort that requires face-to-face contact with the accountant or lawyer. In writing and editing this chapter, I communicated with the editors and staff of the Urban Institute Press only by e-mail. Why couldn't they (or I, for that matter) have been in India? The possibilities are, if not endless, at least vast.

What distinguishes jobs that cannot be offshored from ones that can? I believe it is that some services either *require* personal delivery (e.g., driving a taxi and brain surgery) or are *seriously degraded* when delivered electronically (e.g., college teaching—or so I hope!), whereas other jobs (e.g., call center operations and keyboard data entry) are not.[9] That is the central distinction between *personal services* and *impersonal services,* which I mentioned earlier. To make the distinction more concrete, here are some examples, including both high-end and low-end jobs:

Impersonal services	*Personal services*
Radiologist	Internist
Security analyst	Investment banker
Tax accountant	Auditor (on site)
Computer programmer	Computer repairer
Telemarketer	Retail salesperson
Food packager	Grocery store clerk
Call center operator	Receptionist
Data-entry clerk	Bricklayer

With this distinction in mind, I have three main points to make about preparing our workforce for the brave new world of the future. These three points will set the stage for my discussion of educational reform.

First, the line that divides personal services from impersonal services will move inexorably in only one direction, as technological progress makes it possible to deliver an ever-increasing array of services electronically.

Second, the novel distinction between personal and impersonal jobs differs from, and appears essentially unrelated to, the familiar distinction between jobs that do and do not require high levels of education. For example, it is easy to outsource working in a call center, typing transcripts, writing computer code, and reading X-rays. The first two require little education; the last two require a lot.[10] On the other hand, it is either impossible or very difficult to outsource janitorial services, working in a fast-food restaurant, college teaching, and open-heart surgery. Again, the first two occupations require little or no education, but the last two require a great deal. There seems to be little or no correlation between educational requirements (the old concern) and how easy it is to send a job offshore (the new concern).[11]

This line of thought leads straight to my third point: We need to think about, plan, and probably redesign our educational system with the crucial distinction between personal service jobs and impersonal service jobs in mind. The reason is simple: while many impersonal service jobs will migrate offshore, the personal service jobs will stay here.[12]

The implications seem startling at first. A generation from now, civil engineers (or at least those who must be physically present) may be in greater demand in the United States than computer engineers (who do not need to be physically present). Similarly, there might be more divorce lawyers (not offshorable) than tax lawyers (partly offshorable). Carpenters might earn more than computer programmers. I am not predicting any of these things; lots of factors influence relative demands and supplies for different types of labor. But it all seems within the realm of possibility as technology continues to enhance the ability to send even highly skilled occupations offshore. And the school system should be aware of it.

Adapting Our Educational System to the Job Market of the Future

It is important to note that I am *not* suggesting that education will become a handicap in the job market of the future. On the contrary, to the extent that more education raises productivity, and that better-educated workers are more adaptable or more creative, a wage premium for higher education should remain. So it still makes sense to send more of America's young people to college.

But over the next generation, the *kind* of education our young people receive may prove more important than *how much* education they receive. In that sense, a college degree may lose the exalted "silver bullet" status it acquired over the past generation. Over the past 25 to 30 years, "stay in school longer" was excellent advice for success in the U.S. labor market—almost all the advice you needed. But looking forward over the next 25 to 30 years, more subtle occupational advice may be in order. "Prepare yourself for a high-end personal service occupation that cannot be sent overseas" is a more nuanced message than "stay in school." But it may prove more useful. And notice that many well-paid jobs that cannot be sent overseas—such as carpenters, electricians, and plumbers—do not require college degrees.

The hard question is how to make this more subtle advice concrete and actionable. With educational gestation periods of 13 to 17 years and more, educators and policymakers need to be thinking *now* about the kinds of training and skills that will best prepare today's children for their future working lives. Specifically, the premise with which I opened this chapter implies that it is essential to educate America's youth for the jobs that will actually be available here in 20 to 30 years, not for the jobs that will, by then, have been moved offshore (or be done by machines).

Some of the personal service jobs that will remain in the United States will be very high end (e.g., doctors), others will be less glamorous though well paid (e.g., plumbers), and some will be poorly paid (e.g., janitors). Educational specialists, teachers, principals, and others need to think long and hard about the skills that will best prepare future workers to deliver high-end personal services and about how to teach those skills in our schools. It follows that changes in how we train teachers will likely be necessary.

What might a new K–12 curriculum look like? I do not pretend to have well-thought-out answers, much less a set of detailed lesson plans to offer. But the central principle is pretty simple: we want to emphasize the development of skills that a computer cannot replicate and that an educated worker in a low-wage country will have a hard time doing nearly as well as an American. To me, that suggests emphasizing things like creativity, inventiveness, spontaneity, flexibility, interpersonal relations, and so on—not rote memorization.

Thus I think the fetish with *standardization* is a vestige of the first Industrial Revolution that needs to be (largely) jettisoned as quickly as possible. A team of education scholars from the University of Wisconsin has stated that "theories of learning and instruction embodied in school systems designed to teach large numbers of students a standardized curriculum are dinosaurs in this new world [of free-flowing information technology]" (Shaffer et al. 2005, 110). Saying that does not imply that we should stop teaching our children how to read and write. But I think it does, for example, mean that the central thrust of the federal No Child Left Behind Act is pushing the nation in exactly the wrong direction. I am strongly in favor of accountability. But the nation's school system will not build the creative, flexible, people-oriented workforce we will need in the future by drilling kids incessantly for standardized tests in the vain hope that they will out-memorize a memory chip. If there are to be standardized tests—which we may need for accountability's sake—they will have to differ from the ones to which we are accustomed.

Lesgold, an expert on artificial intelligence, observes that our educational system does not exploit the comparative advantages of humans over machines. Instead, he writes that

almost all of the assessments prevalent in education measure capabilities that machines often have as well. It is not unusual, for example, for a school system to have as its math goals teaching the younger child to emulate a $5 calculator and the older child to emulate a $100 graphing calculator. But, if that's as far as we go, our kids will face stiff competition from machines. Perhaps it's time to think about what our children will need to be more valuable than a computer when they go out into the world.[13]

Lesgold suggests three arenas in which humans outperform computers: "the ability to solve emergent and novel problems," "being a quick learner," and "bridging between different bodies of knowledge." And I'd like to add a fourth, which is encapsulated by that kindergarten grade we all received for "works and plays well with others." The ability to interact productively with other people will become increasingly important in a world of personally delivered services.

What might a new curriculum geared to these emerging job-market realities look like, concretely? I'm a college professor who has never designed a grade-school curriculum, and I'm not about to start now. So I'll stick to some high-level ideas. The task of reform clearly starts in the elementary schools, where we need to develop our youngsters' imaginations and people skills as well as the traditional "reading, writing, and 'rithmetic" that was so essential to the first Industrial Revolution. It is time we recognized that Frederick Winslow Taylor did not foresee the third Industrial Revolution. Although our kids do need to learn basic literacy and numeracy, sitting quietly at ersatz factory benches is probably not the best way to prepare them for the more free-form Information Age, especially when some children have a hard time sitting still anyway.

Instead of rote drills on questions with pat answers that an optical scanner can grade, perhaps we should be posing more novel and even ill-defined problems that have no simple answers—questions that can be wrestled with productively and that, though they have no "right" answers, certainly have better and worse ones. Such questions would, of course, typify the work and social environments in which all of us actually live.

More group activities and interactions may also be essential components of the new curriculum—including, where appropriate, grading the group's performance rather than the individual's. One concrete example, playing sophisticated video games (not zapping aliens or stealing cars, however), may prove to be a useful part of a revised K–12 curriculum. Shaffer and colleagues (2005, 105), for example, have urged educators to "look at [certain types of] video games because they create new social and cultural worlds—worlds that help us learn by integrating thinking, social interaction, and technology." They might have added that children enjoy playing such games and throw much mental energy into them.

In the same spirit, John Seely Brown, the famed computer scientist who for years ran Xerox's remarkable Palo Alto Research Center, has noted that "most folks who write about game play seldom talk about the *social life* around the edge of the game. Yet that's where most of the thinking, planning, trading of arcane knowledge bits, and learning actually occurs" (Brown 2005, 17; emphasis added).[14] As I read thoughts like these, I can't help but think that (a) computers may never be able to do these things well and (b) workers in far-off lands with different cultures will have a hard time competing with homegrown talent on turf like this.

These new types of education probably need to be continued and made more sophisticated in the secondary schools, where, for example, good communication skills also need to be developed. Shaffer and colleagues (2005, 105) emphasize that what they call epistemic games are "personally meaningful, experiential, social, and epistemological all at the same time." These games emphasize learning by doing and experimentation, which are part of the comparative advantage of humans, rather than rote memorization, which is not. Further, playing what they call "massively multiplayer" online games, "in which thousands of players are simultaneously online at a given time, participating in virtual worlds with their own economies, political systems, and cultures" can also be a thoroughly social phenomenon "because playing [them] means developing a set of *effective social practices*" (106).[15]

In the same vein, although he was thinking about college rather than high school students, Brown (2005, 67) argues that "learning by doing with others offers students the opportunity for in-depth enculturation into a particular practice, where one *learns to be* a physicist, social scientist, historian, etc., in contrast to just *learning about* such professions." He advocates de-emphasis of the traditional lecture model for college science classes in favor of "an active learning approach, that is, a highly collaborative, hands-on environment, with extensive use of desktop experiments and educational technology" (73). Again, these sorts of educational practices would exploit and develop the advantages that young Americans have over both computers and young people in, for example, India.

I hasten to add that these ideas for K–12 curriculum reform are by no means mainstream, nor do they represent anything that would be called an emerging consensus. They are best thought of as somewhat renegade ideas that may yet be supplanted by better ones. But I think they merit serious consideration. And, as I've emphasized, the time is now.

As we think about preparing our children for the labor market of the future, more vocational education is probably also in order—maybe much more. After all, nurses, carpenters, and plumbers are already scarce, and we'll likely need many more of them in the future. Since much vocational training now takes place in community colleges, those institutions also need to adapt their curricula to the job markets of the future.

In our present culture, most of these vocations are viewed as a step down from those that require a college degree. But the economics of the labor market might change that. As an example, I have taken to asking audiences to which I speak the following question: In 25 years, who do you think will earn more in the United States, the average computer programmer or the average carpenter? It used to surprise me, but no longer does, that most people choose the latter. The people get it.

As noted above, it is probably still true that we should send more kids to college and increase the numbers who study science, math, and engineering. But we need to focus on preparing more college students for the high-end jobs that are unlikely to move offshore, and on developing a creative workforce that will keep the United States incubating and developing new processes, new products, and entirely new industries. Offshoring is, after all, mostly about following and copying. America needs to lead and innovate instead, just as we have in the past. Brown's ideas, cited above, are relevant here.

Summary

This chapter is predicated on the notion that one main purpose of a nation's school system is to prepare its children for the world of work. That premise implies that the nature of education should evolve along with the nature of the skills demanded of the workforce. Indeed, since there are such long lags between the 5-year-old "inputs" into the school system and the high school and college graduates who emerge 13 to 17 years later, education should be designed with the nature of *future* jobs in mind, as much as possible. That last phrase, however, is a major qualification, because the future will always be elusive.[16]

Yet it is the claim of this chapter that at least two aspects of America's job market future *are* broadly predictable. First, computer and telecommunications technology will continue to advance rapidly, making more and more jobs offshorable. And second, countries such as India and China will continue to produce massive numbers of new skilled workers capable of performing these tasks. These two powerful trends, working in tandem, seem likely to shift the demand for U.S.-based labor strongly away from impersonal services (and manufacturing) and toward personal services.

Unfortunately, the K–12 system still seems mired in the first Industrial Revolution, for which it was well designed to turn out cadres of factory workers—an occupation group that has dwindled to 10 percent of the U.S. workforce and is destined to shrink further. Even as the third Industrial Revolution (the Information Age) proceeds at a breakneck pace, the Tayloristic principles that define so much of factory work are still all too dominant in the design of our nation's school system.

The touchstone principle for a new K–12 curriculum is easy to state but perhaps hard to translate into concrete terms: We need to prepare our children for high-end personal service jobs by developing skills that a computer cannot replicate and that an educated foreign worker will find difficult to emulate. That general idea suggests, among other things, moving away from the rote memorization that current standardized tests so strongly emphasize. Instead, we must focus more on teaching such things as creativity, spontaneity, communication, and interpersonal relations.

The new curriculum for the Information Age must emphasize attributes and skills in which we humans hold comparative advantages over machines and in which Americans hold comparative advantages over off-shore workers. To me, that suggests a style of teaching and a curriculum that features (in addition to reading, writing, and arithmetic) communication and interpersonal skills, group interactions, puzzle solving, learning by doing, experimentation, and perhaps even epistemic video games. Clearly, any such revamp of the K–12 curriculum will also require new ways to test students and new ways to train teachers. All these things will take time to develop and implement, which is unfortunate, because we do not have much time.

As the first Industrial Revolution took hold, the United States radically transformed and democratized its educational system to meet the demands of an emerging industrial society. The effort bore exceptional fruit. But this is not your father's economy, much less your grandfather's. If we are to meet the challenges of the third Industrial Revolution, we may need to do something radical again.

NOTES

1. This is not meant to deny that there is also "reverse feedback" from the nature of the available workers to the mix of the available work.

2. Some historians count three because they consider the changes brought about by electrification and other remarkable technologies in the late 19th and early 20th centuries a second Industrial Revolution. Others call this period the second stage of the first Industrial Revolution. I follow the latter convention, but nothing but the title of this chapter hinges on the count.

3. Taylorism is the theory of management focused on the analyses of workflow processes and the adoption of practices designed to improve labor productivity.

4. Alan Lesgold, "Dean's Blog: Are We Teaching What Our Children Need?," posted August 1, 2006, at http://www.education.pitt.edu/weblogs/weblog.aspx?id=1.

5. Organisation for Economic Co-operation and Development, "Quarterly Labour Force Statistics," various issues, and "Labour Force Statistics," 1985–2005, http://www.sourceoecd.org.

6. A longer version, with appropriate scholarly footnotes and references, appeared as "Fear of Offshoring" (CEPS Working Paper 119, Princeton University, Princeton, NJ, 2005).

7. That said, on January 9, 2008, the radio program *Marketplace* carried a story about remote monitoring of patients in intensive care units (http://marketplace.public radio.org/display/web/2008/01/09/eicu/). And a Chinese-American entrepreneur told me of a Chinese company working on electronic control (from China) of lawnmowers cutting lawns in the United States.

8. The key distinction for this purpose is what workers actually do on their jobs, not whether their employers are classified as manufacturers or service firms. For example, General Motors' lawyers and accountants are service workers. So are the computer programmers at Microsoft, which is classified as a manufacturing firm.

9. In addition, some jobs are tied to a particular geography—for example, you can't work on a farm in Nebraska if you are not actually in Nebraska.

10. Two caveats: First, some call center operators (e.g., technical support operators) must have high levels of skill and education. Second, Frank Levy and Kyoung-Hee Yu ("Offshoring of Professional Services: Radiology Services from India," MIT Industrial Performance Center Working Paper 06-005, Cambridge, 2006) have shown that, while technology permits the offshoring of radiology, U.S. regulations generally prohibit it. But this may change in time.

11. I have explored this relationship systematically in Blinder (2009). In my estimates, the rank correlation between education and ability to send a job offshore is +0.08.

12. Other jobs, including in manufacturing and impersonal services, will also remain here. I do not want to be misinterpreted (as I have been) as arguing that only personal service jobs will be available in the United States. The point is that the *mix* will shift.

13. Lesgold, "Dean's Blog: Are We Teaching What Our Children Need?"

14. Brown was clearly thinking of older children—those in high school or even college.

15. I have one worry: to the extent that the social interactions are electronic, the resulting talents can also be provided by offshore labor.

16. According to a wise old maxim, "One thing you should never predict is the future."

REFERENCES

Blinder, Alan S. 2006. "Offshoring: The Next Industrial Revolution?" *Foreign Affairs* 85(2): 113–28.

———. 2009. "How Many U.S. Jobs Might Be Offshorable?" *World Economics* 10(2): 41–78.

Brown, John Seely. 2005. "New Learning Environments for the 21st Century." Paper presented at the Forum for the Future of Higher Education, Aspen, CO.

Levy, Frank, and Richard J. Murnane. 2004. *The New Division of Labor.* New York: Russell Sage Foundation.

Shaffer, David W., Kurt R. Squire, Richard Halverson, and James P. Gee. 2005. "Video Games and the Future of Learning." *Phi Delta Kappan* 87(2): 104–11.

U.S. Census Bureau. 1975. *Historical Statistics of the United States: Colonial Times to 1970.* Washington, DC: U.S. Government Printing Office.

3

Human Capital Policy and the Quality of the Teacher Workforce

Sean P. Corcoran

Empirical evidence argues that teacher quality is the most valuable input schools contribute to the academic success of their students. Yet for many school officials, recruiting and retaining talented and effective classroom teachers remains an uphill battle. For decades, a small and declining fraction of the most cognitively skilled college graduates has chosen to become teachers, while rigorous national standards and school accountability for student performance have pushed demand for teaching talent to an all-time high.

Recognizing the importance of teacher quality, analysts and policymakers have shown increased interest in the human capital policies and personnel practices of states and local school districts. This attention is sorely needed. In this chapter, I provide a high-level overview of three broad classes of policies that have been proposed to raise the quality of the teacher workforce. I focus in particular on compensation policies targeting the *level* and *structure* of compensation; that is, policies tied to the average level of compensation and the variation in pay across teachers. To a lesser extent, I consider policies on teacher testing, certification, and preparation.

I will define teacher quality and highlight three salient features of the labor market for teachers in the United Sates: the decline in academically talented female graduates who have chosen to become teachers, the uneven distribution of teacher quality across schools, and the annual pay gap between teachers and nonteaching professionals. Given these structural features of the teacher labor market, I then consider evidence on the relative merits of three types of policies designed to improve teacher quality. The chapter concludes with some suggestions and recommendations for policymakers.

The Teacher Quality Problem

Three stylized facts will serve as a point of departure for this discussion of teacher quality in the United States. First, the average quality of public K–12 teachers has declined over the past half-century, and significantly fewer women with high math and verbal abilities are choosing to enter the teaching profession than in years past. Second, teacher quality is unevenly distributed across students and schools, working largely to the disadvantage of poor and minority children. Third, the average earnings of public elementary and secondary teachers fall below those of similarly educated workers who are not teachers, complicating efforts to maintain a high level of teacher quality.

Before reviewing the evidence on these points, it will be useful to establish a working definition of teacher quality. One broad but common definition—that I also adopt here—is the set of teacher skills, knowledge, personal attributes, and pedagogical abilities that yield desired student outcomes (i.e., the level of teacher productivity, or "effectiveness"). Desired outcomes generally consist of student mastery of core academic subjects but should also encompass noncognitive development, civic engagement, educational attainment, life skills, career preparation, and other social goals of education.

How should teacher effectiveness be measured? Formal qualifications, licensure, and tested knowledge serve as crude proxies, but many dimensions of good teaching are difficult to observe, impossible to measure directly, or context-specific. As such, teacher effectiveness ideally would be measured solely as outcomes—that is, a teacher's effectiveness would be measured as her unique contribution to desired educational goals. This indirect approach forms the basis of modern "value added" research and has attracted substantial policy attention (Harris 2009; for examples, see Aaronson, Barrow, and Sander 2007; Kane, Rockoff, and Staiger 2008; and Rockoff 2004).

Unfortunately, indirect measurement of teacher quality in practice falls short of this ideal, for several reasons. First, there is little agreement over the appropriate set of outcomes that should be considered the "output" of teachers' efforts. Even if one restricts this set to standardized test scores, there remains disagreement over which skills or subjects should be tested and how well tests measure these skills. Second, given a choice of output, the complex nature of educational production makes the statistical isolation of teachers' unique contribution exceedingly difficult. (For more detail on this issue, see chapter 9, this volume; Raudenbush 2004; Rivkin 2007; or Rothstein forthcoming). Moreover, in practical terms, one cannot obtain these statistical measures for teachers who have not yet taught or do not teach in a grade or subject in which students are assessed.

As such, practitioners are left with two classes of relatively imperfect measures of effectiveness. On the one hand, we have direct, easily observable proxies such as classroom experience, state licensure, and educational attainment, which have mostly been found to be weak predictors of student outcomes (Hanushek and Rivkin 2006; Wayne and Youngs 2003).[1] On the other hand, we have indirect "value-added" measures that are better able to explain variation in student achievement but face considerable statistical hurdles, especially in the application to individual teachers.

More troubling is the finding that these two categories of teacher quality are not strongly correlated (Nye, Konstantopoulos, and Hedges 2004; Rivkin, Hanushek, and Kain 2005). For example, state licensure and a master's degree have been shown to be weakly if at all related to value-added measures.[2] Fortunately, a few observable teacher characteristics appear to be exceptions. Experienced teachers, teachers who majored in their subject matter, and teachers who themselves scored higher on standardized tests systematically produce better student outcomes than other teachers (Aaronson et al. 2007; Clotfelter, Ladd, and Vigdor 2007; Ehrenberg and Brewer 1994, 1995; Goldhaber 2007; Goldhaber and Anthony 2007; Goldhaber and Brewer 1997, 2000; Harris and Sass 2007; Rockoff 2004).

In the sections that follow, I adopt the elusive "value added" concept of teaching effectiveness as the object of ultimate interest to policymakers. Operationally, however, my discussion relies on specific characteristics— such as subject matter expertise, experience, and cognitive ability—that, although imperfect, have been found to be most closely aligned with value-added measures of effectiveness.

The Decline in the Relative Quality of Teachers

As described above, few easily measured characteristics adequately capture the quality of the teaching force. Even fewer are measured in such a way as to allow for comparisons across states or over time. One possible exception is teacher test scores. Not surprisingly, teachers with a stronger mastery of math and verbal skills are generally more effective in instilling these skills in their own students (Goldhaber 2007). Comparable measures of these abilities are available over a relatively long period, and their trend is not overly optimistic.[3]

As shown in table 3.1, the average verbal and math aptitude of new female teachers—as measured by their percentile rank on a standardized test—fell steadily between 1964 and 2000, from 67.2 to 63.7.[4] (These per-

Table 3.1. Trends in the Average Cognitive Ability of New Female Teachers, 1964–2000

Characteristic	Data Source and Year of Observation				
	WLS 1964	Project Talent 1971–74	NLS-72 1979	HSB 1992	NELS 2000
Mean age of cohort at time of follow-up survey (years)	25.0	26.8	26.1	27.5	26.1
Mean percentile rank of new female teachers in their high school cohort	67.2	69.5	66.4	64.8	63.7
Percentage of new female teachers scoring in the top decile of their high school cohort	20.3	24.2	15.3	15.2	11.2
Percentage of new female teachers scoring in the bottom third among college graduates	41.2	44.4	44.4	54.6	38.8

Sources: Data are from five longitudinal surveys of high school students: the Wisconsin Longitudinal Survey (WLS), Project Talent, the National Longitudinal Survey of the High School Class of 1972 (NLS-72), High School and Beyond (HSB), and the National Education Longitudinal Survey (NELS).

Note: All teachers were observed in a follow-up survey that occurred at approximately age 26. For details, see Corcoran, Evans, and Schwab (2004).

centile ranks are relative to the teachers' own high school cohort and are calculated with data from Corcoran, Evans, and Schwab 2004. Each of the five cohorts of teachers is observed at approximately age 26.)

This relatively small decline observed in the average aptitude of new female teachers masks stark changes in other parts of distribution. Most striking, for example, is the decline in women scoring in the top decile of their graduating cohort who elected to teach. In 1964, more than 20 percent of new female teachers ranked in the top decile of their high school cohort; by 2000, this had fallen to 11.2 percent. Figure 3.1 illustrates how this loss of highly skilled women from the teaching profession has changed the composition of new teachers; also apparent is the corresponding rise in the fraction of teachers who scored in the bottom half of the test score distribution.

Comparable analyses of the National Longitudinal Survey of Youth by Murnane and colleagues (1991) and Bacolod (2007a) corroborate these

Figure 3.1. Distribution of Teachers across High School Class Deciles, 1964–2000

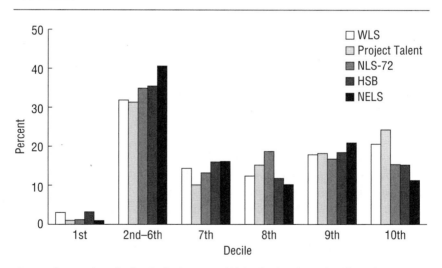

Sources: Data are from five longitudinal surveys of high school students: the Wisconsin Longitudinal Survey (WLS), Project Talent, the National Longitudinal Survey of the High School Class of 1972 (NLS-72), High School and Beyond (HSB), and the National Education Longitudinal Survey (NELS).

Notes: All teachers were observed in a follow-up survey that occurred at approximately age 26. For details, see Corcoran, Evans, and Schwab (2004).

trends.[5] They find that the greatest decline in teaching as an occupational choice between 1967 and 1989 occurred among graduates who scored highest on the Armed Forces Qualifying Test or attended the most selective colleges. Bacolod (2007a) shows this trend is evident across all race and gender categories but finds it is particularly pronounced among high-aptitude women and African Americans.

Recent reports on the academic achievement of new teachers suggest a possible reversal of this trend. Gitomer (2007) compares the academic aptitude of teachers taking the *Praxis*—one of the most common teacher certification exams—in 2002–05 to those taking the test a decade earlier and finds that the aptitude of new teachers has improved, as measured by SAT scores and grade-point average.[6] However, the 2 to 3 percent increase in mean SAT scores—while substantial relative to the population of test takers—is small relative to the long-run decline in teacher aptitude. Further, this report applies only to *Praxis* test takers (mostly prospective new teachers), not to the entire workforce, and may reflect a one-time shift in response to minimum standards embodied in the federal No Child Left Behind Act.

National programs like Teach For America and the New Teacher Project that offer alternate routes into the teaching profession have shown promise and have demonstrated an appeal to top graduates of elite universities (Glazerman, Mayer, and Decker 2006; Xu, Hannaway, and Taylor 2008). But Teach For America–like programs staff only a minuscule number of teaching positions nationwide and are unlikely to fully satisfy competing goals of expansion and selectivity. For example, the Teach For America corps in 2007 consisted of 3,000 new teachers nationwide. This represents 0.09 percent of the 3.2 million public elementary and secondary teachers in the United States (based on the *2007 Digest of Education Statistics*—see Snyder, Dillow, and Hoffman 2008). Whether these recent developments in the aptitude of new teachers are signs of a trend reversal, or just a one-time adjustment, remains to be seen.

The Inequitable Distribution of Teacher Quality

In addition to the long-run decline in the aptitude of new teachers, recent evidence shows that teachers are unevenly distributed across districts and schools, with less-qualified teachers disproportionately located in schools with more low-income families or racial and ethnic minorities (Clotfelter, Ladd, and Vigdor 2005, 2006; Corcoran and Evans 2008; Lankford, Loeb, and Wyckoff 2002). For example, in North Carolina,

Clotfelter, Ladd, and Vigdor (2005, 2006) show that the average black student in 2000–01 was 54 percent more likely to face a novice teacher than the average white student. In New York, Lankford, Loeb, and Wyckoff (2002) find that teachers with better qualifications, more experience, high licensure test scores, degrees from selective colleges, and advanced certification from the National Board for Professional Teaching Standards are much more likely to be found in schools with fewer minorities and students eligible for subsidized lunches.

Table 3.2 summarizes select black–white gaps in exposure to teacher characteristics during the 1990s. Each figure in the first five columns of this table represents the gap between mean teacher characteristics in schools attended by the average black student and mean teacher characteristics in schools attended by the average white student. Most of these gaps are statistically significant and growing over time. For example, in 2004 the average black student attended a school where 17.5 percent of teachers had three or fewer years of experience, a 5 percentage-point larger share than in schools attended by the average white student. Similar gaps exist for turnover, certification, master's degrees, and job satisfaction, and most of these gaps have grown since the late 1980s.[7]

This structural gap in exposure to high-quality teachers is unlikely to be easily reversed. Teacher labor markets are remarkably local (Boyd et al. 2005),[8] and enrollment is not becoming more racially integrated over time (Clotfelter 2004; Clotfelter, Ladd, and Vigdor 2008; Orfield and Lee 2006). Teacher decisions about where to work depend in part on the class and racial composition of students, and the distribution of teachers across schools will in large part reflect these preferences and seniority privileges extended to experienced teachers (Bacolod 2007b; Hanushek, Kain, and Rivkin 2004; Scafidi, Sjoquist, and Stinebrickner 2007).

The Low Relative Earnings of Teachers

One of the most popular explanations for public education's struggle to attract and retain high-quality teachers is the relatively low base salaries the profession has to offer (Moulthrop, Calegari, and Eggers 2005; Stronge, Gareis, and Little 2006; Temin 2003). This pay difference partly reflects the shorter work year available to teachers (discussed more below), but it persists even when adjusting for annual weeks of work (although there is some disagreement on this—see Podgursky and Tongrut 2006).[9]

Teaching has long struggled to match earnings growth in other skilled professions, and its unique experience as a field dominated by women

Table 3.2. Black–White Differences in Exposure to Teacher Characteristics, 1988–2004

Teacher characteristic	Gap (percentage points)					Change, 1987–2004	Mean for average black student, 2004
	1988 gap	1991 gap	1994 gap	2000 gap	2004 gap		
First-year teacher	0.0	0.4	0.4	1.3*	1.8*	1.8*	6.0%
≤ 3 years of experience	0.7	1.1*	2.4*	3.3*	5.0*	4.2*	17.5%
Years of experience	0.2*	−0.1	−0.4*	−0.8*	−1.5*	−1.7*	13.2
Years at current school	−0.8*	−1.0*	−1.3*	−1.4*	−1.7*	−0.8*	6.7
Master's degree or higher	2.5*	2.3*	1.4	−1.5	−3.8*	−6.3*	44.6%
Mathematics degree (for secondary school)	0.5	1.9	−1.3	−3.6*	—	—	29.0%
Traditional state certification	−2.5*	−1.4*	−1.9*	−3.4*	−5.8*	−3.3*	83.5%
Planning to exit teaching as soon as possible	1.2*	0.7*	2.0*	2.2*	0.5*	−0.6	2.5%
Agree that student behavior interferes with teaching	12.4*	14.9*	14.7*	17.9*	17.8*	5.5*	50.2%
Do not believe principal supports them	1.4*	2.9*	3.5*	6.9*	3.4*	2.0*	14.7%

Source: Corcoran and Evans (2008), using data from the Schools and Staffing Surveys.

Note: Gaps are calculated as the difference between mean teacher characteristics in schools attended by the average black student and mean teacher characteristics in schools attended by the average white student.

*α = .05

undergirds this challenge. Perhaps like no other occupation, teaching has been profoundly affected by improvements in work opportunities for women. For decades, schools enjoyed a captive labor pool in academically talented women who had few career options outside teaching, nursing, and social work. As opportunities have improved, college-educated women are now more likely to pursue medicine, law, science, and management than to enter a traditionally female-dominated profession like teaching (Black and Juhn 2000; Goldin 2006).

Along with increased professional options have come lucrative earnings opportunities, particularly for the most skilled female graduates. Wage growth for college-educated women has outpaced that for men for decades, both in the aggregate and within traditionally male-dominated professions (Bacolod 2007a; Murphy and Welch 2001). Given the high economic returns possible in the most rewarding of these occupations, the declining proportion of academically talented women choosing to teach seen in figure 3.1 is not surprising. After all, these women have the most to gain economically from such opportunities.

Figures 3.2 and 3.3 illustrate how mean annual earnings of public school teachers compared with that of other full-time workers between 1968 and 2004, based on the Bureau of Labor Statistics' March Current Population Survey. For the first 18 years of this period, the average elementary or secondary teacher earned approximately 80 to 82 percent of the average college graduate's annual wage. After a brief rise, relative teacher salaries suffered in the late 1990s, falling below 70 percent in 2002 and to 66.5 percent in 2004.[10] This long-run gap between earnings in teaching and other professions has been well documented in a variety of surveys (Allegretto, Corcoran, and Mishel 2004, 2008; Hanushek and Rivkin 1997; Temin 2002).

Some suggest that generous pensions or other nonwage benefits in teaching are sufficient to offset the pay gap between teaching and other professions (Podgursky 2003; Podgursky and Tongrut 2006; Roza 2007).[11] But these claims may be overstated (Allegretto et al. 2008) and, regardless, are less relevant to new teachers who do not intend to spend a career in teaching.

Strategies for Improving the Quality of the Teacher Workforce

I have highlighted three salient features of the labor market for teachers in the United States: (1) a long-run decline in the academic aptitude of

Figure 3.2. Real Annual Earnings of Teachers, College Graduates, and All Workers, 1968–2005

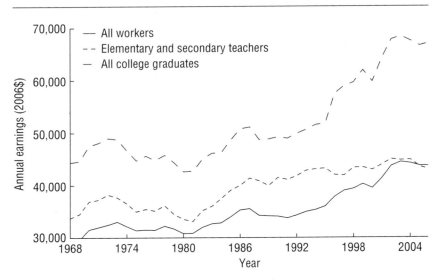

Sources: March Current Population Survey, 1968–2005.

Figure 3.3. Ratio of Teacher Annual Earnings to Selected Workers, 1968–2005

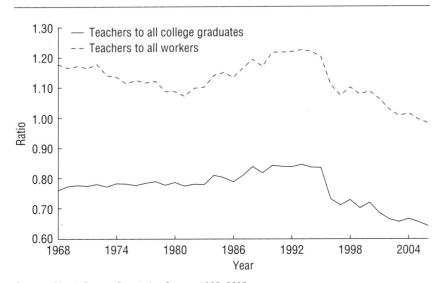

Sources: March Current Population Survey, 1968–2005.

new teachers, (2) an inequitable distribution of qualified teachers across schools, and (3) a sizable gap between the earnings of teachers and those of other professions. None of these features is new, and none is unique to the United States. (For a more in-depth discussion of this point, see chapter 5.) But policymakers charged with increasing the human capital of the teacher workforce must recognize that—in the context of these three powerful forces—their task is a formidable one.

In thinking about strategies for improving the quality of the teacher workforce, I rely on the occupational choice model of labor economics. Put simply, this model states that young people weigh the expected benefits and costs of alternate career paths and choose an occupation that—to them—provides the highest net benefit. The perceived benefits of a career include its financial and nonpecuniary rewards, and these benefits will vary across individuals.[12] Costs associated with a career choice involve monetary and time costs because of required education, training, and licensing; these costs will also be person-specific. Individuals consider the entire future stream of benefits and costs in each occupation and have incomplete information about the future.

Policies aimed at recruitment and retention of high-quality teachers generally target one or more components of this model. An obvious example is the level of base compensation. Calls for higher salaries in teaching recognize that—other things being equal—higher salaries will raise the attractiveness of teaching relative to other professions and increase the likelihood that a graduate will choose to teach. Further, to the extent higher-skilled individuals have more attractive alternatives to teaching, higher salaries may raise the average quality of graduates willing to teach. A second example is the cost of certification and licensing. A higher cost of preparation for an occupation will *lower* its attractiveness relative to other professions, other things being equal.

I refer to the above framework to consider several classes of human capital policies aimed at raising the quality of the teacher workforce. I focus in part on compensation policies, specifically those targeting the *level* or *structure* of compensation. To a lesser extent, I also consider policies for teacher testing, certification, and preparation.

Increasing Base Compensation

Figures 3.2 and 3.3 show how average earnings in teaching fall below those of the typical college graduate. This gap has led many to ask whether the level of teacher pay is sufficient to attract and retain the desired level of quality, *irrespective of how pay is structured* (Allegretto et al. 2008; Temin 2003). Calls for higher base pay inevitably generate two critiques. The first one is that there is no empirical evidence of a relationship between the level of teacher pay and teacher quality (Ballou and Podgursky 1995, 1997). The second is that teacher compensation is comparable to that of other professions once wages are adjusted to reflect differences in work schedules (Greene and Winters 2007; Podgursky and Tongrut 2006; Vedder 2003).

There appears to be some truth to the first of these claims, at least in the short run. Hanushek, Kain, and Rivkin (1999), for example, document a weak relationship between shifts in the teacher salary schedule in Texas and teacher quality as measured by state licensure scores. Likewise, Figlio (2002) finds no statistically significant relationship between increases in district-level salaries in the short run and the aptitude of new hires in unionized districts, as proxied by college selectivity. Yet, Figlio (1997) and Murnane and colleagues (1991) find evidence that higher salaries attract better teachers, and the salary effects on teacher *retention* appear even stronger (Dolton and van der Klaauw 1999; Guarino, Santibañez, and Daley 2006; Imazeki 2005).

Several reasons may explain the weak link observed between across-the-board pay increases and quality. First, in practice most increments to teacher salaries are modest and potentially too small to detect sizable effects on quality. Second, salary increases and benefits are often "back-loaded," or weighted toward experienced teachers, such that effects on the quality of *new* teachers will be minimal (Lankford and Wyckoff 1997).[13] Third, the quality measures in these studies (such as licensure scores or college selectivity) may be poorly suited for this purpose.[14] Fourth, *potential* teacher quality may rise in response to higher pay, but to the extent school districts are poor at identifying and hiring high-quality applicants, the observed level of quality may remain flat (Ballou 1996).[15]

It may take years for changes in relative teacher pay to be reflected in the quality of the teaching force. Studies of the long-run relationship between teacher compensation and quality more clearly and convincingly demonstrate this. Bacolod (2007a), for example, explicitly links the trends in teacher quality observed in figure 3.1 to relative earnings opportunities between 1970 and 1990. She finds that where relative earnings outside teaching increased the most, graduates were less likely to make teaching their occupational choice. She also finds that the highest-aptitude graduates are the most responsive to outside wage opportunities.[16]

The second critique of across-the-board pay increases is that teacher pay is comparable to other occupations once adjustments are made for differing work schedules (most teachers are contracted to work 9 to 10 months of the year; see Greene and Winters 2007 and Vedder 2003). However, these comparisons are relevant only to the extent potential teachers consider *rates* of pay, as opposed to the full work-leisure and compensation package available to them during the course of a year or lifetime. Lower annual salaries surely reflect a "compensating differential" for the summer months, but the relevant question for policy is whether the profession's traditional offering of part-year employment holds the same attraction to academically talented women that it did in the past. I argue that it does not.

Improving the Structure of Compensation

Another approach to teacher pay reform plays down the importance of base pay and emphasizes the *structure* of teacher compensation (Hoxby and Leigh 2004; Leigh and Mead 2005; Podgursky and Springer 2007; Solmon and Podgursky 2000). This approach asks whether the traditional teacher salary schedule (1) properly rewards effective teachers, (2) should better reward teachers with scarce skills (such as mathematics or science), (3) should vary according to the student population served (so-called combat pay), and (4) is optimally structured over the life cycle of a teacher.[17]

Since the early 20th century, most public school teachers have been paid according to a "uniform" or "single" salary schedule with pay levels and steps dictated strictly by education and experience (Odden and Kelley 2002). These schedules may disproportionately reward experienced teachers with a back-loaded salary schedule or pension that rewards long careers (Costrell and Podgursky 2008; Lankford and Wyckoff 1997), or they may offer attractive starting salaries that lag behind as teachers grow more experienced (Allegretto et al. 2008; Goldhaber et al. 2007). Aside from these differences, salary schedules usually vary little.

Evidence on the first of the above questions—whether the traditional salary schedule properly rewards effective teachers—is clear and nearly tautological. Uniform pay schedules do not reward teachers who are demonstrably more effective or who possess observable traits associated with teacher quality (such as subject matter expertise). As a result, the monetary return on productivity—or aptitude, as a proxy for productivity—has been found to be low or nonexistent in teaching (Goldhaber et al. 2007; Hoxby and Leigh 2004; Sander 2008).

Critics of the uniform salary schedule argue that the weak relationship between productivity and pay deters talented graduates, who are better rewarded elsewhere. As potential teachers weigh returns on skill across occupations, the "compressed" teacher pay schedule is unlikely to appeal to highly skilled graduates. There is little empirical evidence on this deterrence effect, but Hoxby and Leigh (2004) offer some evidence of "pushing out." Their analysis suggests that wage compression contributed to a loss of high-aptitude women from teaching in the 1970s and 1980s. Using more recent data, Goldhaber and colleagues (2007) show that older teachers in particular experience a low return on aptitude.

Traditional salary schedules fail to recognize that attracting teachers in competitive fields such as math, science, and technology requires a higher level of pay for a given skill level. One recent review finds that pay premiums in these fields remain exceedingly rare (Odden and Kelley 2002). Studies of teacher shortages have found that math and science positions are perennially the hardest to fill, and that turnover is highest among the most academically talented in these fields (Podgursky, Monroe, and Watson 2004).

Providing higher salaries for teachers working in hard-to-staff schools has received widespread support among teachers but remains scarce in practice (Goldhaber 2006). Experiments with modest bonus programs in high-need areas have shown promise (Clotfelter, Glennie, et al. 2008), but research also suggests that the pay premium necessary to retain effective teachers in high-need schools is likely substantial (Hanushek et al. 2004).

Finally, some critics of the current structure of teacher compensation argue that built-in pay increases for experience over the career cycle are inefficient and unnecessary (Roza 2007). These critiques warrant further study and are mostly based on differences in interpretation of value-added studies on teaching experience.[18] There is no reason to presume that teacher earnings should rise lockstep with productivity over the course of a career, and the implicit contracts literature in labor economics offers many examples from the private sector where earnings do not follow the same time pattern as productivity (Carmichael 1989).

Minimum Standards, Testing, and Teacher Preparation

A naïve approach to raising the quality of the teacher workforce would be simply to impose higher barriers to entry, by raising minimum standards for certification, for example, or by requiring more extensive testing of subject knowledge. But as Angrist and Guryan (2004) point out, more stringent standards will not necessarily raise average teacher quality.[19] In fact, it may be the case that tougher licensing requirements will sufficiently increase the cost of preparation such that some potential teachers will be discouraged from pursuing licensure. Higher entry standards by definition raise the *minimum* level of quality but may in fact result in a drop in *average* quality if higher-quality candidates are disproportionately dissuaded by these costs. In one empirical test of this hypothesis, Angrist and Guryan (2004) find—using the Schools and Staffing Survey—that states with more rigorous teacher testing do not, on average, have higher-aptitude teachers.

Teacher preparation programs are an important example of barriers to entry into teaching. These programs may consist of a degree or a proscribed set of courses, as determined by the states. (No Child Left Behind's mandate that teachers be "highly qualified" includes a requirement that teachers satisfy their state's criteria for certification, but allows state education agencies to determine what those criteria are.) On the surface, preparation programs would appear to be a relatively easy way of regulating the quality of incoming teachers. But these requirements can influence potential teachers in varying and unexpected ways.

In a recent paper, Wiswall distinguishes between "general" skills (in a subject matter, for example) and teaching-specific skills and suggests that individuals with high general skills are less willing to invest in teaching-specific skills that are not transferable to other occupations. In other words, young people who do not anticipate a lifelong career in the classroom will find it less worthwhile to invest in teacher training. If highly skilled graduates are more likely to make career transitions, teacher quality could suffer from more onerous training requirements. In his empirical investigation, Wiswall finds that stronger licensing requirements do reduce overall teacher supply and the average quality of teachers.[20]

The possible unintended consequences of teacher training and licensure requirements suggest that policymakers should pay close attention to these mandates and their potential effects on quality. Flexible paths into teaching also warrant consideration and closer study. Teach For

America and the "teaching fellow" programs sponsored by the New Teacher Project, for example, have shown promise and a popular appeal to highly skilled graduates. Still, the research on the effectiveness of alternate-path teachers remains mixed (Boyd et al. 2006; Glazerman et al. 2006; Xu et al. 2008). The cost of higher turnover and mobility in alternative certification programs must also be weighed against any potential gains in teacher quality.

Finally, rigorous and voluntary certification programs like the National Board Certification (NBC) may serve an important role in identifying effective teachers. In many districts, teachers who successfully satisfy NBC requirements are rewarded with higher salaries (Odden and Kelley 2002). An advantage of this form of certification is its voluntary nature; teachers are not required to obtain licensure but may use NBC as a method of demonstrating their effectiveness. Indeed, research by Goldhaber and Anthony (2007) shows that teachers with National Board Certification are more effective in raising student achievement than those without such credentials, although there is nothing about the credentialing process per se that enhances productivity.[21]

Concluding Thoughts

I have considered three broad classes of human capital policies that have been proposed to raise the quality of the teacher workforce: (1) increasing base compensation, (2) altering the structure of compensation, and (3) increasing minimum standards, testing, or teacher preparation requirements. While these three categories encompass many of the policies under consideration for improving teacher quality, many policies have been omitted. One important example relates to school working conditions. The occupational choice model recognizes that potential teachers weigh both financial and nonpecuniary costs and benefits of available career choices. Job conditions—such as class size, student demands, parental involvement, and autonomy—all play an important role in the level of teacher quality and its distribution across schools (Bacolod 2007b; Hanushek et al. 2004; Scafidi et al. 2007). Policymakers must pay close attention to these indirect influences on teacher quality. Another policy, discussed more in depth by Jennifer King Rice in chapter 11, is the role that professional development might play in enhancing teacher effectiveness.

A defining feature of the teaching profession is that its structure, compensation, and entry requirements are a product of another era, in many ways incompatible with the modern labor market for skilled professionals. The September-to-June school calendar (and its nine-month teacher contract) worked well for agrarian communities or cities seeking to implement a common system of age-graded schooling (Fischel 2006) but makes less sense today. For most of the 20th century, schools relied on a steady supply of well-educated women who had few opportunities outside teaching or who found the shorter work year compatible with raising children. As such, schools had little trouble staffing classrooms with high-quality teachers for annual salaries that fell well below those of other professionals.

Changes in the labor market mean that schools today are not operating in conditions that allow them to hire large numbers of high-quality teachers at relatively low pay. Educated women have markedly better opportunities than in years past, and this shift in the labor market has affected the composition of teachers over time. Policymakers should recognize that a considerable increase in the overall level of compensation will be an important first step toward modernizing the profession. Policy analysts will continue to quibble over the compensating benefits of a three-month summer "vacation," but there is little evidence that our most highly skilled graduates have a demand for part-year employment.

It is also clear that greater recognition of talent is needed in the teacher pay structure. The challenge, of course, will be to determine how best to measure and recognize teacher effectiveness. Current proposals are tied to measures of "value added," or a teacher's contribution to student progress on standardized tests. Although this corresponds to our definition of "quality" (at least on a narrow set of educational outcomes), in practice, as Steven G. Rivkin outlines in chapter 9, it is exceptionally difficult to statistically identify a teacher's contribution to student learning. Educational production is complex, involving student, teacher, school, family, and community inputs, such that isolating true teacher value added is a very complicated task.

When labor economists refer to young people weighing the "return on skill" across occupations, they generally assume that graduates understand (1) how effort and ability translate into output or "success" in each occupation, and (2) how "success" translates into reward. That is, graduates know what it takes to be productive in each occupation, have a sense of how productivity will be rewarded, and are able to assess their own likely productivity in each occupation. Statistical models may bring us closer to identifying teacher effectiveness in the classroom, but in order for performance pay to ultimately affect new-teacher quality, candidates must have a clear picture of how their contribution will be measured and rewarded. Although we have made progress on this front, my sense is that, to date, individual value-added estimates of teacher productivity do not provide this clear picture.

Finally, higher barriers to entry into teaching are generally not advisable as a tool for improving the level of teacher quality. A minimal level of screening is necessary to assure parents that working teachers are qualified to work in the classroom, but overly restrictive certification requirements are likely to have adverse consequences on teacher quality in the long run. Today's skilled graduates will make multiple career transitions during their lifetimes and are less willing to invest in teaching-specific skills that cannot be taken with them. Alternative routes to teaching such as Teach For America and Teaching Fellows have shown promise in attracting talented students and professionals into teaching, and their selectivity may have positive spillover effects on the profession's prestige. These programs will never supply more than a minuscule fraction of the whole teaching force, and cannot be relied upon to raise the overall level of quality, but they may have important impacts in targeted, high-need schools.

NOTES

1. The federal No Child Left Behind definition of a "highly qualified teacher" continues to rely exclusively on observable credentials. Of course, that traditional measures of teacher quality have not been found to have strong systematic relationships with student outcomes should not be taken as evidence that these credentials have *no* value. Some of these credentials—state licensure, for example—may serve only as assurance of a *minimum* level of quality.

2. In a new paper, Boyd and colleagues (2008) find that the correlation between teacher qualifications and value added may be considerably understated due to the role of measurement error in value-added measures.

3. While measured teacher aptitude is not the same thing as value added, it is one of the stronger predictors of value added (Goldhaber 2007). As long as the correlation between teacher aptitude and value added is relatively unchanged over time, an analysis of trends in teacher aptitude should remain very informative.

4. I focus on female teachers here given the traditionally large fraction of teachers that are women. According to the 2005 March Current Population Survey, 72.8 percent of elementary and secondary public school teachers were female, a fraction that has remained relatively fixed since 1968, when 68.5 percent of teachers were female.

5. See also Jora Stixrud, "U.S. Teacher Quality from 1960 until Today: A Supply and Demand Analysis," mimeo, University of Chicago Department of Economics, 2007.

6. See Gitomer, Latham, and Ziomek (1999) for the earlier analysis.

7. Corcoran and Evans (2008) show that these changes in differential exposure to high-quality teachers occurred predominately at the elementary school level. They speculate that large-scale class size reduction policies in grades K–3 over this period contributed to these growing gaps, as schools sought large numbers of new teachers to fill new classroom positions.

8. Boyd et al. (2005) find in New York State that an extraordinarily high proportion of teachers accept their first teaching position in the same district in which they attended high school.

9. A back-of-the-envelope calculation demonstrates this gap. Assuming teachers only devote an average of 38 contracted teaching weeks to their profession, teachers might be expected to earn 73 percent (38/52) the annual rate of other professions. In fact, on average teachers earn an annual pay that is 66.5 percent of average college graduate compensation (43,420/65,213, based on the 2005 March Current Population Survey). This rough calculation likely understates the teacher pay gap to the extent teachers are more likely to hold advanced degrees or devote more than 38 weeks to their work, and it overstates the gap to the extent the average teacher has less work experience than the average college graduate.

10. Flyer and Rosen (1997) show that the increase in relative pay during the 1980s can be attributed almost entirely to the aging of the teacher workforce. After controlling for demographic differences, they find that the relative wage of elementary teachers fell more than 15 percent from 1967 to 1989. Part of the decline after 1994 observed in figures 3.2 and 3.3 was likely due to the redesign of the Current Population Survey. On this, see Allegretto, Corcoran, and Mishel (2004).

11. See chapter 10 by Costrell, Johnson, and Podgursky for a discussion of the role of teacher retirement benefits and teacher quality.

12. Even the expected monetary returns to a career choice will vary by individual if job-specific productivity varies by person, which it surely does.

13. Goldhaber and colleagues (2007) and Allegretto and colleagues (2008) find from nationally representative data that teacher salary schedules on net may be *front-loaded*—that is, they may offer attractive starting salaries that fail to keep up with outside options in later years.

14. Take college selectivity, for example. To the extent future teachers do not perceive additional returns for attending a selective college, they may opt to attend a less-selective (and less costly) college or university. If this is the case, college selectivity measures will underestimate the average academic aptitude of teachers.

15. DeArmond, Shaw, and Wright discuss the role of teacher selection and teacher quality in chapter 4 of this volume.

16. See also Stixrud, "U.S. Teacher Quality from 1960 until Today."

17. The traditional salary schedule has also been criticized for providing weak incentives for performance, to the extent compensation is not explicitly tied to student outcomes. Although this is an important and rapidly growing area of policy interest, it is only tangentially related to teacher recruitment and retention. Interested readers should see Podgursky and Springer (2007) for a review.

18. The research on this question typically observes that teacher value added rises in the early years of teaching but plateaus after two to three years. (There are some exceptions—see Clotfelter and colleagues 2007, Harris and Sass 2007, and Rockoff 2004.) Some interpret this pattern to mean that older teachers are *less* productive or that a continual turnover of inexpensive, less experienced teachers would be as productive as a system that rewards experience. But the evidence finds diminishing *returns* on experience, not diminishing productivity.

19. See also Matthew Wiswall, "Licensing and Occupational Sorting in the Market for Teachers," mimeo, New York University Department of Economics, 2007.

20. Wiswall, "Licensing and Occupational Sorting."

21. Harris and Sass (2007) do not find NBC teachers more effective; see also Clotfelter and colleagues (2007); and Steven Cantrell, Jon Fullerton, Thomas J. Kane, and Douglas O. Staiger, "National Board Certification and Teacher Effectiveness: Evidence from a Random Assignment Experiment," mimeo, Dartmouth University Department of Economics, 2007.

REFERENCES

Aaronson, Daniel, Lisa Barrow, and William Sander. 2007. "Teachers and Student Achievement in the Chicago Public High Schools." *Journal of Labor Economics* 25(1): 95–135.

Allegretto, Sylvia A., Sean P. Corcoran, and Lawrence Mishel. 2004. *How Does Teacher Pay Compare? Methodological Challenges and Answers.* Washington, DC: Economic Policy Institute.

———. 2008. *The Teaching Penalty: Teacher Pay Losing Ground.* Washington, DC: Economic Policy Institute.

Angrist, Joshua D., and Jonathan Guryan. 2004. "Teacher Testing, Teacher Education, and Teacher Characteristics." *American Economic Review* 94(2): 241–46.

Bacolod, Marigee. 2007a. "Do Alternative Opportunities Matter? The Role of Female Labor Markets in the Decline of Teacher Quality." *Review of Economics and Statistics* 89(4): 737–51.

———. 2007b. "Who Teaches and Where They Choose to Teach: College Graduates of the 1990s." *Educational Evaluation and Policy Analysis* 29(3): 155–68.

Ballou, Dale. 1996. "Do Public Schools Hire the Best Applicants?" *Quarterly Journal of Economics* 111(1): 97–133.

Ballou, Dale, and Michael J. Podgursky. 1995. "Recruiting Smarter Teachers." *Journal of Human Resources* 30(2): 326–38.

———. 1997. *Teacher Pay and Teacher Quality.* Kalamazoo, MI: W. E. Upjohn Institute for Employment Research.

Black, Sandra E., and Chinhui Juhn. 2000. "The Rise of Female Professionals: Are Women Responding to Skill Demand?" *American Economic Review* 90(2): 450–55.

Boyd, Donald J., Hamilton Lankford, Susanna Loeb, and James H. Wyckoff. 2005. "The Draw of Home: How Teachers' Preferences for Proximity Disadvantage Urban Schools." *Journal of Policy Analysis and Management* 24(1): 113–32.

Boyd, Donald J., Pamela L. Grossman, Hamilton Lankford, Susanna Loeb, and James H. Wyckoff. 2006. "How Changes in Entry Requirements Alter the Teacher Workforce and Affect Student Achievement." *Education Finance and Policy* 1(2): 176–216.

———. 2008. "Measuring Effect Sizes: The Effect of Measurement Error." Working Paper 19. Washington, DC: National Center for Analysis of Longitudinal Data in Education Research, The Urban Institute.

Carmichael, H. Lorne. 1989. "Self-Enforcing Contracts, Shirking, and Life Cycle Incentives." *Journal of Economic Perspectives* 3(4): 65–83.

Clotfelter, Charles T. 2004. *After Brown: The Rise and Retreat of School Desegregation.* Princeton, NJ: Princeton University Press.

Clotfelter, Charles T., Helen F. Ladd, and Jacob L. Vigdor. 2005. "Who Teaches Whom? Race and the Distribution of Novice Teachers." *Economics of Education Review* 24(4): 377–92.

———. 2006. "Teacher-Student Matching and the Assessment of Teacher Effectiveness." *Journal of Human Resources* 41(4): 778–820.

———. 2007. "How and Why Do Teacher Credentials Matter for Student Achievement?" Working Paper 2. Washington, DC: National Center for Analysis of Longitudinal Data in Education Research, The Urban Institute.

———. 2008. "School Segregation under Color-Blind Jurisprudence: The Case of North Carolina." Working Paper 16. Washington, DC: National Center for Analysis of Longitudinal Data in Education Research, The Urban Institute.

Clotfelter, Charles T., Elizabeth Glennie, Helen F. Ladd, and Jacob L. Vigdor. 2008. "Would Higher Salaries Keep Teachers in High-Poverty Schools? Evidence from a Policy Intervention in North Carolina." *Journal of Public Economics* 92(5/6): 1352–70.

Corcoran, Sean P., and William N. Evans. 2008. "The Role of Inequality in Teacher Quality." In *Steady Gains and Stalled Progress: Inequality and the Black-White Test Score Gap,* edited by Katherine Magnuson and Jane Waldfogel (212–49). New York: Russell Sage Foundation.

Corcoran, Sean P., William N. Evans, and Robert M. Schwab. 2004. "Women, the Labor Market, and the Declining Relative Quality of Teachers." *Journal of Policy Analysis and Management* 23(3): 449–70.

Costrell, Robert M., and Michael J. Podgursky. 2008. "Peaks, Cliffs, and Valleys: The Peculiar Incentives of Teacher Pensions." *Education Next* 8(1): 22–28.

Dolton, Peter, and Wilbert van der Klaauw. 1999. "The Turnover of Teachers: A Competing Risks Explanation." *Review of Economics and Statistics* 81(3): 543–50.

Ehrenberg, Ronald G., and Dominic J. Brewer. 1994. "Do School and Teacher Characteristics Matter? Evidence from High School and Beyond." *Economics of Education Review* 13(1): 1–17.

———. 1995. "Did Teachers' Verbal Ability and Race Matter in the 1960s? Coleman Revisited." *Economics of Education Review* 14(1): 1–21.

Figlio, David N. 1997. "Teacher Salaries and Teacher Quality." *Economics Letters* 55(2): 267–71.

———. 2002. "Can Public Schools Buy Better-Qualified Teachers?" *Industrial and Labor Relations Review* 55(4): 686–99.

Fischel, William A. 2006. "'Will I See You in September?' An Economic Explanation for the Standard School Calendar." *Journal of Urban Economics* 59(2): 236–51.

Flyer, Fredrick, and Sherwin Rosen. 1997. "The New Economics of Teachers and Education." *Journal of Labor Economics* 15(1): S104–39.

Gitomer, Drew H. 2007. "Teacher Quality in a Changing Policy Landscape: Improvements in the Teacher Pool." Policy information report. Princeton, NJ: Educational Testing Service.

Gitomer, Drew H., Andrew S. Latham, and Robert Ziomek. 1999. "The Academic Quality of Prospective Teachers: The Impact of Admissions and Licensure Testing." Princeton, NJ: Educational Testing Service.

Glazerman, Steven, Daniel Mayer, and Paul Decker. 2006. "Alternative Routes to Teaching: The Impacts of Teach for America on Student Achievement and Other Outcomes." *Journal of Policy Analysis and Management* 25(1): 75–96.

Goldhaber, Dan. 2006. *Teacher Pay Reforms: The Political Implications of Recent Research.* Washington, DC: Center for American Progress.

———. 2007. "Everyone's Doing It, but What Does Teacher Testing Tell Us about Teacher Effectiveness?" *Journal of Human Resources* 52(4): 765–94.

Goldhaber, Dan, and Emily Anthony. 2007. "Can Teacher Quality Be Effectively Assessed?" *Review of Economics and Statistics* 89(1): 134–50.

Goldhaber, Dan, and Dominic J. Brewer. 1997. "Evaluating the Effect of Teacher Degree Level on Educational Performance." In *Developments in School Finance 1996,* edited by William J. Fowler, Jr. (197–210). Washington, DC: U.S. Department of Education, Office of Educational Research and Improvement, National Center for Educational Statistics.

———. 2000. "Does Teacher Certification Matter? High School Teacher Certification Status and Student Achievement." *Educational Evaluation and Policy Analysis* 22(2): 129–45.

Goldhaber, Dan, Michael M. DeArmond, Albert Liu, and Daniel Player. 2007. "Returns to Skill and Teacher Wage Premiums: What Can We Learn by Comparing the Teacher and Private Sector Labor Markets?" School Finance Redesign Project Working Paper 8. Seattle: University of Washington.

Goldin, Claudia. 2006. "The Quiet Revolution That Transformed Women's Employment, Education, and Family." *American Economic Review* 96(2): 1–21.

Greene, Jay P., and Marcus A. Winters. 2007. "How Much Are Public School Teachers Paid?" Civic Report No. 50. New York: Manhattan Institute.

Guarino, Cassandra M., Lucrecia Santibañez, and Glenn A. Daley. 2006. "Teacher Recruitment and Retention: A Review of the Recent Empirical Literature." *Review of Educational Research* 76(2): 173–208.

Hanushek, Eric A., and Steven G. Rivkin. 1997. "Understanding the Twentieth-Century Growth in U.S. School Spending." *Journal of Human Resources* 32(1): 35–68.

———. 2006. "Teacher Quality." In *Handbook of the Economics of Education, Volume 2,* edited by Eric A. Hanushek and Finis Welch (1051–78). Amsterdam: Elsevier.

Hanushek, Eric A., John F. Kain, and Steven G. Rivkin. 1999. "Do Higher Salaries Buy Better Teachers?" Working Paper 7082. Cambridge, MA: National Bureau of Economic Research.

————. 2004. "Why Public Schools Lose Teachers." *Journal of Human Resources* 39(2): 326–54.

Harris, Douglas N. 2009. "The Policy Uses and 'Policy Validity' of Value-Added and Other Teacher Quality Measures." In *Measurement Issues and the Assessment of Teacher Quality,* edited by Drew H. Gitomer (99–130). Thousand Oaks, CA: SAGE Publications.

Harris, Douglas N., and Tim R. Sass. 2007. "Teacher Training, Teacher Quality, and Student Achievement." Working Paper 3. Washington, DC: National Center for Analysis of Longitudinal Data in Education Research, The Urban Institute.

Hoxby, Caroline M., and Andrew Leigh. 2004. "Pulled Away or Pushed Out? Explaining the Decline of Teacher Aptitude in the United States." *American Economic Review* 94(2): 236–40.

Imazeki, Jennifer. 2005. "Teacher Salaries and Teacher Attrition." *Economics of Education Review* 24(4): 431–49.

Kane, Thomas J., Jonah E. Rockoff, and Douglas O. Staiger. 2008. "What Does Certification Tell Us about Teacher Effectiveness? Evidence from New York City." *Economics of Education Review* 27(6): 615–31.

Lankford, Hamilton, and James H. Wyckoff. 1997. "The Changing Structure of Teacher Compensation, 1970–94." *Economics of Education Review* 16(4): 371–84.

Lankford, Hamilton, Susanna Loeb, and James H. Wyckoff. 2002. "Teacher Sorting and the Plight of Urban Schools: A Descriptive Analysis." *Educational Evaluation and Policy Analysis* 24(1): 37–62.

Leigh, Andrew, and Sara Mead. 2005. "Lifting Teacher Performance." Policy report. Washington, DC: Progressive Policy Institute.

Moulthrop, Daniel, N., Anive Clements Calegari, and Dave Eggers. 2005. *Teachers Have It Easy: The Big Sacrifices and Small Salaries of America's Teachers.* New York: The New Press.

Murnane, Richard J., Judith D. Singer, John B. Willett, James J. Kemple, and Randall J. Olsen. 1991. *Who Will Teach? Policies That Matter.* Cambridge, MA: Harvard University Press.

Murphy, Kevin M., and Finis Welch. 2001. "Wage Differentials in the 1990s: Is the Glass Half-Full or Half-Empty?" In *The Causes and Consequences of Increasing Inequality,* edited by Finis Welch (341–64). Chicago, IL: University of Chicago Press.

Nye, Barbara, Spyros Konstantopoulos, and Larry V. Hedges. 2004. "How Large Are Teacher Effects?" *Educational Evaluation and Policy Analysis* 26(3): 237–57.

Odden, Allan, and Carolyn Kelley. 2002. *Paying Teachers for What They Know and Do: New and Smarter Compensation Strategies to Improve Schools.* Thousand Oaks, CA: Corwin Press.

Orfield, Gary, and Chungmei Lee. 2006. *Racial Transformation and the Changing Nature of Segregation.* Cambridge, MA: The Civil Rights Project, Harvard University.

Podgursky, Michael J. 2003. "Fringe Benefits." *Education Next* 3(3): 71–76.

Podgursky, Michael J., and Matthew G. Springer. 2007. "Teacher Performance Pay: A Review." *Journal of Policy Analysis and Management* 26(4): 909–49.

Podgursky, Michael J., and Ruttaya Tongrut. 2006. "(Mis-)Measuring the Relative Pay of Public School Teachers." *Education Finance and Policy* 1(4): 425–40.

Podgursky, Michael J., Ryan Monroe, and Donald Watson. 2004. "The Academic Quality of Public School Teachers: An Analysis of Entry and Exit Behavior." *Economics of Education Review* 23(5): 507–18.

Raudenbush, Stephen W. 2004. "What Are Value-Added Models Estimating and What Does This Imply for Statistical Practice?" *Journal of Educational and Behavioral Statistics* 29(1): 121–30.

Rivkin, Steven G. 2007. "Value-Added Analysis and Education Policy." Policy Brief 1. Washington, DC: National Center for Analysis of Longitudinal Data in Education Research, The Urban Institute.

Rivkin, Steven G., Eric A. Hanushek, and John F. Kain. 2005. "Teachers, Schools, and Academic Achievement." *Econometrica* 73(2): 417–58.

Rockoff, Jonah E. 2004. "The Impact of Individual Teachers on Student Achievement: Evidence from Panel Data." *American Economic Review* 94(2): 247–52.

Rothstein, Jesse. Forthcoming. "Teacher Quality in Educational Production: Tracking, Decay, and Student Achievement." *Quarterly Journal of Economics.*

Roza, Marguerite. 2007. "Frozen Assets: Rethinking Teacher Contracts Could Free Billions for School Reform." Washington, DC: Education Sector.

Sander, William. 2008. "Teacher Quality and Earnings." *Economics Letters* 99(2): 307–09.

Scafidi, Benjamin, David L. Sjoquist, and Todd R. Stinebrickner. 2007. "Race, Poverty, and Teacher Mobility." *Economics of Education Review* 26(2): 145–59.

Snyder, Thomas D., Sally A. Dillow, and Charlene M. Hoffman. 2008. *Digest of Education Statistics 2007.* NCES 2008-022. Washington, DC: U.S. Department of Education, Institute of Education Sciences, National Center for Education Statistics.

Solmon, Lewis C., and Michael J. Podgursky. 2000. "The Pros and Cons of Performance-Based Compensation." Santa Monica, CA: Milken Family Foundation.

Stronge, James H., Christopher R. Gareis, and Catherine A. Little. 2006. *Teacher Pay and Teacher Quality: Attracting, Developing, & Retaining the Best Teachers.* Thousand Oaks, CA: Corwin Press.

Temin, Peter. 2002. "Teacher Quality and the Future of America." *Eastern Economic Journal* 28(3): 285–300.

———. 2003. "Low Pay, Low Quality." *Education Next* 3(3): 8–13.

Vedder, Richard. 2003. "Comparable Worth." *Education Next* 3(3): 7–19.

Wayne, Andrew J., and Peter Youngs. 2003. "Teacher Characteristics and Student Achievement Gains." *Review of Educational Research* 73(1): 89–122.

Xu, Zeyu, Jane Hannaway, and Colin Taylor. 2008. "Making a Difference? The Effects of Teach for America in High School." Working Paper 17. Washington, DC: National Center for Analysis of Longitudinal Data in Education Research, The Urban Institute.

4

Zooming In and Zooming Out
Rethinking School District Human Resource Management

Michael M. DeArmond, Kathryn L. Shaw,
and Patrick M. Wright

In August 2007, just weeks before the start of the school year, the *New York Times* ran a front-page story about how school districts across the country were struggling to hire enough teachers to fill their classrooms. Kansas Commissioner of Education Alexa Posny told the paper that finding enough teachers in her state was "an acute problem that is becoming a crisis."[1] To anyone who has paid attention to public education over the past decade, this sounds very familiar. Ten years ago, back-to-school stories about a looming teacher shortage filled the *New York Times* and other newspapers. Then, as now, they described schools and districts struggling to hire teachers, punctuated by an alarming statistic: that the country would need to hire 2 million new teachers in the coming decade. Then, as now, people referred to the situation as a "crisis."[2]

But not everything was the same. Ten years ago, newspapers largely placed the blame for shortages outside of school districts. It was simply a matter of supply and demand: a thriving economy decreased supply, and a baby boomlet, an imminent retirement wave, and class size reduction policies increased demand. Recent accounts still mention some of these factors (e.g., retirements), but they also highlight something different. They point out that part of the problem comes from the way school districts approach staffing. As Tim Daly, the president of the New Teacher Project, told the *New York Times,* many districts "have no coherent hiring strategy. . . . There isn't any maliciousness in this, it's just a conspiracy of dysfunction." When chaotic hiring practices put new teachers in difficult assignments at the last minute, Daly said, it is no wonder that attrition rates among new teachers are high or that districts have to scramble to fill vacancies at the last minute.[3]

In other words, when it comes to the struggle to staff schools, many districts have met the enemy, and it is themselves. Or, more specifically, they have met the enemy, and it is the way they approach human resource management (HRM). This "conspiracy of dysfunction" is made up of nuts-and-bolts functions—the policies and practices that school districts use to acquire, deploy, develop, evaluate, and reward human capital. Although human resource management is often in the background in public education, policymakers, researchers, philanthropists, and others who want to improve human capital in schools can no longer afford its shortcomings—or its potential.[4]

Why Is Human Resource Management Important?

Debates about teachers and human capital have long focused on licensing standards (e.g., Darling-Hammond 2001; Walsh 2001), teacher education policies (e.g., Leal 2004; Levine 2006), and teacher compensation (e.g., Goldhaber 2006b). Human resource management has, by contrast, received little notice (Odden, Milanowski, and Heneman 2007). The failure to pay serious attention to human resource management in education is a mistake for two reasons.

First, there is a straightforward functional argument. Recruitment, selection, placement, induction, and other human resource management practices greatly influence who ends up teaching in the classroom and what happens to them once they get there. As Tim Daly pointed out in the *New York Times,* if basic human resource management functions do not work—if human resources departments fail to welcome applicants or track application materials; if they fail to mentor and induct new hires—districts have trouble attracting and keeping teachers (DeArmond and Goldhaber 2005).

Second, and more subtly, human resource management is important because of the mystery of good teaching. Despite substantial empirical evidence that effective teachers make a big difference in how much students learn as measured by standardized test scores (Ferguson 1998; Goldhaber 2002; Hanushek 1992; Rivkin, Hanushek, and Kain 2005; Rockoff 2004; Sanders and Rivers 1996), researchers struggle to understand what makes someone a good teacher. On balance, research suggests that the relationship between individual teacher characteristics and quality is highly contingent on context and intangible personal characteristics. Mathematics teachers with master's degrees *in mathematics,* for example, appear to be more effective (Goldhaber and Brewer 1997), but this is not the case in other subjects; additional years of experience seem to matter at the beginning of a teacher's career, but not later (Boyd et al. 2006; Goldhaber 2006a; Rockoff 2004). Most important, the objective characteristics that researchers can measure explain only a tiny fraction of the differences in student test scores that are attributable to teachers (Goldhaber 2002; Rivkin et al. 2005).

Given the elusiveness and complexity surrounding teacher quality, human resource management practices provide the best opportunity for schools to look deeper at candidates and to make more subtle judgments about their potential, especially compared with licensure and teacher testing policies.[5] Whether through structured interviews, sample lessons, or other real-time interactions between schools and candidates, the face-to-face interactions associated with many human resource management practices offer opportunities for "information-rich" exchanges (Liu and Johnson 2006). They provide a chance for school personnel to make more fine-drawn evaluations of the "fit" between a candidate and a given school and to provide appropriate support and training once they are hired.[6]

Unfortunately the evidence suggests that school districts, especially large urban districts, often fail to make the most of human resource management and its potential. Job interviews are generally information-poor (Liu and Johnson 2006). Hiring timelines are often pushed late into the summer with unfavorable effects (Levin and Quinn 2003). Many on-the-job policies and practices are also problematic: induction and mentoring programs (Johnson et al. 2001) and professional development (Corcoran 1995; Guskey 1986) have been criticized for lacking focus and continuity; teacher evaluation policies are often ineffective;[7] dismissal policies can be time consuming and costly.[8]

In this chapter, we argue that improving this state of affairs requires approaching human resource management from two perspectives, neither of which is common in public education. First, researchers and policymakers need to zoom in and confront the dysfunction associated with individual human resource management practices. In doing this they need to search inside and outside of education for alternative approaches that can improve the quality of the teacher workforce. There is much to learn here from the private sector, where human resource management practices have shifted dramatically in the past 30 years toward innovation and higher levels of performance. We illustrate this point by looking at two important functions at the front end of the human resource management chain: teacher recruitment and teacher selection. We consider where they fall short in public education and what districts can learn from the private sector about improving them. Second, researchers and educators need to zoom out and take a broader, strategic view of human resource management that considers how *systems* of HRM practices work together and affect school and district performance. In the end, policymakers who reform single human resource management practices (e.g., introducing performance pay) without considering what they imply for complementary practices (e.g., teacher evaluations and dismissal policies) will miss HRM's potential to build human capital in schools.

Zooming In: Two Examples of the "Conspiracy of Dysfunction"

Recruitment Practices

Like all organizations, districts engage in recruitment activities to identify and attract job applicants. Recruitment activities include everything from search activities (e.g., advertising) to the strategic targeting of nontraditional applicants (e.g., alternatively certified teachers) and inducements to make jobs more attractive (e.g., signing bonuses; Rynes and Barber 1990). A closer look at school district recruitment practices highlights the following problem: school districts, in stark contrast to the private sector, tend to be passive and provincial when it comes to identifying and attracting applicants.

The most detailed information about district search practices comes from a small number of surveys in a few states.[9] In one of the most recent surveys, researchers at Syracuse University collected information on human resource management practices in 488 school districts in New York State (Balter and Duncombe 2005). On balance, they found that most districts used fairly traditional search techniques, such as posting job announcements on the district's web site, in local newspapers, and on college bulletin boards; presenting at education job fairs; and working with college faculty to identify potential candidates. With the exception of working with college faculty, these practices are fairly passive; districts simply post job announcements and then wait to see who applies. An earlier survey in Pennsylvania produced similar results; districts said that they relied on traditional advertisements in local newspapers, local colleges of education, state-level education trade publications, bulletin boards in the local district, and word of mouth to attract applicants (Strauss et al. 2000).[10]

In the private sector, by contrast, firms are increasingly taking a proactive approach to recruitment. They actively reach out to applicants, even poaching the most talented people from their competitors (Gardner 2005). Firms also proactively court applicants throughout the recruitment process (Boswell et al. 2003). Rather than simply take applications, set up interviews, and then inform applicants of their decisions, many firms emphasize constant and consistent communications with applicants throughout recruitment. They do this to show that they value applicants and to communicate a culture of care and professionalism.[11]

Firms also use a broader set of recruitment activities than what is typical of school districts. For example, when they build relationships and partnerships with universities (just as districts do), they use a wider variety of methods: they sponsor centers, scholarships, and other events to boost their visibility with the student applicant pool; they have executives guest lecture in classes to additionally gain visibility. Firms often advertise their campus recruiting visits in student newspapers and post detailed advertisements about the company around campus. These and other proactive recruitment activities assessed by Collins and Han (2004) are listed in table 4.1. Some of these activities (e.g., funding scholarships) may have little application to school districts. But others closely echo proposals from reformers that call on school districts to be more aggressive recruiters (e.g., see The Aspen Institute 2008).

As they take a proactive approach to recruitment, the most competitive firms in the private sector also search widely for candidates. In the so-called war for talent, the battlefield is large. By contrast, school district search efforts are highly localized. The Syracuse survey, for example, suggests that only a quarter of districts in New York advertise in newspapers outside their local area; only 1 percent advertise in out-of-state newspapers. Fewer than one-third of the districts make recruiting trips to nonlocal colleges (30%), compared with a solid majority (68%) for local colleges. (Larger districts appear more likely to conduct wider searches than smaller ones, though wide searches are still in the minority.) This localism is consistent with other studies of New York that find

Table 4.1. Proactive Recruitment Practices

General recruitment advertisements	Sponsorship	Detailed recruitment advertisements	Employee endorsements
• Place banner advertisements on web sites frequently visited by student job seekers. • Place ads in student newspapers to communicate general information about who we are as an employer. • Place posters containing general images and company logos in classroom hallways on campus.	• Contribute money to the university in exchange for naming rights (e.g., classrooms, endowed chairs, buildings). • Donate equipment that students will work on as part of their studies. • Sponsor events on campus (e.g., concerts, tailgate parties). • Fund scholarships for students to complete their education.	• Post job listings on career web site that detail positions for new graduates. • Distribute recruitment brochures with detailed information about jobs and the company in the career services office. • Place job postings in career services offices (or on their web site) that communicate details about open positions.	• Send recent alumni back to campus on recruiting trips to discuss their experiences as employees. • Encourage recent alumni and interns to share their experiences with other students on campus. • Provide a forum for student interns or co-ops to share their experiences with other students on campus. • Send executives to campus to talk to students about what it is like to work at this company.

most people entering the teaching profession take jobs very close to where they grew up and, to a lesser extent, where they went to college (Boyd et al. 2005). Strauss and colleagues' study of Pennsylvania districts reached a similar conclusion: "a high proportion of hired teachers are simply those that the district knows best, their own graduates" (2000, 405).

When a district's demand for teachers outstretches its local supply (as is often the case in city districts), these local recruitment efforts will, by definition, fail to attract enough applicants, regardless of talent.[12]

Combined with passive search, this is especially problematic when it comes to hard-to-staff subject areas, such as special education, math, science, and English as a second language, or for positions in a district's most impoverished and chaotic schools.

Of course, some school districts and education policy analysts recognize these problems and are responding. Indeed, recent evidence suggests that when districts pursue more aggressive strategies—such as continuously searching, recruiting earlier, aggressively targeting the top schools of education, enlisting teachers as part-time recruiters, and tracking the results of recruitment efforts—they can attract many more applicants than they have vacancies (Levin and Quinn 2003).[13] Unfortunately, even when districts develop a large applicant pool, their selection and hiring practices can stand in the way of moving the best applicants into the classroom.

Selection and Hiring

Once districts have identified and attracted job applicants, they assess and evaluate them before deciding whether to make a job offer. These selection activities propel a complicated process in which prospective teachers move from being applicants to candidates, finalists, and, finally, new hires. On balance, critics have singled out selection activities as the poster child of the "conspiracy of dysfunction" in school district human resource management. They portray teacher selection as an overly centralized and bureaucratic process in which schools, in fact, do not select teachers at all. Instead, new hires

> find themselves selecting schools that they know little about from a limited list of vacancies during late July and August, and even into the start of the school year. They typically arrive at the schoolhouse door to be greeted by administrators and colleagues whom they have never met before (and who have never met them) . . . Most schools have little choice over the assignment of veteran teachers to their buildings; these teachers have the automatic right to fill a vacancy (in an area for which they are qualified), based on seniority. (Useem and Farley 2004, 2)

As compelling as this picture is, most districts actually do not organize hiring this way. Instead, they use a mix of centralized and decentralized action, with central administrators conducting initial assessments that reduce the pool of applicants (e.g., by screening teaching credentials) and school-based personnel making hiring decisions (Wise et al. 1987). A recent survey of first- and second-year teachers in four states finds that school-based interviews and job offers—not centrally arranged matches—are the norm (Liu and Johnson 2006). The surveys of Pennsylvania and New York mentioned above also find that, in the vast majority of cases, school principals interview candidates (Balter and Duncombe 2005; Strauss et al. 2000).[14] But this happy picture is misleading. Even in ostensibly decentralized hiring systems, selection decisions are heavily constrained. Beyond the obvious constraints created by state certification policies (Hess 2001; Podgursky 2004), several important local constraints affect who eventually ends up teaching in which classrooms.

In large districts, centralized human resources departments typically conduct initial assessments to select candidates from the applicant pool. Like most organizations, these departments review application materials and background checks to eliminate applicants who do not possess the minimum qualifications required (e.g., they do not have a teaching certificate). In many cases, districts also use substantive assessments to narrow the pool of qualified applicants before they apply for jobs in schools. One popular assessment, the Gallup TeacherInsight Assessment, is designed to "assess the talents that result in teacher excellence that are difficult or nearly impossible to teach . . . [and produce] a score that is predictive of an applicant's potential for teaching success based on his or her talent."[15] Districts use these assessments to "clear" teachers for hire, sometimes greatly reducing the pool of qualified applicants. (One district administrator told us that she sometimes selects only 20 applicants to "clear for hire" from a pool of 350.) Despite their prevalence, very little is known about how districts use these personnel assessments or how they shape the teacher workforce (Jacob 2007).[16] Anecdotally, central administrators appear to use them flexibly, lowering the score in hard-to-staff shortage areas or ignoring the score as a courtesy for student teachers.

Even after a district has cleared enough applicants to fill its vacancies, individual schools may face severe supply constraints. Within the same district, some schools may have a surplus of applicants while others face chronic shortages. Although it is hard to obtain data on school-level applicant pools, it should come as no surprise that even when big-city districts like Chicago receive as many as 20 applicants for each teaching position, the most impoverished and chaotic schools in the system may have very few applicants (Jacob 2007).[17] Indeed, in interviews with principals in Milwaukee (a district with school-based interviewing), a principal of a high-need school told us that when "you don't have an interest [among teachers], you don't have a pool to select from."[18] Another added, "We can't compete with the specialty schools [elsewhere in the district]. They might get 30 candidates for one vacancy; that tells you everything."[19]

A host of complicated factors creates these inequities (including the structure of teacher compensation), but part of the problem stems from the way districts manage their internal labor markets. Transfer provisions that typically guarantee placements to incumbent teachers, for instance, can make it much harder for schools to hire the teachers they want by allowing teachers to move away from difficult schools, or by forcing schools to hire incumbents before considering external hires. A recent report from the New Teacher Project on hiring practices in five urban districts concludes that transfer policies force schools to hire large numbers of incumbent teachers—an average of 40 percent of all hires (Levin, Mulher, and Schunck 2005). Whether this is a problem depends on the teachers and schools involved. Unfortunately, principals in the New Teacher Project study report that transfer candidates are often poor performers who were "passed around" the district.

Indeed, surveys in other districts suggest that principals think forced hires are low performers compared with their other teachers (Van Cleef 2005). Moreover, teachers involved in the placements appear far less satisfied with their positions than teachers who are selected by school-based interview teams (New Teacher Project 2007). These transfer provisions, coupled with other policies (e.g., late notification requirements and lengthy budgeting timelines), further interfere with hiring by pushing district hiring decisions into mid- and late summer (Levin and Quinn 2003). As a result, even when districts have a large pool of initial applicants, the slowness of the hiring process alienates many of the most attractive candidates. By the time an urban district makes job offers in August, the strongest applicants may have already accepted jobs elsewhere.

Late-summer hiring also makes it difficult for principals and school-level personnel to engage in information-rich interview practices with the applicants they do have (Liu and Johnson 2006). Exchanging information during the hiring process takes time: to engage in school-based interviews, to set up demonstration teaching lessons, and so on. When districts compress hiring decisions into the final urgent weeks of summer, there is little time for applicants to interact with school-based personnel. Sometimes there is no interaction at all: one-fifth of teachers in Florida report that they did not participate in *any* interviews as part of the hiring process (Liu and Johnson 2006). As Liu and Johnson conclude, "Just because certain schools have control over hiring does not mean that they conduct hiring in ways that take advantage of this control. Decentralized hiring can still be information poor" (340).[20]

The problems with teacher selection and deployment in school districts are multilayered and complex. And, to be sure, the private sector is not immune from dysfunction in these areas. A recent study on the assessment practices of 10 multinational organizations finds, for example, that few have a strong grip on the recruitment and assessment practices implemented across their business units and geographies. Some firms have no control over or knowledge of the practices used in individual business units. Some firms mandate standards for assessment practices (e.g., that they be validated) but give autonomy to the units to decide the actual practices. Only one organization mandates the actual assessment practices and requires annual reports on the use of those practices to be submitted to corporate headquarters (Rollinson and Wright 2008).

Even so, two important lessons from selection in the private sector point the way toward more sophisticated practice: the use of systematic assessment instruments and, importantly, the evaluation of how well they work.

A large body of research has demonstrated the validity of several types of formal testing in candidate selection (general mental ability, work sample, personality, etc.). Although many organizations still hesitate to use general mental ability testing (despite it being perhaps the most valid selection device—see Rynes, Giluk, and Brown 2007), most have at least implemented formal and systematic skill- or competency-based assessments. For instance, a large-scale study of 959 firms in 20 countries finds that applicants undergo two to four interviews as part of the application process. Firms, on average, use five different tests to evaluate applicants. The most popular tests are work samples, medical screens, and cognitive ability tests (Ryan et al. 1999).

In addition to testing, firms are increasingly being more systematic and structured in the way they interview candidates. Although the level of structure may vary from situational interviews (where all questions are read from a script with benchmark example answers provided for interviewers to score) to patterned behavior description interviews (where initial questions are scripted but interviewers are encouraged to follow up with additional, probing questions), firms recognize the superiority of structured over unstructured interviews. At a minimum, effective interviewing requires that firms base all their interview questions on a thorough job analysis and design them to capture an interviewee's skill or ability to perform the job.

Many large school districts use testing and structured interviewing to assess candidates. It is less clear, however, if they assess the validity of these practices. Most large private-sector firms require some form of validity evidence for their formal assessment practices. Initially the interest in validation stemmed from the risk of litigation, but as business leaders increasingly recognized the importance of human capital to their firms' success, validity evidence has provided the business case for the selection practices. The validation technique varies depending upon the nature of the test. For instance, interviews may be validated through content validation, that is, having experts assess whether each question captures an important part of the job. Psychological tests (either mental ability or personality), on the other hand, may more often require criterion-related evidence, that is, demonstrating that scores on the test are empirically related to scores on some relevant performance metrics. Such validation evidence may be collected and demonstrated by the firm or the test vendor. The point is that when human capital is critical to firm success, the techniques used to assess it cannot be left to chance. They must be systematic and evaluated systematically on the basis of evidence about their effectiveness.

The Role for Research

Whether we look at recruitment, selection, or other human resource management practices, school districts would benefit by being more proactive and deliberate. As we have noted, assessing what works and what does not work is key. Doing so will be easier in some areas than in others. For example, it may be relatively easy for school districts to evaluate the effectiveness of recruitment practices by measuring the number of applicants from each recruitment source and the "yield" (number of hires) each source produces. This information could then help districts eliminate ineffective or inefficient recruitment sources. It is, however, far less likely that a school district would have the capacity or incentives to evaluate the more complex effects of screening tests, interview protocols, or compensation reforms. In these and other, more complicated areas, the research community has an important role to play in helping examine and improve individual human resource management practices.

In the private sector, researchers produce empirical estimates of the value of alternative human resource management practices. They closely study businesses, with quantitative and qualitative methods, to understand how human resource management practices affect specific production processes. They focus on narrow production processes that can be modeled empirically; visit a significant sample of work sites; conduct field research to understand the process thoroughly; interview a range of people to develop alternative views of the process and practices; gather accurate panel data on production, technology, and organizational practices from the broadest possible sample of work sites; and estimate empirical models of the effects of human resource practices on performance (see, e.g., Ichniowski, Shaw, and Prennushi 1997). Researchers have used this "insider econometrics" approach to examine the effects of a wide range of human resource management practices, including everything from incentive pay (e.g., Lazear and Shaw 2007) to teamwork (e.g., Mas and Moretti 2006). Admittedly, the first step in this methodology— identifying a narrow production process that functions consistently across school contexts—presents serious challenges in education. An alternative approach would be to focus on how various human resource management practices affect the composition of the teacher workforce (rather than the "production" of learning). In any event, a sophisticated examination of human resource management practices and their effects— especially given advances in state data systems that allow for more sophisticated measures of teacher effectiveness—is needed to provide research-based guidance for reform.

Assessing individual human resource management practices can be a useful first step in understanding where there are problems and opportunities for improvement, but it is not enough. Experience in the private sector suggests that making the most of human resource management requires stepping back and thinking about how an array of policies, acting together, can support or hinder a school district's overall strategy for improvement.

Zooming Out: Strategic Human Resource Management

In some ways, public education is about twenty years behind the noneducation world when it comes to thinking about human resource management systems and their impact on organizations. Early on, human resource management researchers in the private sector focused most of their attention on how single practices (e.g., selection) affected individuals' quality, productivity, or job satisfaction (Wright and Boswell 2002). Rooted in the tradition of industrial and organizational psychology, this line of "micro" human resource management research has produced a large body of evidence about recruitment, selection, training, and other functional areas of human resources (HR) that has direct bearing on the menu of methods organizations use to acquire, deploy, and retain staff today (e.g., Heneman and Judge 2006). When education policymakers or researchers call for developing better ways to recruit or select job applicants, as we did in the first part of this chapter, they are appealing to this tradition.

There is, however, a second tradition in human resource management research that takes a broader view. Instead of focusing on individual practices, it examines sets of practices—the human resource management *system.* And rather than focusing on how human resource management affects individual workers, it considers impacts on the organization (Wright and Boswell 2002). This second tradition emphasizes that human resource management systems have an important relationship to organizational strategies for performance and, reciprocally, that organizational strategy has important implications for HRM policy design (Wright and McMahan 1992). Both traditions are important for understanding how human resource management can improve human capital in education. The latter perspective, however, is rarely taken in education.

One exception is Heneman and Milanowski's "HR alignment model," which presents the alignment of multiple school district HRM practices (e.g., recruitment, selection, induction, mentoring, training) with a specific model of teacher competency: Danielson's (1996) Framework for Teaching. Heneman and Milanowski explain that

> Imbedded within the [HR alignment] model are two types of alignment—vertical and horizontal. Vertical alignment represents the degree of linkage between a particular HR functional practice and teacher performance competency. . . . Horizontal alignment represents the linkages among HR practices such that the practices are internally consistent and reinforcing. (2004, 115)

For selection practices to be vertically aligned, for instance, certification, assessment, and hiring standards must ensure that candidates are proficient in the desired competencies through licensing tests (certification), structured behavioral interviews or work samples (assessment), and high standards that ensure only the best applicants are hired (hiring). For human resource management practices to be horizontally aligned, they need to be coherent. If a district has high standards for hiring, for example, it needs compensation packages that will attract high-quality applicants—a sophisticated screening protocol will do little good if salaries are too low or poorly structured to attract a large pool of high-quality candidates.

In other words, school districts should think of human resource management practices as complements, where doing more of one of them increases the return to doing more of the others. Indeed, research in the private sector suggests that when a new human resource management practice is introduced, it often requires supporting practices to be successful. For example, teams are more productive when workers are thoroughly trained, given team-based incentive pay, and selected for complementary skills. If a firm does not introduce all these practices, its teams may be less productive. Ichniowski and colleagues' (1997) detailed study of human resource management practices in 35 steel mills, for example, finds the introduction of *systems* of innovative HRM practices (e.g., group-based incentive pay, teamwork, careful hiring, high communication with workers, implicit job security, extensive training, and job flexibility) is far more effective than the introduction of a limited set of innovations.

Such synergy is rare in education. When Heneman and Milanowski (2004) evaluated human resource management systems in two districts that ostensibly use Danielson's Framework (Cincinnati, Ohio, and Washoe County, Nevada), they found that orientation, mentoring, and professional development activities were the most aligned with the Framework for Teaching, whereas compensation and leadership development policies were the least aligned. As their application suggests, an HR alignment model in education provides a useful framework for thinking about both the evaluation and design of HRM systems (not just individual HRM practices). Rather than looking at one HRM function in isolation, it can highlight the relative strengths and weaknesses in a district's approach to human capital.

At the same time, thinking about strategic human resource management solely in terms of alignment has some important limitations. Some scholars, for example, dispute the notion that a district can actually identify a system-wide model of teacher competency:

> Despite nearly two decades of reform initiatives, we still do not know how to provide effective schools for millions of poor and minority students. . . . We also do not know exactly what all youngsters will need in order to meet the demands of

the fast-changing global economy. . . . these realities demand new educational approaches that allow for various types of schools that have the freedom to innovate to meet students' unique needs. (Hill 2006, 1)

If the type of uncertainty Hill describes makes any single model of competency in a school district hard to imagine, another important limitation of the alignment model is its assumption that district policymakers can specify human resource management practices and control the system's implementation. This is problematic given that HRM practices and possibilities in schools are directly affected by other important factors, such as labor unions and collective bargaining agreements (Hannaway and Rotherham 2006) as well as state and federal policy (e.g., the highly qualified teacher provisions of the No Child Left Behind Act). School district central offices may also be too fragmented or lack the capacity to pursue tightly aligned HRM practices (Campbell, DeArmond, and Schumwinger 2004; Murphy and DeArmond 2003).

In short, knowledge constraints, labor politics, bureaucracy, and structural inertia present serious barriers to the application of a rational, strategic model of human resource management in schools. This is not to say that educators and policymakers cannot benefit from zooming out and thinking about HRM strategically. But it suggests that doing so means they need a more flexible approach to the development of a strategic system.

Flexibility in Strategic Human Resource Management

Wright and Snell (1998) argue that the challenge for HRM in organizations is to align strategically relevant HRM practices in the way Heneman and Milanowski suggest while building "generic organizational capabilities that can be applied toward both discovering and implementing a variety of diverse strategic initiatives" (767). Rather than see strategic alignment and flexibility in conflict, organizations thinking strategically about HRM need to consider how *practices* fit together and how the *organization* can be flexible enough to adapt. Three elements seem critical for a more flexible HRM system.

First, despite the fact that decentralized human resource management practices in schools have often failed to live up to their potential, giving schools the authority to develop HRM practices (around selection in particular) is a logical part of a flexible, strategic HRM system. Rather than abandoning the idea of providing schools with authority over hiring, educators and researchers need to revisit how decentralized hiring unfolds in practice and, in particular, how it is affected by different constraints and variation in local capacity.

Rollinson and Wright (2008) find that firms in the private sector seek to achieve a balance between centralization and decentralization by having the corporate headquarters develop the basic selection techniques (e.g., mental ability tests, assessment centers, and structured interview protocols)[21] while allowing local units to decide where in the selection process each assessment falls. Local units might also be allowed to tailor some of the interview questions to their unique culture, climate, or strategy.[22]

Second, if school districts are to approach strategic human resource management with flexibility, they need a much stronger feedback system to identify effective practices. Investments in data collection and analysis are difficult to make. They are costly and can be politically difficult to sell, because they seem removed from the work of the classroom. Nevertheless, they are critical if school districts are to gauge the effects of HRM practices, especially if school-based actors have the freedom to explore different strategies tailored to their individual needs. At the same time, investments in technology might also improve teacher productivity, by providing systematic information about students' academic needs. In the private sector, HR innovation and technological innovation often go hand in hand as complements, each making the other more productive (Bresnahan, Brynjolfsson, and Hitt 2002). Where districts lack the capacity to provide feedback and manage detailed information, external analytical support may be needed, either in the form of multi-district cooperatives or some other institution along the lines of the Chicago Consortium on School Research (Brooks and Hill 2004), as well as external (i.e., state-level) resources. Moreover, as Hill discusses in chapter 7, interest groups may actively work against using technology in innovative ways if it is seen as threatening.

Third, flexibility requires rethinking the skills needed in the teacher workforce. More than 20 years ago, Wise (1986) suggested a "two-tiered" model of teaching in which schools would be staffed with a mix of "professional" and "enlisted" teachers, with different skill sets, reward structures, and career expectations.[23] Others have suggested redesigning teaching jobs so some teachers specialize in higher-order skills while others specialize in basic skills (Hannaway 1992). Regardless of the details, to the degree that districts and schools can develop more differentiated roles among teachers and the flexibility for teachers to move through different roles, they can marshal a wider range of responses to the challenge of improving school performance, an issue that Frederick M. Hess delves into more deeply in chapter 6.

In sum, as human resource management gains more attention in education, educators and researchers need to consider rethinking specific HRM functions. They also need to consider the macro-level, strategic HRM picture. When it comes to strategic HRM, however, the combination of uncertainty and inertia in school districts requires that leaders consider not only how coherent and aligned the components of the HRM system are, but also, paradoxically, how flexible the system is. As with much else in education, this requires that districts have the analytical capacity to take a more evidence-based approach. Such an approach provides opportunities for constant monitoring of the effectiveness of the HRM system, as well as a platform for experimentation and knowledge sharing (Wolfe, Smart, and Wright 2006).

Conclusion

Human capital is at the center of the performance challenge in public education. Rethinking human resource management is a useful way to examine the issue if we look closely at individual HRM practices and take a more integrated view that encompasses the entire HRM system. Thinking about new approaches to dysfunctional practices and about the broader strategic role of HRM in a dynamic and uncertain environment focuses educators' and researchers' attention on a few key challenges, some of which we have already mentioned.

Examining and Improving Individual Human Resource Management Practices

School districts struggling with staffing need to experiment with alternatives, such as more aggressive recruitment practices or more information-rich selection processes, and invest in the analytical capacity to evaluate their effects on the workforce. A systematic improvement of these and other functional areas of human resource management would not only make districts more effective employers; it might also change the incentives surrounding the preparation of teachers in colleges of education.

Understanding the Impact Human Resource Management Systems Have on Schools

Public education would benefit from more studies of human resource management that take a systems approach, especially when they bridge the divide between traditional HR functions (e.g., hiring) and other important HRM functions that are often treated separately (e.g., training and compensation). In cases of HRM reform, it is also particularly important to study how HRM designs are identified and translated into practices. Compelling models about the complicated links between HRM and their organizational and performance effects already exist in the private sector (e.g., Bowen and Ostroff 2004).

Identifying Which HRM Practices Should Be "Tight" and "Loose"

As we have argued, total alignment is unlikely in organizations as complex and fraught with uncertainty as school districts. Deciding what should be "tight" and what should be "loose" across complicated organizations is an old theme in education and public administration in general. Researchers and educators need to look more carefully at which practices are best set centrally (i.e., tight) and which practices require variation and multiple drafts in schools (i.e., loose). States and districts, for example, might be best at providing certain information about teaching candidates (e.g., teacher testing results), and local actors might be best at evaluating that information along with other, more detailed information gathered through interviews or work samples.

Improving Feedback about HRM Practices and Labor Markets in General

Being proactive requires being analytical. Some districts may be able to analyze their human resource management practices themselves. But other districts may need new departments that report directly to superintendents and that are responsible for coordinating flows of information throughout the system, including the integrated analysis of both student performance and human capital information. There may be a role for third-party analytical organizations as well. States arguably have a critical role to play here, both in providing information to localities and in collecting information that can be analyzed regionally and statewide.

Understanding How District Central Offices Affect HRM Implementation

Finally, understanding human resource management implementation requires that we better understand the district central office bureaucracy. To date, "the district" has been framed mainly by how centralized *policy* affects HRM. Far less is known about the role of those who work in central HR offices—their capabilities, interests, and the informal structures and organizational politics in which they work.

What Will It Take?

For too long, educators and policymakers have assumed human resource management functions were either disconnected from each other or, more truthfully, beside the point when it came to human capital. Continuing to ignore HRM functions will not make their influence go away, however. Indeed, if we continue to leave HRM and its impact on the workforce out of discussions about human capital in public education, well-intended reforms of certification requirements, pre-service training, and other areas of teacher policy will fail to bring (and keep) good teachers into the classrooms where they are needed the most.

As is often the case, building our understanding of how to improve human resource management is not enough. What will it take for school districts to adopt more innovative and productive HRM practices? Although the private sector does not have all the answers, the experience of firms that have adopted innovative HRM practices can be instructive, if daunting. There is ample evidence, across many firms and industries, that it often takes a crisis (e.g., the threat of a plant closing due to competition from imports) for a firm to change and adopt new HRM practices. A crisis has the advantage of forcing firms to consider implementing an entire set of new, complementary HRM practices instead of tinkering around practices' edges (e.g., introducing performance pay).[24]

Adopting systems of human resource management practices rather than individual practices is costly, both for firms and for individuals who have to transition into a new system of pay, seniority, or skills. It may indeed take a breakpoint for school districts to adopt HRM systems. In some districts, this breakpoint may stem from the threat of school choice or sanctions from No Child Left Behind. In other districts, outsider superintendents may come in and pull districts into the 21st century. More broadly, an increasingly competitive global workforce among both highly educated and less-educated workers may, in the long run, create enough pressure for change (if not on school districts directly, then on those who can influence them). Whether these or other factors provide the spur, policymakers and researchers need to adopt an inquiring frame of mind—zooming in and out on HRM practices, their problems, and their potential—if they hope to improve the acquisition and development of human capital at the front of our nation's classrooms.

NOTES

1. Sam Dillon, "Schools Scramble for Teachers Because of Spreading Turnover," *New York Times,* August 27, 2007, A1.

2. Jacques Steinberg, "As Students Return, Schools Cope with Severe Shortage of Teachers," *New York Times,* August 31, 1999, A1.

3. Sam Dillon, "Schools Scramble for Teachers."

4. Because urban school districts face some of the most acute human capital challenges in public education and are the subject of many of the emerging concerns about human resource management in schools, they are our main focus.

5. If these "gateway" policies are imprecise at identifying good teachers (and it appears that they are), then they will produce both false positives and, importantly, false negatives that eliminate candidates who may actually be better in practice (Goldhaber 2004). In the end, teacher quality's complexity makes it an elusive target for high-level policy instruments designed to regulate who may and may not teach and under what conditions.

6. Teacher–school "fit" is a particularly important issue in light of the intuition and evidence that cooperative and trusting working relationships among adults are related to school effectiveness (Bryk and Schneider 2002; Newmann and Associates 1996). And, after teachers are hired, HRM policies play an important role in shaping their professional lives through induction, development, evaluation, and dismissal policies. (These last two functions are especially important given that most teachers receive tenure after a few years on the job.)

7. In general, evaluation in education is time consuming and has few impacts on teacher effectiveness (Medley and Coker 1987; Peterson 2000). There is a small amount of intriguing evidence that principals may have a difficult time evaluating the majority of teachers they supervise. Jacob and Lefgren (2005) studied how well principals' subjective assessments of 202 elementary teachers predicted student achievement in a mid-sized Midwestern district. Overall, principals were good at distinguishing high- and low-performing teachers but had a far more difficult time identifying the middle of the distribution.

8. Most school districts grant teachers tenure protection (automatic contract renewal) after three to five years. These protections can make dismissal an expensive proposition. The New York State School Board Association released estimates in 1994 that it costs an average of $177,000 and takes approximately 455 days to dismiss a teacher; if the teacher appeals the decision, the cost rises to $317,000 (D. M. McVicar, "Firing Teachers Is Costly, Arduous—and Rare," *Providence Journal-Bulletin,* May 4, 1998). More recently, Michael Podgursky at the University of Missouri at Columbia has examined data on dismissals from the 1999–2000 Schools and Staffing Survey and found that overall, traditional public schools dismiss about 1.1 percent of the total teaching workforce; by comparison, the dismissal rates in charter schools and private schools are 7.5 and 3.7 percent, respectively (Podgursky 2006).

9. The only nationally representative data on recruitment practices come from the U.S. Department of Education's Schools and Staffing Survey (SASS). The SASS recruitment items, however, tend to focus on incentives—for example, on whether or not districts offer signing bonuses (Q14a in the 2003–04 SASS) or student loan forgiveness (Q14b in the 2003–04 SASS), not on search practices.

10. The New York survey also asked districts *when* they started advertising for candidates and found that most do not typically begin advertising until the spring. This recruitment calendar can be a source of frustration among district human resource directors. "I know I'm going to have to hire 200 teachers this year," one HR director explained to us in a prior study, "But my staff doesn't want to do anything until they have those positions on paper and in the budget. But by that time, it's too late" (Murphy and DeArmond 2003, 47).

11. Being proactive about recruitment also involves planning. Firms typically frame recruitment activities around their long-term human capital needs to ensure that they have access to new employees when they need them. While the number of employees firms hire certainly fluctuates over time, most successful firms develop systematic processes for either constantly or cyclically processing applicants to ensure that they have access to people when they need them. Rather than waiting until a position opens to begin a search process, many firms are constantly advertising and processing applicants for jobs where they can predict some need. If turnover in key jobs averages 8 percent, for instance, the firm can predict that it might need to hire between 6 and 10 employees for its 100 full-time-equivalent positions over the next 12 months. Or, if the firm's hiring process is cyclical, it can predict that it will need between 6 and 10 employees in the next cycle. In either case, the firm can develop recruitment processes and sources ahead of time. By analyzing employee flows from the past, firms can reasonably predict future needs and build processes around those predicted needs.

12. Urban districts face the dual challenge of overcoming nonlocal teachers' preferences for home as well as all the aspects of teaching in a city school that make it relatively less attractive, such as salary, working conditions, or disadvantaged student populations (Boyd et al. 2005). National data show that, compared with suburban districts, urban districts are more likely to have vacancies in critical subject areas and are far more likely to fill them with someone who is not a fully qualified teacher (Jacob 2007).

13. The New Teacher Project uses such strategies in partnership with districts to recruit teachers into hard-to-staff schools.

14. This echoes national data from the U.S. Department of Education's Schools and Staffing Survey: 88.6 percent of principals in the 2003–04 SASS reported that they had a "major influence" on hiring new full-time teachers verses only 29.4 percent who reported that school district staff had a "major influence" on hiring new full-time teachers (U.S.

Department of Education, National Center for Education Statistics, Schools and Staffing Survey, 2003–04, Public School Principal Data Files).

15. Gallup, Inc., "Education Practice," http://education.gallup.com/content/default. aspx?ci=22093.

16. Metzger and Wu's synthesis of 24 studies of the precursor to the Gallup instrument, called the Teacher Perceiver Interview, concludes that the Teacher Perceiver Interview "best predicts which teachers will show up regularly and will be most esteemed by their administrator-evaluators" rather than teaching ability (2008, 925).

17. This is unsurprising given that we know that schools serving higher proportions of minority, low-income, and low-performing students have the biggest teacher retention problems (Guarino, Santibañez, and Daley 2006).

18. Interview with principal, February 26, 2007.

19. Interview with principal, March 2, 2007.

20. Another constraint on teacher hiring has less to do with district policy and more to do with the capacity of school administrators. What little we know about selection suggests that school administrators make decisions based more on the personal characteristics of candidates than their professional characteristics; they also appear less inclined to hire teachers with strong academic backgrounds (Ballou 1996). When it comes to identifying teachers who "fit" their school, they appear more interested in the demographic mix of their staff (e.g., age and experience) than they are in finding teachers with complementary teaching philosophies or skills (Harris et al. 2006). Whether these approaches lead to the selection of good teachers is debatable. There is, for example, evidence that the general bias against cognitive ability in candidates should be cause for concern (e.g., see Ehrenberg and Brewer 1995; Ferguson and Ladd 1996; and Strauss and Vogt 2001).

21. This stems largely from the economies of scale: it is much more efficient to amortize the cost of developing the system across a larger number of units rather than have each unit pay to develop and validate its own set of assessments.

22. This division of labor assumes that local units are also given the decision-making authority and possess the problem-solving capacity they need to serve students well. In private firms, the advent of HRM innovations (e.g., job rotations, careful screening and selection of workers, incentive pay) along with advances in information technology have put a premium on putting decisionmaking at lower levels in the organization (Jensen and Meckling 1992).

23. Although some have suggested that the second tier in such a system be made up of people limited to delivering "teacher-proof" curricula, others have argued that partial career teachers might bring more to the classroom (Brooks and Hill 2004).

24. Some evidence suggests that adopting single HRM practices can hurt performance if it disrupts the general work environment enough (Roberts 2004).

REFERENCES

Aspen Institute, The. 2008. *Human Capital Framework for K–12 Urban Education: Organizing for Success.* Aspen, CO: The Aspen Institute.

Ballou, Dale. 1996. "Do Public Schools Hire the Best Applicants?" *Quarterly Journal of Economics* 111(1): 97–133.

Balter, Dana, and William Duncombe. 2005. *Teacher Hiring Practices in New York State School Districts.* Albany, NY: Education Finance Research Consortium, Center for Policy Research, Rockefeller College of Public Affairs, University at Albany-SUNY.

Boswell, Wendy R., Mark V. Roehling, Marcie A. LePine, and Lisa M. Moynihan. 2003. "Individual Job-Choice Decisions and the Impact of Job Attributes and Recruitment Practices: A Longitudinal Field Study." *Human Resource Management* 41(2): 23–49.

Bowen, David E., and Cherie Ostroff. 2004. "Understanding HRM–Firm Performance Linkages: The Role of the 'Strength' of the HRM System." *Academy of Management Review* 29(2): 203–21.

Boyd, Donald J., Hamilton Lankford, Susanna Loeb, and James H. Wyckoff. 2005. "The Draw of Home: How Teachers' Preferences for Proximity Disadvantage Urban Schools." *Journal of Policy Analysis and Management* 24(1): 113–32.

Boyd, Donald J., Pamela L. Grossman, Hamilton Lankford, Susanna Loeb, and James H. Wyckoff. 2006. "How Changes in Entry Requirements Alter the Teacher Workforce and Affect Student Achievement." *Education Finance and Policy* 1(2): 176–216.

Bresnahan, Timothy F., Erik Brynjolfsson, and Lorin M. Hitt. 2002. "Information Technology, Workplace Organization, and the Demand for Skilled Labor: Firm-Level Evidence." *Quarterly Journal of Economics* 117(1): 339–76.

Brooks, Sarah, and Paul T. Hill. 2004. "Taking Advantage of Teacher Turnover." In *Making School Reform Work: New Partnerships for Real Change,* edited by Paul T. Hill and James Harvey (52–64). Washington, DC: Brookings Institution Press.

Bryk, Anthony S., and Barbara Schneider. 2002. *Trust in Schools: A Core Resource for Improvement.* New York: Russell Sage Foundation.

Campbell, Christine, Michael M. DeArmond, and Abigail Schumwinger. 2004. *From Bystander to Ally: Transforming the District Human Resources Department.* Seattle: Center on Reinventing Public Education, University of Washington.

Collins, Christopher J., and Jian Han. 2004. "Exploring Applicant Pool Quantity and Quality: The Effects of Early Recruitment Practice Strategies, Corporate Advertising, and Firm Reputation." *Personnel Psychology* 57(3): 685–717.

Corcoran, Thomas B. 1995. "Helping Teachers Teach Well: Transforming Professional Development." RB-16. New Brunswick, NJ: Consortium for Policy Research in Education, Rutgers University.

Danielson, Charlotte. 1996. *Enhancing Professional Practice: A Framework for Teaching.* Alexandria, VA: Association for Supervision and Curriculum Development.

Darling-Hammond, Linda. 2001. *The Research and the Rhetoric on Teacher Certification: A Response to "Teacher Certification Reconsidered."* Washington, DC: National Commission on Teaching and America's Future.

DeArmond, Michael M., and Dan Goldhaber. 2005. "The Back Office: The Neglected Side of Teacher Quality." *Education Week* 24(22): 31–32.

Ehrenberg, Ronald G., and Dominic J. Brewer. 1995. "Did Teachers' Verbal Ability and Race Matter in the 1960s? Coleman Revisited." *Economics of Education Review* 14(1): 1–21.

Ferguson, Ronald F. 1998. "Can Schools Narrow the Black-White Test Score Gap?" In *The Black-White Test Score Gap,* edited by Christopher Jencks and Meredith Phillips (318–74). Washington, DC: Brookings Institution Press.

Ferguson, Ronald F., and Helen F. Ladd. 1996. "How and Why Money Matters: An Analysis of Alabama Schools." In *Holding Schools Accountable: Performance-Based Reform in Education,* edited by Helen F. Ladd (265–99). Washington, DC: Brookings Institution Press.

Gardner, Timothy M. 2005. "Interfirm Competition for Human Resources: Evidence from the Software Industry." *Academy of Management Journal* 48(2): 237–56.

Goldhaber, Dan. 2002. "The Mystery of Good Teaching." *Education Next* 2(1): 50–55.

———. 2004. "Why Do We License Teachers?" In *A Qualified Teacher in Every Classroom? Appraising Old Answers and New Ideas,* edited by Frederick M. Hess, Andrew J. Rotherham, and Kate Walsh (81–100). Cambridge, MA: Harvard Education Press.

———. 2006a. "Everyone's Doing It, but What Does Teacher Testing Tell Us about Teacher Effectiveness?" Working Paper 2006-1. Seattle: Center on Reinventing Public Education, University of Washington.

———. 2006b. *Teacher Pay Reforms: The Political Implications of Recent Research.* Washington, DC: Center for American Progress.

Goldhaber, Dan, and Dominic J. Brewer. 1997. "Evaluating the Effect of Teacher Degree Level on Educational Performance." In *Developments in School Finance 1996,* edited by William J. Fowler (197–210). Washington, DC: U.S. Department of Education, Office of Educational Research and Improvement, National Center for Education Statistics.

Guarino, Cassandra M., Lucrecia Santibañez, and Glenn A. Daley. 2006. "Teacher Recruitment and Retention: A Review of Recent Empirical Literature." *Review of Educational Research* 76(2): 173–208.

Guskey, Thomas R. 1986. "Staff Development and the Process of Teacher Change." *Educational Researcher* 15(5): 5–12.

Hannaway, Jane. 1992. "Higher Order Skills, Job Design, and Incentives: An Analysis and Proposal." *American Educational Research Journal* 29(1): 3–21.

Hannaway, Jane, and Andrew J. Rotherham, eds. 2006. *Collective Bargaining in Education: Negotiating Change in Today's Schools.* Cambridge, MA: Harvard Education Press.

Hanushek, Eric A. 1992. "The Trade-Off between Child Quantity and Quality." *Journal of Political Economy* 100(1): 84–117.

Harris, Douglas N., Stacey A. Rutledge, William K. Ingle, and Cynthia C. Thompson. 2006. "Mix and Match: What Principals Look For When Hiring Teachers and Implications for Teacher Quality Policies." Paper presented at the annual conference of the American Education Research Association, San Francisco, April 7–11.

Heneman, Herbert G. III, and Timothy A. Judge. 2006. *Staffing Organizations.* 5th ed. Burr Ridge, IL: McGraw-Hill Irwin.

Heneman, Herbert G. III, and Anthony T. Milanowski. 2004. "Alignment of Human Resource Practices and Teacher Performance Competency." *Peabody Journal of Education* 79(4): 108–25.

Hess, Frederick M. 2001. *Tear Down This Wall: The Case for a Radical Overhaul of Teacher Certification.* Washington, DC: Progressive Policy Institute.

Hill, Paul T. 2006. *Put Learning First: A Portfolio Approach to Public Schools.* Washington, DC: Progressive Policy Institute.

Ichniowski, Casey, Kathryn Shaw, and Giovanna Prennushi. 1997. "The Effects of Human Resource Management Practices on Productivity: A Study of Steel Finishing Lines." *American Economic Review* 87(3): 291–313.

Jacob, Brian A. 2007. "The Challenges of Staffing Urban Schools with Effective Teachers." *The Future of Children* 17(1): 129–53.

Jacob, Brian A., and Lars Lefgren. 2005. "Principals as Agents: Subjective Performance Measurement in Education." Working Paper RWP05-040. Cambridge, MA: Kennedy School of Government, Harvard University.

Jensen, Michael C., and William H. Meckling. 1992. "Knowledge, Control and Organizational Structure." In *Contract Economics,* edited by Lars Hijkander and Hans Werin (251–74). Cambridge, MA: Basil Blackwell.

Johnson, Susan Moore, Sarah Birkeland, Susan M. Kardos, David Kauffman, Edward Liu, and Heather G. Peske. 2001. "Retaining the Next Generation of Teachers: The Importance of School-Based Support." *Harvard Education Letter* 17(4).

Lazear, Edward P., and Kathryn L. Shaw. 2007. "Personnel Economics: The Economist's View of Human Resources." *Journal of Economic Perspectives* 21(4): 91–114.

Leal, David L. 2004. "Assessing Traditional Teacher Preparation: Evidence from a Survey of Graduate and Undergraduate Programs." In *A Qualified Teacher in Every Classroom? Appraising Old Answers and New Ideas,* edited by Frederick M. Hess, Andrew J. Rotherham, and Kate Walsh (101–17). Cambridge, MA: Harvard Education Press.

Levin, Jessica, and Meredith Quinn. 2003. *Missed Opportunities: How We Keep High-Quality Teachers Out of Urban Classrooms.* New York: The New Teacher Project.

Levin, Jessica, Jennifer Mulher, and Joan Schunck. 2005. *Unintended Consequences: The Case for Reforming the Staffing Rules in Urban Teachers Union Contracts.* New York: The New Teacher Project.

Levine, Arthur. 2006. *Educating School Teachers.* Washington, DC: The Education Schools Project.

Liu, Edward, and Susan Moore Johnson. 2006. "New Teachers' Experiences of Hiring: Late, Rushed, and Information-Poor." *Educational Administration Quarterly* 42(3): 324–60.

Mas, Alexandre, and Enrico Moretti. 2006. "Peers at Work." Working Paper 12508. Cambridge, MA: National Bureau of Economic Research.

Medley, Donald M., and Homer Coker. 1987. "The Accuracy of Principals' Judgments of Teacher Performance." *Journal of Educational Research* 80(4): 242–47.

Metzger, Scott A., and Meng-Jia Wu. 2008. "Commercial Teacher Selection Instruments: The Validity of Selecting Teachers through Beliefs, Attitudes, and Values." *Review of Educational Research* 78(4): 921–40.

Murphy, Patrick, and Michael M. DeArmond. 2003. *From the Headlines to the Frontlines: The Teacher Shortage and Its Implications for Recruitment Policy.* Seattle: Center on Reinventing Public Education, University of Washington.

New Teacher Project, The. 2007. *Hiring, Assignment, and Transfer in Milwaukee Public Schools.* New York: The New Teacher Project.

Newmann, Fred M., and Associates. 1996. *Authentic Achievement: Restructuring Schools for Intellectual Quality.* San Francisco, CA: Jossey-Bass Publishers.

Odden, Allan, Anthony Milanowski, and Herbert G. Heneman III. 2007. "Policy and Professionals: Commentary, Discussion of the Chapters." In *The State of Education Policy Research,* edited by Susan H. Fuhrman, David K. Cohen, and Fritz Mosher (337–45). Mahwah, NJ: Lawrence Erlbaum Associates.

Peterson, Kenneth D. 2000. *Teacher Evaluation: A Comprehensive Guide to New Directions and Practices.* 2nd ed. Thousand Oaks, CA: Corwin Press.

Podgursky, Michael J. 2004. "Improving Academic Performance in U.S. Public Schools: Why Teacher Licensing Is (Almost) Irrelevant." In *A Qualified Teacher in Every Classroom? Appraising Old Answers and New Ideas,* edited by Frederick M. Hess, Andrew J. Rotherham, and Kate Walsh (255–78). Cambridge, MA: Harvard Education Press.

———. 2006. "Teams versus Bureaucracies: Personnel Policy, Wage-Setting, and Teacher Quality in Traditional Public, Charter, and Private Schools." Paper prepared for the National Conference on Charter School Research. Nashville, TN: National Center on School Choice, Vanderbilt University.

Rivkin, Steven G., Eric A. Hanushek, and John F. Kain. 2005. "Teachers, Schools, and Academic Achievement." *Econometrica* 73(2): 417–58.

Roberts, John. 2004. *The Modern Firm: Organizational Design for Performance and Growth.* Oxford: Oxford University Press.

Rockoff, Jonah E. 2004. "The Impact of Individual Teachers on Student Achievement: Evidence from Panel Data." *American Economic Review* 94(2): 247–52.

Rollinson, Elizabeth, and Patricia M. Wright. 2008. "Assessment Practices in Large Multinational Organizations: A Technical Report." Center for Advanced Human Resource Studies working paper. Ithaca, NY: Cornell University School of Industrial and Labor Relations.

Ryan, Anne Marie, Lynn McFarland, Helen Baron, and Ron Page. 1999. "An International Look at Selection Practices: Nation and Culture as Explanations for Variability in Practice." *Personnel Psychology* 52(2): 359–92.

Rynes, Sara L., and Alison E. Barber. 1990. "Applicant Attraction Strategies: An Organizational Perspective." *Academy of Management Review* 15(2): 286–310.

Rynes, Sara L., Tamara L. Giluk, and Kenneth G. Brown. 2007. "The Very Separate Worlds of Academic and Practitioner Periodicals in Human Resource Management: Implications for Evidence-Based Management." *Academy of Management Journal* 50(5): 987–1008.

Sanders, William L., and June C. Rivers. 1996. *Cumulative and Residual Effects of Teachers on Future Student Academic Achievement.* Knoxville: University of Tennessee Value-Added Research and Assessment Center.

Strauss, Robert P., and William B. Vogt. 2001. "It's What You Know, Not How You Learned to Teach It: Evidence from a Study of the Effects of Knowledge and Pedagogy on Student Achievement." Paper presented at annual meeting of the American Educational Finance Association, Cincinnati, Ohio, March 22–24.

Strauss, Robert P., Lori R. Bowes, Mindy S. Marks, and Mark R. Plesko. 2000. "Improving Teacher Preparation and Selection: Lessons from the Pennsylvania Experience." *Economics of Education Review* 19(4): 387–415.

Useem, Elizabeth, and Elizabeth Farley. 2004. *Philadelphia's Teacher Hiring and School Assignment Practices: Comparisons with Other Districts.* Philadelphia, PA: Research for Action.

Van Cleef, Victoria. 2005. "Half Empty or Half Full? Challenges and Progress in Hiring Reform." In *Urban School Reform: Lessons from San Diego,* edited by Frederick M. Hess (177–98). Cambridge, MA: Harvard Education Press.

Walsh, Kate. 2001. *Teacher Certification Reconsidered: Stumbling for Quality.* Baltimore, MD: The Abell Foundation.

Wise, Arthur E. 1986. "Three Scenarios for the Future of Teaching." *Phi Delta Kappan* 67(9): 649–52.

Wise, Arthur E., Linda Darling-Hammond, Barnett Berry, David C. Berliner, E. Haller, Amy Praskac, and Phillip C. Schlechty. 1987. *Effective Teacher Selection: From Recruitment to Retention.* Santa Monica, CA: RAND Corporation.

Wolfe, Richard, Dennis L. Smart, and Patrick M. Wright. 2006. "Radical HRM Innovation and Competitive Advantage: The Moneyball Story." *Human Resource Management* 45(1): 111–44.

Wright, Patrick M., and Wendy R. Boswell. 2002. "Desegregating HRM: A Review and Synthesis of Micro and Macro Human Resource Management Research." *Journal of Management* 28(3): 247–76.

Wright, Patrick M., and Gary C. McMahan. 1992. "Theoretical Perspectives for Strategic Human Resource Management." *Journal of Management* 18(2): 295–320.

Wright, Patrick M., and Scott A. Snell. 1998. "Toward a Unifying Framework for Exploring Fit and Flexibility in Strategic Human Resource Management." *Academy of Management Review* 23(4): 756–72.

5

Lessons from Abroad

Exploring Cross-Country Differences in Teacher Development Systems and What They Mean for U.S. Policy

Dan Goldhaber

International comparisons show that America's students fall somewhere in the middle of the pack when it comes to test performance, and compared to the world's top performers—students in Finland, Korea, and Japan, for example—our students lag far behind.[1] Our relative mediocrity is cause for some concern, not just embarrassment. In a world where capital flows freely across borders (see chapter 2 by Blinder) and where the competition for skilled labor knows no boundaries, middling American students are less competitive as employees. Moreover, lagging cognitive skills among students (in math and science) are closely tied to lower economic growth (see chapter 8).

What is behind America's undistinguished performance? Given what we know about the import role teacher quality plays in explaining student achievement, it's natural to assume that part of the answer has to do with cross-country differences in teacher quality. Indeed, a recent report by McKinsey and Company (Barber and Mourshed 2007) finds that most countries scoring in the top tier of international test comparisons draw teachers from the upper end of the academic achievement distribution, whereas in the United States this tends not to be the case (Goldhaber and Liu 2003; see chapter 3 by Corcoran).[2]

In this chapter, I consider teacher development systems and policies in several other countries to see how they attract people into teaching and train them once they are in the system, and what we in the United States might learn from them.[3] By "teacher development systems," I mean a host of important policies: compensation and employment security policies that influence the front end of the teacher pipeline; policies that govern the selection of applicants into teacher training; the quality and type of training received by individuals who enter the teacher pipeline; and the mechanisms that determine the selection of those judged qualified to teach and their distribution into schools.

I begin by describing what is a relatively sparse (but growing) literature on how teacher development systems vary from one country to the next and how they influence the caliber of a country's teacher workforce. Included is a discussion of new work on teacher training by William Schmidt, who served as project coordinator and executive director of the U.S. National Research Center for the influential Trends in International Mathematics and Science Study.[4] Schmidt studied the training of middle school (or lower secondary school, internationally) mathematics teachers in six countries: Bulgaria, Germany, Korea, Mexico, Taiwan, and the United States. I also report on new in-depth case study findings about human capital systems for teachers in two countries: Germany and Korea. These case studies were completed by scholars from each country (Ludger Woessmann and Hunseok Oh, respectively).[5] Germany and Korea are interesting cases because both are highly industrialized countries with well-educated populaces that, on average, pay their teachers relatively well. And yet the average academic proficiency of their teachers and student performance on international assessments diverges: Korean teachers tend to be more academically capable relative to the Korean workforce than German teachers, and Korean students tend to outperform those from Germany.[6]

Of course, drawing strong inferences based on cross-national comparisons is always a risky business. Institutional and cultural differences between countries mean that policies and practices that work well in one place may not work well in another. Nevertheless, such comparisons can help put the U.S. teacher development system in perspective. I try to provide some of that perspective. Finally, such comparisons provide important lessons about the kind of reforms that might work in the United States, as well as those that are probably infeasible. I discuss both types of reforms.

Cross-National Differences in Teacher Development Systems

It would be nice to be able to look at the international evidence on teacher policies and identify the type of teacher development system that produces the highest-caliber teachers. Unfortunately, it is not that easy.[7] As the examples below suggest, differences between countries do not point toward a consensus about the types of policies—or even sets of policies—that might ensure a high-quality teacher workforce. Instead, they gesture toward some of the characteristics that might be necessary, but not sufficient, for an effective teacher development system.

Despite similarities (e.g., the great majority of people entering the teacher workforce do so immediately after completing postsecondary education training in most industrialized countries),[8] the countries approach teacher development somewhat differently. Four areas of difference stand out: how teachers are paid, the types of selection mechanisms (e.g., national tests) used to determine who can pursue a teaching career, the training that prospective teachers receive, and how teachers enter into the workforce.

How Are Teachers Paid?

Teacher salaries vary considerably from one country to the next and comparisons can be difficult to make. Ideally, one would like information about teaching salaries relative to other occupations (OECD 2008).[9] Lacking good within-country occupational comparisons that can stand up to cross-country comparisons, probably the best way to compare the financial desirability of compensation in different countries is to see how teacher salaries compare relative to gross domestic product (GDP) per capita.[10] Figure 5.1 shows this for teachers at the primary level at two points in the salary scale: starting salaries with minimum required training and salaries after 15 years of experience and minimum training (the cross-nation findings at the secondary level are roughly comparable).[11]

In addition to differences in salary levels, salary structures differ from country to country, which is readily apparent from looking at figure 5.1. For each country, the height of the darker portion of the bar relative to the total height of the bar shows the ratio of starting salaries to those after 15 years of teaching experience. Countries like Germany have relatively "flat" salary structures, in the sense that the top salary a teacher can

Figure 5.1. Ratio of Primary-School Teacher Salaries to GDP Per Capita

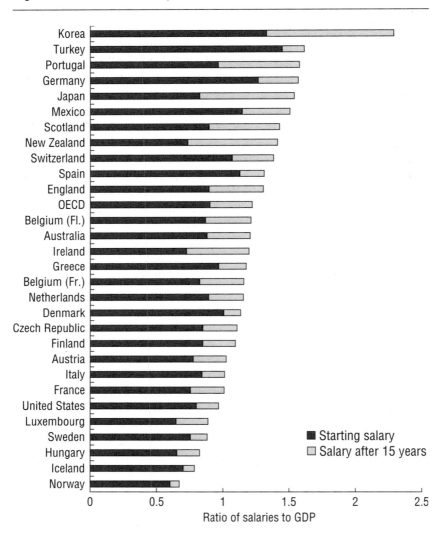

Sources: OECD (2005) and web table supplements.

receive (not shown) only exceeds starting salaries by about 30 percent. Other countries, like Korea, have far "steeper" structures, such that the top salary is nearly three times the starting salary. Not surprisingly, given these differences, the number of years it takes to move from a starting salary to the top of the scale varies considerably—from 6 years in Scotland to 40 years in Hungary. There exists little detailed cross-national information on other aspects of salary structure—for example, whether rewards are allocated for teacher performance or specialization—but in most industrialized countries, the structure of salaries is similar to that in the United States in the sense that they are determined primarily by experience and educational level (Murnane and Steele 2007), and individual teacher performance is not part of negotiated compensation agreements (OECD 2004).[12]

It would be natural to jump to the conclusion that differences between countries in the academic caliber of the teacher workforce that translate into differences in student performance are driven by investments in teacher compensation. Surprisingly, we know very little from empirical evidence about the connection between teacher compensation and teacher quality. U.S. research by Figlio (1997) finds that districts offering higher salaries tend to hire teachers with stronger subject matter qualifications and from more-selective colleges, and new research by Leigh (2009) shows that increases in average teacher salaries in Australia increase the aptitude of those entering teacher education. The recent McKinsey report (Barber and Mourshed 2007) explicitly notes that most of the top-performing school systems paid starting salaries that were above the average for OECD nations. This is certainly true for standout performers like Japan and Korea. But a broader lens reveals a much more muddled picture.

The four panels of figure 5.2 plot out the relationship between (1) starting salaries relative to GDP against international measure of student achievement in math (panel A) and science (panel B) and (2) salaries for teachers with 15 years of experience relative to GDP versus achievement in math (panel C) and science (panel D).[13] What stands out about these figures is that there appears to be little or no consistent relationship between teacher salaries and student achievement. While some countries, like Korea, have high salaries and achievement results that far exceed those of the United States (countries whose scores fall between the horizontal lines have achievement results that are not statistically distinct from those in the United States) and the international average (for OECD

Figure 5.2. Salary Plotted against Student Achievement, International Comparison

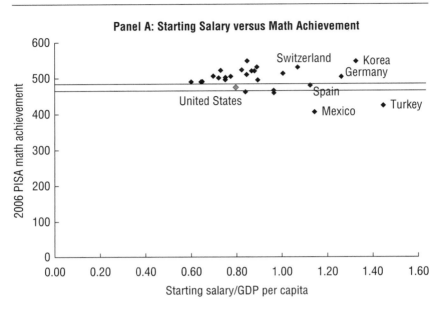

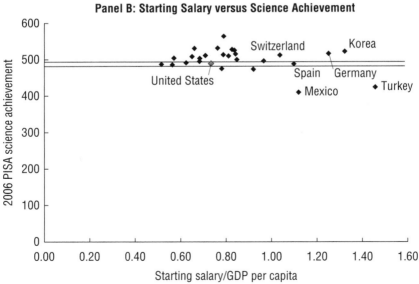

Figure 5.2. *(Continued)*

Panel C: Salary after 15 Years Experience versus Math Achievement

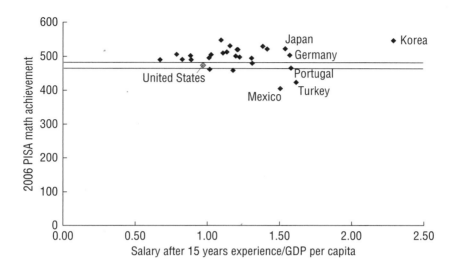

Panel D: Salary after 15 Years Experience versus Science Achievement

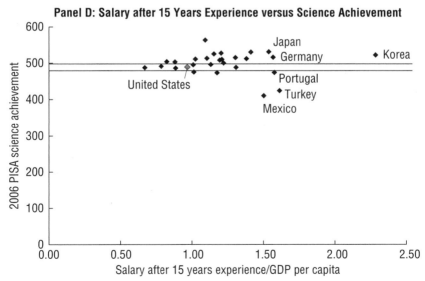

Sources: OECD (2005) web table supplements and Baldi et al. (2007).

countries), there are counter examples. Switzerland and Turkey, for instance, have relatively high salaries but mediocre achievement results, and Austria and the Czech Republic have below-average salaries but above-average achievement results. These teacher salary–student achievement comparisons are, admittedly, quite simplistic. They do not take into account the many other country factors that no doubt influence achievement, but they also suggest that countries that provide high salaries to teachers are not guaranteed good student achievement results. This finding is reflected in a significant amount of U.S.-based research that finds little or no direct relationship between teacher salaries and student achievement (e.g., Betts 1995; Grogger 1996; Hanushek 1997).

One reason for this is that salaries are only one of many factors individuals consider when deciding upon an occupation or specific job. Workload, working conditions, job security, and the prestige of the profession can vary considerably from one country to the next and will all influence the desirability of becoming a teacher. Mexico, for example, is an outlier in the figure 5.2; salaries are high, but student achievement is low. But in Mexico, the average number of teaching hours (hours teachers spend in the classroom) is about 1,000, among the highest of OECD countries, so the per-hour wage of Mexican teachers is far lower than the annual salary might suggest. In the case of Germany and Korea, the simple salary calculations shown in figure 5.2 may understate the desirability of teaching relative to other occupations (even considering the fact that, by the salary-relative-to-GDP standard, both these countries appear to have teacher pay that exceeds the OECD average and far exceeds that in the United States). In particular, in both countries, the number of teaching hours a year, about 800 at the primary level, is far lower than in the United States, which, like Mexico, has an average closer to 1,000 a year (OECD 2008).

Clearly, the more that salary and working conditions result in individuals having a greater interest in and propensity to pursue a career in teaching, the more selective a teacher development system can be at the point that individuals are applying to teacher training.

How Are Teachers Selected into Training Programs?

There is a growing (though largely anecdotal) body of evidence that, relative to the United States, many countries that do well on international assessments have more individuals with top-tier academic credentials applying to teacher training programs and are also more deliberate and selective on who they allow into these programs. Schmidt (2008) reports that, because teaching is a relatively prestigious, well-compensated occupation, many countries have an abundance of individuals seeking entry into teacher preparation programs. In Singapore, for instance, roughly five times as many students are applying to teacher training than are admitted into a program (Barber and Mourshed 2007).

The economic returns for teaching shown in figure 5.1 are certain to play a role in who opts to pursue a teaching career. But it is also worth noting that countries have different policies when it comes to *who pays* for teacher training, which will also affect who opts to pursue teaching. For example, in Korea, teachers' colleges receive considerable public subsidies and are required to keep tuition relatively low;[14] in Singapore, prospective teachers are paid a salary while being trained (Barber and Mourshed 2007). Moreover, the number of people who are admitted into training relative to the number of teaching positions varies from country to country, and this will no doubt influence the desirability of teaching by making it more or less likely that a job will be available to those who become trained.

Germany and Korea are particularly interesting because both countries offer relatively attractive compensation levels (see figure 5.1) and grant civil-service protections that afford a high degree of job security.[15] Despite these similarities, the two countries diverge in the academic caliber of teacher training applicants.

In Germany, the basic requirement for entry into a teacher training institution is that students pass the final examination after secondary education, the *Abitur*.[16] There are no other formal entrance requirements and Woessmann reports that, in general, universities cannot reject any individual with an *Abitur* degree.

Unfortunately, there does not appear to be good data on the academic performance of teacher trainees, but Woessmann does report on the academic performance of teachers who are in the workforce. Overall, using *Abitur* grades as a metric for academic proficiency, Woessmann finds that other occupations competing in the German labor market for college graduates tend to employ people with stronger academic skills than does the teaching profession. Not surprisingly, however, there is also some evidence that the prestige of a particular teaching position influences the academic caliber of those in the position. For example, *Abitur* grades are dependent on teacher assignment, with teachers assigned to the highest-track secondary school type (*Gymnasium*) having demonstrated academic proficiency comparable to those trained in technical subjects, such as engineering and natural sciences, business, and economics, and only slightly lower than those trained in law and medicine. But the majority of teachers—those teaching at other secondary schools and in primary schools—were found to have significantly lower *Abitur* grades, lower in fact than those who obtained degrees from the German equivalent of a technical college.[17]

By contrast, the arrangement in Korea of both institutional design and who pursues a career in teaching appears to be quite different from Germany. Entry into teacher training, at either the primary or secondary levels, is based upon high school grades, performance on a college entrance exam, and an interview. Although this sounds broadly similar to the systems in Germany and the United States, two things distinguish the Korean model. First, Korea mandates that institutions consider college entrance exams. Second, there are only 12 universities that prepare primary-level teachers (11 of which are public), with about 6,000 available slots.[18] Those wishing to receive secondary-level teacher training can do so at 258 training institutions that have more than 40,000 slots. Consequently, the relatively small number of slots for those training to teach at the primary level means there is a close match between supply and demand for new teachers at that level, and those who graduate have a high likelihood of securing a job, far better than at the secondary level (Barber and Mourshed 2007). For example, in recent years, the ratio of credentialed individuals to open teaching slots has been in the 1.2:1 to 2:1 range at the elementary level, but between 8.50:1 and 20:1 at the secondary level.

It is not possible to know for sure what institutional or cultural features of the Korean system might lead to differences in the academic caliber of those entering teacher training, but the McKinsey report singles out Korea as drawing some of the most academically proficient people into teaching. This is consistent with statistics cited in Oh's case study. He finds that, in contrast with the situation in Germany, teacher training institutions appear to enroll individuals with top-tier academic records. Specifically, college admission scores to teacher training institutions were roughly comparable to those applying to study law and were higher than those applying to study business administration, computer engineering, and physics.

Of course, these country-level average differences in the academic proficiency of teacher candidates mask a considerable level of individual heterogeneity. Unfortunately there is, to my knowledge, no detailed cross-national data on the variation in test scores (or any other measure of academic proficiency) of individuals entering teacher training. But it is almost surely the case that, as in the United States (where we do have good data), training institutions in other countries enroll many academically proficient individuals as well as many who are not as academically competent. Heterogeneity in the academic skills of teacher trainee applicants, however, does not imply that differences in averages are irrelevant. Average differences in the academic preparation of those entering teacher training have potentially important implications for the training received, as it is quite likely that the level of instruction will vary depending on the average readiness to learn of teacher candidates and that the experiences while in teacher training will be shaped in part by the academic caliber of fellow students. These are key factors to keep in mind as I describe cross-nation variation in teacher training systems.

How Are Teachers Trained?

In many respects, the broad structure of teacher training looks roughly the same across most industrialized countries. Virtually all industrialized countries require prospective teachers to complete a college degree that includes multiple courses in pedagogy, educational theory, and subject areas; they also require them to have firsthand experiences student teaching and observing classroom teachers (Ladd 2007; OECD 2005; Wang et al. 2003).[19] But the emphasis on different elements of a program can vary, both from country to country and perhaps more important, in some countries, from one training institution to the next.

Wang and colleagues (2003) study the teacher pipeline in the United States and seven other industrialized countries (Australia, England, Hong Kong, Japan, Korea, the Netherlands, and Singapore) and report that it is only in the United States and Australia where the approval of the teacher training curriculum resides at the state level.[20] In the rest, approval is required by a centralized national agency. It is reasonable to infer that in countries with more-centralized control of their training institutions, there will be more standardization across institutions, especially in countries where there are few providers of teacher education. This is an area where the United States appears to be an outlier: the number of training providers varies from one nation to the next, and by intended level (primary or secondary) of preparation, but the United States has more than *1,500 providers,* which exceeds the *combined number of providers in the other seven countries.*

The length of postsecondary education training, of course, depends on whether a prospective teacher is pursuing a baccalaureate or a higher degree, and there is some variation in requirements for entry into the workforce (e.g., in Singapore, all prospective teachers must complete a graduate program to be qualified to teach). In the United States, the typical length of undergraduate teacher training is four years, consisting of over 130 credit hours (51 of general studies, 38 of work in a subject area, 28 of professional studies in education courses, and 14 of student teaching or other field-based experiences) (Wang et al. 2003). Although the breakdown of credit hours varies from institution to institution, it is not common in the United States to vary the length of postsecondary training on the basis of the intended area of teaching specialization—for example, grade level or subject area.

Considerable international variation is seen in the relative emphasis of courses in pedagogy, educational theory, and subject areas (OECD 2005; Wang et al. 2003), but it appears that other OECD countries are far more likely than the United States to differentiate the length of training programs depending on the focus of the training. For example, the average program length for primary school teachers is 3.9 years, for lower secondary school teachers it is 4.4 years, and for upper secondary teachers it is 4.9 years (Ladd 2007).

Another area with large differences across nations in teacher training is the required duration of field experiences. The Netherlands, for instance, requires a minimum of 48 weeks, whereas Korea requires only 4 weeks, and Japan requires only 3. The typical requirement for 12 weeks of field experiences in the United States is similar to the requirements in Australia (16 weeks), Singapore (10 weeks), and Hong Kong(8 weeks) (Wang et al. 2003). It is interesting to note that while OECD countries—the United States included (Huling 1998; Maxie 2001)—are increasing opportunities for pre-service classroom experiences (Ladd 2007), the countries in the Wang and colleagues sample with shorter field requirements than the United States—Singapore, Hong Kong, Korea, and Japan—all have average student achievement that exceeds that of U.S. students on international assessments (Baldi et al. 2007; Gonzales et al. 2004).

Do differences in teacher training translate into important differences in teacher knowledge of subject or pedagogical techniques? In practice, it is difficult, if not impossible, to draw strong conclusions about how training is affecting teachers because, as I discussed above, there are significant cross-national differences in the people who opt to pursue teacher training. Although it is not possible to causally determine whether it is training related, Schmidt and colleagues (2007) illustrate that there are significant cross-country differences in the academic preparation of *future* middle-school mathematics teachers in a sample of six countries, Bulgaria, Germany, Korea, Mexico, Taiwan, and the United States. Specifically, as part of the Mathematics Teaching in the 21st Century (MT21) study, he and colleagues surveyed pre-service teachers to assess what they learned in training.

The MT21 study shows that there are significant differences across surveyed countries in the proportion of advanced mathematics topics (abstract algebra, calculus, multivariable calculus, differential equations, functional analysis, the theory of complex functions, differential geometry, and topology) covered in training. Future U.S. teachers, on average, were found to receive less training in these areas than teachers in all the other countries except Mexico. For instance, the proportion of advanced mathematics topics covered by the average future U.S. teacher is 40 to 60 percent, depending on topic—slightly less than the proportion of future German teachers, but typically only half of that in Taiwan and South Korea, where future teachers were found to study more than 80 percent of advanced mathematics topics.[21]

Because the MT21 study sampled multiple teacher training institutions in the United States, Schmidt and colleagues were also able to assess the variation between institutions and whether there were significant differences based on their orientation toward elementary, middle, or secondary teacher training (all three types train future middle school teachers). It is perhaps not surprising, given the decentralized system of teacher training in the country, that the MT21 study shows there is considerable variation between institutions in the proportion of mathematics topics covered in training, with institutions with a middle school focus appearing to be much more similar to those with an elementary-level focus than to those with a high school focus.

Differences between countries in training both in general pedagogy and in mathematics education were also found. Here, "general pedagogy" refers to a future teacher's perception of learning about classroom management strategies, using data, and how to contribute to the whole school, and "mathematics education" refers to a number of practical aspects of teaching middle school mathematics. In these comparisons, the average future teacher in the United States ranked in the middle in terms of general pedagogy, but lower than all other countries except Germany when asked about their satisfaction with opportunities to learn about these topics.

Schmidt and colleagues (2007, 41) are careful not to draw overreaching conclusions, but they do note that

> Those countries whose students have performed well in previous international comparative studies demanded a different level of preparation on the part of their future teachers than was provided in the United States. In Taiwan and Korea, the level of mathematics preparation was very strong and, in both countries, the amount of emphasis given to the practical issues of mathematics pedagogy was also extensive. In general pedagogy, there was a difference between the two top performing countries. In Taiwan, there was also extensive emphasis given to the practical aspects of general pedagogy such as classroom management, which was not the case for Korean future teachers. Apart from that difference, it is clear that the future teachers in those two countries have extensive coverage of two of the areas (and in the case of Taiwan all three areas). In none of the six countries was the preparation of teachers done without at least some level of coverage associated with each of the three broad areas.

Another theme that emerges from our review of Schmidt's work, the country case studies,[22] and other cross-nation studies of teacher training is the heterogeneity of training programs in the United States (Boyd et al. 2008; Cochran-Smith 2005) compared with those in other countries (OECD 2005; Wang et al. 2003)—a finding that is not surprising given the decentralization of approval of teacher training to the state level. Finally, it is worth highlighting the seeming lack of connection between the length of field experiences and country average levels of student achievement. The length of experiences is surely a crude measure of the quality of those experiences, but the finding is still rather striking given some of the current thinking in the United States that restructuring and extending field experiences may be a key mechanism for upgrading the skills of new teachers.

How Do Teachers Enter the Teacher Workforce?

The great majority of teachers in the United States and other OECD countries enter the profession soon after having completed traditional teacher training. There is a trend in the United States and some other industrialized nations (e.g., England) toward allowing lateral entry into the teacher labor market through alternative routes, but these typically constitute only a fraction of new entrants (OECD 2005; Wang et al. 2003). In the United States, for example, only about 20 percent of new teachers in recent years have entered the profession through alternative routes (Walsh and Jacobs

2007). Thus, the discussion below is focused on the systems that govern the movement of teachers from traditional teacher training institutions into school systems and particular schools.

A number of countries have no formal requirements beyond graduation from an approved teacher training institution. This is true of Finland, Hong Kong, and Singapore (OECD 2005; Wang et al. 2003), which are lauded for the high achievement of their students on international assessments.

Other countries test prospective teachers before they are allowed to enter the labor market. But in many of these countries, there is no threshold requirement for entry into the teacher labor market. Instead, test performance is a factor in determining which prospective teachers obtain which teaching positions (OECD 2005; Schmidt 2008). In Korea, for example, prospective teachers take three different examinations and the pool of prospective teachers is winnowed after each. The first is a multiple-choice test (encompassing both education theory and subject area), the second is an essay test, and the third is a combination interview and evaluation of a comprehensive lesson plan geared toward the intended teaching subject and level. The exams are given by region within Korea, but most are quite similar, differing more on the weight applied to each of the three stages than the substance of the exams themselves.[23]

Finally, in a few countries, the teacher pipeline is narrowed via a licensure system. Typically this system requires the completion of teacher training but also requires testing of prospective teachers after they have received training, and unlike the use of tests in Korea described above, prospective teachers must attain threshold scores to be eligible to compete in the teacher labor market. In general, licensure systems are more common in OECD nations where there is a greater diversity of teacher training institutions and less centralized control over them (OECD 2005).

The U.S. Teacher Development System in Perspective

From the 30,000-foot level, the teacher development systems in some of the high-performing countries that have been studied look a lot like the U.S. system for training doctors: There are relatively few training providers, there is a high degree of standardization across programs, and program graduates are likely to obtain a relatively high-paying job upon graduation. The U.S. teacher development system looks quite different.

Teacher salaries (for teachers with at least 15 years of experience) in the United States fall in the middle of pack among OECD nations in absolute terms; they are far below (by about $10,000 annually) those of some high-paying industrialized countries like Korea and Germany but far above (also by roughly $10,000) many lower-paying industrialized countries like Italy and Sweden.[24] When judged relative to GDP per person, a more apt comparison, U.S. teacher salaries are further back (see figure 5.1). For instance, the ratio of average teacher salaries in the United States to GDP per capita was about 1:1 (at both the primary and secondary levels) compared with an OECD average of about 1.2:1 at the primary level and 1.3:1 at the secondary level. This puts teacher salaries in the United States roughly on par with Italy, but far below those in Korea (about 2.3:1), Germany (about 1.6:1), and Japan (about 1.5:1). In fact, of the 29 OECD countries for which there were data, the United States ranked 21st on relative starting salaries and 24th on relative salaries for teachers with 15 years of experience.

The structure of the U.S. teacher pipeline also makes it relatively unappealing to enter teaching before receiving training. Across the United States, many more individuals graduate with a teaching credential than there are available teaching slots. Precise estimates of the supply of teachers (trained, licensed, and certified) is difficult to obtain because national datasets do not track recipients of non-educational degrees who complete requirements for certification (Boe and Gilford 1992; Ingersoll 2003). However, conservative estimates suggest that only 40 to 50 percent of new recipients of bachelor's degrees in education end up teaching within a year of finishing (Belcheir 1998; Ingersoll 2003).

As a consequence of having a highly decentralized (state-level) system of program approval and a large number of training institutions, training itself appears to be far more diverse in the United States relative to other countries that have been studied (Schmidt 2008; Wang et al. 2003). Given these conditions, it is not surprising that training institutions, on the whole, have applicants with mediocre academic skills (Goldhaber and Liu 2003; Hanushek and Pace 1995) and that the training of U.S. teachers often does not cover the same breadth of advanced subject matter as training in countries with more academically capable recruits (Schmidt 2008).

Given the diversity of teacher training programs, it makes sense that a final step would be required of prospective teachers before they are eligible to participate in the labor market, a common practice in countries with considerable variation in training (Murnane and Steele 2007). In the United States, in addition to having graduated from an approved training program, licensure typically requires that teacher candidates pass a test of knowledge or teaching skills. Licensure tests typically winnow out very few teacher candidates, and they can differ substantially from state to state. Such tests vary in topic and substance, depending on the grade level and subject area in which teachers intend to work, and there is also a significant amount of cross-state variation in the threshold requirement to pass these tests. For example, in states that use common licensure tests, the "cut-score" threshold can vary by more than a full standard deviation (Goldhaber 2007).[25]

In many ways, Germany appears reflective of the institutional arrangement in the United States. Specifically, Germany also has a relatively large number of training institutions, each of which has wide latitude in deciding whom to admit, and German states require prospective teachers to be licensed. In addition, the similarity of these structures appears to create similar problems. Guidelines for cross-state recognition of teacher licenses exist, but the fact that each state has its own system of examinations can create often severe restrictions in geographic mobility; in fact, cross-state hiring tends only to happen when there is severe understaffing of teachers in one state or another.[26]

In theory, the post-training licensure system might serve the purpose of placing a floor on the skill set of new entrants into the teacher workforce, but in practice, it looks incoherent because the specific requirements are left up to the states. As a result, the system as a whole creates barriers to cross-state mobility. We do not know the extent to which limitations in cross-state portability of a teaching credential dissuade people from getting this credential. Nor do we know how many teachers are lost to the profession, because of hurdles associated with getting licensed in a new state after a cross-state family move, for example. Although the magnitude of these issues is unknown, it is clear that the decentralization of the licensure system in the United States is one factor making teaching a less desirable occupation.

On the whole, there appear to be important differences in the desirability of the teaching occupation in the United States and elsewhere (Barber and Mourshed 2007).[27] As one point of comparison, Oh notes that surveys of Korean students and parents indicate that adolescents and parents of adolescents both rank teacher as their ideal job (16 percent of students say this and 25 percent of parents).[28] There are not perfectly comparable surveys of United States students and parents, but research suggests a long-term downward trend in interest in becoming a teacher. In the late 1960s, more than 20 percent of freshmen reported an interest in a teaching career; this figure declined to less than 5 percent by 1982 (Astin et al. 1997). Corcoran, for instance, in chapter 3 shows that the share of female entrants into the teacher labor market who graduated from the top decile of their high school class dropped by about half, from 20 percent in 1964 to about 10 percent in 2000.[29]

Lessons for Teacher Development Systems in the United States

This review of teacher development systems in countries around the world suggests that the U.S. system is one of the more decentralized among industrialized countries. It is also a system where the narrowing of the teacher pipeline happens only after teacher training. As a consequence of these features of the U.S. system, there are significant political and structural hurdles to crafting cost-effective teacher development policy reforms along the lines of making the U.S. system look more like, for instance, systems in high-achieving Asian countries (Barber and Mourshed 2007). I discuss this in greater detail and suggest some alternative reforms that I argue would have a better chance of being implemented given the structure of the U.S. teacher development system.

Cost, Politics, and What Probably Won't Fly in the United States

In contrast with relative earnings in the 1960s, in the United States today, most college-educated women and about two-thirds of college-educated men earn more than teachers (Hanushek and Pace 1995; Hanushek and Rivkin 2006).[30] The relative decline of U.S. teacher salaries is surely one factor explaining the finding that the most academically proficient college graduates in the United States tend to opt for nonteaching careers. Few would argue that public schools would be better off if the United States were able to attract more proficient graduates and that raising teacher salaries is a straightforward way to do this.[31]

The international evidence makes it clear that teachers in the United States, relative to many other nations, are poorly paid. While this argues for more education spending to raise U.S. teacher salaries, this is a very costly strategy to implement on a national scale, particularly in the United States. The reason is that teacher salaries are not low because of a low national level of investment in education; they are low because of the investment choices that U.S. schools make.

Public expenditures on primary and secondary schools by the United States is higher in dollar terms than the majority of OECD countries and, as a percentage of GDP, is just about equal to the OECD average.[32] In fact, U.S. spending on students is also higher than some of the countries with the highest teacher salaries in the world, like Korea and Japan. In these countries, spending on high salaries is offset by having larger classes. Korea, for instance, has the largest average class size amongst OECD nations, averaging well over 30 students at both the elementary and secondary levels.[33]

The trajectory in the United States over the past couple of decades has been to reduce class sizes (Hanushek and Rivkin 1997) so that today they average less than 25 students in both primary and secondary schools (OECD 2008). But it is not the small class size that explains high U.S. educational expenditures; despite the investment in smaller classes, the U.S. average, while lower than those of Korea and Japan, is actually slightly larger than the average in OECD countries. Instead, high U.S. educational expenditures are the result of an investment in specialist teachers and staff. The United States has some of the lowest ratios of students to teaching staff (not class size) among OECD nations.[34] These ratios, unlike class size, include teachers who might, for instance, be involved with pull-out programs (such as supplemental reading instruction or English as a second language).

The relatively large size of the U.S. teacher workforce makes raising U.S. teacher salaries *across the board* relatively costly, which is illustrated by the following back-of-the-envelope calculation. Assume that the United States wanted to raise teacher salaries across the board to be in the same ballpark as salaries in Germany and Japan. This would require salary increases of 50 to 60 percent. Given that in the typical school district teacher salaries account for 50 to 60 percent of educational expenditures (Ballou 1996; Guthrie and Rothstein 1999; Monk, Pijanowski, and Hussain 1997), the increase would require K–12 spending per pupil to rise from roughly $9,000 today to between $11,000 and $12,000, an increase that would cost between $150 and $200 billion nationwide.[35]

I may be wrong, but I see little indication that the United States is set to make educational investments of this magnitude, at least in the short run. Moreover, it is worth remembering that the international evidence shows that offering relatively high teacher salaries does not guarantee that schools will attract more-capable teachers. As discussed above (in relation to figure 5.2), there does not appear to be a strong relationship internationally between teacher salaries and student achievement, which is consistent with research evidence from the United States showing no significant relationship between the teacher salaries and student achievement (Hanushek and Rivkin 2006).

There are certainly other financial incentives that might be tried to make teaching a more desirable profession—the subsidization of teacher training, for instance, as is done in Korea and Singapore. However, I would argue that this strategy is unlikely to be a cost-effective national strategy in the United States in the absence of radical changes to the country's teacher development system.[36] The reason is that, unlike countries where this type of subsidy is typical, the narrowing of the teacher pipeline occurs after teacher training in the United States, not before training, as is typical in countries that subsidize it. Thus, in any given year, across the whole country, many more teachers are prepared than will receive job offers. Furthermore, many of those who actually do enter the teacher workforce are likely to leave—either of their own volition or because they are counseled out of the profession. Thus, the character of the U.S. teacher pipeline is such that teacher training subsidies are likely to be paid out to many individuals who do not teach or do not teach for very long, and this makes the wholesale subsidization of training quite costly.

One can certainly imagine ways of narrowing the teacher pipeline to make teaching more desirable up front and subsidization of training more economical, but my guess is this is unlikely to happen. There is simply no easy way to adopt this as a *national strategy* since, unlike the situation in many countries, the policies governing teacher training are controlled in 50 different states. Moreover, training providers (universities) have vested interests in maintaining education programs, in that they are, at least in some places, "cash cows"—with tuition and subsidies exceeding the cost of training (Darling-Hammond 2000; Twombly and Ebmeier 1989; Zeichner 2002), and universities have political clout with governors and legislatures, making changes to the system difficult. In essence, the large number of teacher education programs, combined with the decentralization, work to maintain the current structure.

There may be other nonfinancial ways to make teaching a more desirable profession. Teach For America (TFA), for instance, has developed a model that attracts some of the most academically capable college students into teaching. I do not wish to wade into debates about the value of TFA for the education system, but the evidence clearly shows that (1) TFA attracts applicants with strong academic records, (2) far more apply to TFA than are admitted into the program, and (3) TFA has built a strong national brand name.[37] The branding is such that TFA corps members often use the TFA credential when applying for jobs, and the credential is widely recognized and respected within and outside of the teaching profession.

The TFA example shows that teaching can be made prestigious, but I rather doubt that one can simply "talk up" the prestige of the profession as a whole. Lawyers are often the subject of jokes, but law is regarded as a prestigious and desirable profession. Teaching, though considered a noble profession, is not terribly prestigious.[38] I doubt very much that the prestige of teaching can be elevated to that of being a lawyer without big changes in pay. Right or wrong, in the United States in particular, job prestige and compensation are tied together (Goyder and Frank 2007; Weaver 1977).

What Might Work

As I described above, some features of the U.S. teacher development system—decentralization and the large number of training providers— make changes to the teacher pipeline and training politically difficult. That said, the decentralization of teacher training is, in itself, not necessarily a bad strategy. There is no policy consensus on precisely what constitutes effective training (Cochran-Smith 2005; Wilson, Floden, and Ferrini-Mundi 2001). It is entirely plausible that there is no one best set of training experiences, rather that the benefits associated with the training teachers receive are dependent on the particular students and teaching environments in which they find themselves.

Notwithstanding the considerable rhetoric surrounding teacher education, I would argue that we do not know much at this stage about the value of teacher training, and that research is only now at the beginning stages of exploring connections between the features of teacher training and student achievement (Boyd et al. 2008). Thus, clearly one strategy for improving the teacher pipeline is to take advantage of the decentralization and diversity of providers—the thousand flowers blooming—to determine what seems to work.

Another way to take advantage of the U.S. teacher training system is to transform it into more of a continuous learning system.[39] There are a variety of reasons it is not such a system today—data limitations being one of the key inhibitors (Loeb and Plank 2008)—but a large part of the problem is that education schools have little incentive, other than good-will, to improve the rigor of their training programs. States such as Florida and Texas have considered ways to hold teacher training programs accountable for their graduates,[40] but this is clearly a nascent idea.

Of course, improvements to teacher training may do little to improve the desirability of the teaching profession. And if a lack of raw talent in the teacher pipeline limits the quality of the workforce, then improvements in training are likely to have only marginal effects on the effectiveness of the nation's teachers.

I offer three divergent strategies for attracting more talent into the teaching profession: elevating the profession, opening the profession, and experimenting with incentives. The first strategy, to elevate the profession, could be approached from many different angles. I don't doubt, for instance, that higher teacher salaries or a narrowing of the front end of the teacher pipeline would make teacher training more desirable, but, as I describe above, I do harbor doubts about the political feasibility of these approaches. Thus, instead I argue for elevating the profession by creating a national entry-level teacher credential. This credential would mitigate the problem of non-portability, making it more valuable than any state-level license, and, if the requirements to obtain this credential were seen as rigorous, it could help recast the public perception of the teaching profession.

In a sense, there are already movements toward the national credentialing of teachers. Specifically, there are now two teaching credentials recognized across some state borders: certification by the National Board for Professional Teaching Standards (NBPTS) and certification by the American Board for Certification of Teacher Excellence (ABCTE). More than 30 states recognize NBPTS certification, but this credential is only available to those with at least three years of experience in the classroom. The newer ABCTE credential is available to new entrants into the labor market, but only a handful of states currently recognize it.[41]

I'm not advocating that these particular credentials should be recognized in all states, but simply that a national credential would go a long way toward making teaching more desirable. The federal government has already shown itself willing to venture into state teacher policy by requiring, as part of the No Child Left Behind Act, that school districts employ "highly qualified teachers" in core academic subjects.[42] (Ironically, this provision does little to standardize teaching credentials across states because the core elements of what it means to be a highly qualified teacher are based on states' policies.[43]) So, it is not inconceivable to imagine that the federal government could specify that teachers who graduate from one or more (presumably rigorous) programs and meet one or more licensure test standards would be granted a national teacher license. Moreover, were such a system to be carefully thought out, it could help subjects for which it is difficult to attract and retain teachers (such as math, science, or special education).

The second, and quite different, strategy to attract more talent is to open up the profession to a greater number of people by bypassing traditional teacher training requirements and making teaching desirable to a broader segment of the U.S. workforce. In theory, this is a strategy already under way in the United States, where most states have some sort of alternative certification program on their books, but in practice, only some states and school systems extensively use these alternative routes to recruit new teachers. It clearly has not been a real national strategy, as many programs on the books do not reduce the time it takes for a college graduate to move into a teaching position (Rotherham 2008), which research suggests is the main appeal of alternative route programs (Johnson, Birkeland, and Peske 2005).

I won't describe the potential advantages or disadvantages of alternative routes in any detail here, since they have been extensively debated elsewhere. It is sufficient to say that the value of alternative licensure rests on how many individuals who would be talented teachers are dissuaded from doing so by the time and expense of traditional teacher preparation programs, the value of those programs, and the ability of local hiring officials to make sound judgments about prospective teachers who come through traditional and alternative routes.[44] Further, it is clear that making this a real national strategy would almost certainly require reconceptualizing what constitutes a typical career in teaching (see chapter 6) and would clearly set the U.S. teacher development system apart from most other industrialized countries.[45]

A third strategy that could complement either of the two above would be to experiment more extensively with incentives. Although the public is unlikely to support large, across-the-board increases in salary, targeted salary increases may be politically feasible.[46] The nub of the problem, of course, is figuring out systems that determine which teachers would receive salary increases. They could take the form of a new type of career ladder (hierarchy) in schools or differentiated teaching roles (as exists in the nursing profession, for instance). They could also be linked to teacher performance. Of course, any departure from the single salary schedule tends to be subject to great debate,[47] and there is little to go on from the international evidence since most other industrialized countries rely on an experience and educational level schedule for paying teachers (Murnane and Steele 2007).[48]

Again, this is an area where we see a willingness to experiment. The federal government is encouraging this with its Teacher Incentive Fund, and prominent localities like Denver have adopted salary structure reforms. While I applaud these efforts, believing that we need to try alternatives, I worry that the magnitudes of the incentives are too small, and the sustainability of the reforms too much in question, to have any significant impact on the careers that people opt to pursue. Unfortunately, it is not clear to me that the sustainability issue can be easily addressed.

The available literature on cross-nation differences in teacher development systems suggests that the U.S. teacher development system is not drawing in the same talent as a number of other countries, but that only one strategy—the national credential—would bring the United States more in line with these countries. The other options—creating a continuous teacher training learning system or expansion of alternative routes and restructuring of compensation—while largely untested in international terms, are, to my mind, reforms of necessity given the unique decentralized nature of the U.S. teacher development system. Thus, somewhat ironically, the review and analysis presented here argues that a significant upgrading of the quality of the U.S. teacher workforce is only likely if the United States exploits what is now a somewhat incoherent system to create a more uniquely American teacher development structure.

NOTES

1. Findings from the Trends in International Mathematics and Science Study (TIMSS) (Gonzales et al. 2004) and the Program for International Student Assessment (PISA) show somewhat divergent results. The test performance of U.S. students in mathematics and science was slightly higher than the average of students from nations participating in the TIMSS assessments but below the average of nations participating in the PISA assessments. However, in both assessments, U.S. students were found to perform significantly less well than students from many industrial competitor nations.

2. Moreover, in the United States, this problem has grown worse over time. However, it is worth noting that a recent report shows a slight increase in the demonstrated academic competence of those who opt to take a common teacher licensure test, suggesting a possible change in this long-term trend (Gitomer 2007).

3. One could also focus on cross-nation differences related to in-service training. I opt not to do that here, as research suggests that teacher workforce quality is determined more by who enters the profession than by policies targeting those who are already in it.

4. TIMSS is one of the studies that highlights the poor performance of U.S. students in mathematics and science relative to those from other nations around the world.

5. See Ludger Woessmann, 2008, "Entering the Teacher Labor Force in Germany," background paper prepared for the Urban Institute's Gates Human Capital Reform of Teaching Project, Washington, D.C.; and Hunseok Oh, 2008, "The Teacher Training System and Teaching Profession in Korea," background paper prepared for the Urban Institute's Gates Human Capital Reform of Teaching Project, Washington, D.C.

6. According to the most recent PISA results, Korean students outscore German students in mathematics and have roughly comparable achievement levels in science.

7. Even were it the case, I would caution readers against drawing strong conclusions about the attributes of an effective teacher development system, given the many institutional and cultural differences between countries.

8. The number of alternative routes by which people enter teaching, such as Teach For America in the United States, are increasing, but individuals entering through these routes still represent only a fraction of the new entrants into the teacher workforce.

9. In some countries, like the United States, Korea, and Japan, compensation decisions are made locally; in others, like Singapore, England, and the Netherlands, these decisions are made nationally (Wang et al. 2003).

10. More ideal would be comparisons for each country of teacher salaries to salaries in occupations that compete in the labor market for teachers. Unfortunately such data do not seem to exist. But Woessmann ("Entering the Teacher Labor Force in Germany") shows that, in contrast to the situation in the United States, the salaries in Germany are such that female teachers earn substantially more than female college graduates in other occupations, and male teachers earn roughly the same as male college graduates who enter an alternate field.

11. The OECD data break grades up into primary, lower secondary, and upper secondary; these roughly correspond to elementary, middle, and high schools in the United States. See OECD (2008), indicator D3, table D3.1, available from http://www.oecd.org/edu/eag2008.

12. Oh ("The Teacher Training System and Teaching Profession in Korea"), for instance, reports that, while there are bonuses for teacher performance in Korea, nearly all teachers receive these bonuses—de facto, the most important influence on salary is years of teaching experience.

13. The measure of student achievement we use is the 2006 performance on the PISA mathematics and science literacy scores. For more on these, see Baldi et al. (2007). Ladd (2007) shows similar results for earlier years of data.

14. The teachers' college in Seoul, for example, charges tuition of about $1,300 annually, a figure only 20 to 30 percent of the typical tuition at a South Korean private university (Oh, "The Teacher Training System").

15. Woessmann, "Entering the Teacher Labor Force"; Oh, "The Teacher Training System."

16. The *Abitur* consists of a set of written and oral exams that students take after 12 to 13 years of schooling (depending on the German state) and that vary according to the specialization that students choose while in the last few years of secondary school.

17. Woessmann reports that these patterns are consistent with a number of other studies of the German workforce showing that, with the exception of those assigned to *Gymnasium,* nonteachers have higher demonstrated cognitive skills than teachers, as measured by tests of verbal and numerical ability.

18. Oh, "The Teacher Training System."

19. See also Woessmann, "Entering the Teacher Labor Force"; Oh, "The Teacher Training System."

20. These countries were selected based on the fact that their students outperformed U.S. students on the 1999 TIMSS mathematics or science assessments.

21. Perhaps not surprisingly, U.S. teachers reported relatively high dissatisfaction with their opportunities to study mathematics (Schmidt et al. 2007).

22. Woessmann, "Entering the Teacher Labor Force"; Oh, "The Teacher Training System."

23. Oh, "The Teacher Training System."

24. These salary figures are converted to U.S. dollars using purchasing power parity.

25. There are four basic types of tests—basic skills, liberal arts and general knowledge, subject-matter knowledge, and pedagogic skills—and some tests cover various combinations of these areas in various forms, from multiple-choice questions to constructed-response essay-type questions (Goldhaber forthcoming). In some states, teachers have to reach performance thresholds on multiple tests to be eligible to receive a full state teaching credential, though most states allow teachers to teach for a specified period without full state credentials.

26. Woessmann, "Entering the Teacher Labor Force."

27. Economic considerations certainly will influence the desirability of teaching, but the importance of culture in influencing prestige should not be undersold. In Korea, for instance, there exists an old saying that the monarch, teacher, and father are at the same level, and Koreans are thought to have great respect for teachers (Oh, "The Teacher Training System").

28. Oh, "The Teacher Training System."

29. It is likely no coincidence that this corresponds roughly to a period in the United States of declines in relative teacher salaries, particularly for women (Corcoran, Evans, and Schwab 2004; Hanushek and Rivkin 2006).

30. For a more comprehensive discussion of this issue, see chapter 3.

31. This strategy would no doubt make the profession more attractive in the long term, but in the short run the effects of increases in salary are theoretically ambiguous (Ballou and Podgursky 1997).

32. See chart C2.2 of the web supplement to OECD (2008), available from http://www.oecd.org/edu/eag2008.

33. Oh, "The Teacher Training System."

34. See tables D2.1 and D2.2 of OECD (2008), available from http://www.oecd.org/edu/eag2008.

35. In the 2006–07 school year, the United States spent approximately $600 billion on primary and secondary schools (Snyder, Dillow, and Hoffman 2008).

36. U.S. interest in this strategy appears to be growing, though it tends to be more targeted; for example, some states provide tuition subsidies to teachers in harder-to-staff subjects like math and science (Goldhaber 2008).

37. In a way, TFA represents "the narrow the pipeline early strategy" described above as this pathway into teaching relies on recruitment from very selective colleges.

38. Studies of occupational prestige (e.g., Nakao and Treas 1994) typically find teaching to be far less prestigious than law.

39. There are some efforts to change the system in this direction; see, for instance, the Carnegie Corporation's Teachers for a New Era initiative at http://www.teachersforanewera.org/.

40. Robert Johnston, "Texas Boosts Accountability for Teacher Preparation," *Education Week* online article, 1997, http://www.edweek.org/ew/articles/1997/10/15/07accred.h17.html.

41. See http://www.abcte.org/how-we-help/passport-to-teaching for more information on this credential.

42. The federal government has softened these regulations in response to the difficulties that districts have had in employing teachers that satisfy their provisions. See http://www.ed.gov/nclb/methods/teachers/hqtflexibility.html.

43. The highly qualified teacher provision requires that teachers (1) have attained at least a bachelor's degree in their subject area, (2) be fully licensed in their state, and (3) have demonstrated knowledge in the subjects taught. Two (and arguably all three) of the core elements of the provision leave states a significant amount of discretion. For example, states have discretion over what constitutes being licensed and over the tests and standards used to judge demonstrated knowledge in a subject.

44. See Goldhaber (2004) for a more comprehensive discussion of these issues.

45. One cannot glean much about the effects of this strategy by looking at the international evidence because, outside of a few countries (e.g., England), most do not allow individuals to enter the teacher labor market without having completed formalized teacher training (Barber and Mourshed 2007; Ladd 2007; OECD 2008; Wang et al. 2003).

46. As I said above, I doubt that the United States will fund large, across-the-board increases in salary.

47. See Goldhaber (2006) for an overview of restructuring teacher salaries.

48. One exception to this rule is Singapore, which provides teachers with large bonuses (equivalent to one to three months of pay) based on subjective evaluations of both current teacher performance and future potential (Sclafani 2008).

REFERENCES

Astin, Alexander W., Sarah A. Parrott, William S. Korn, and Linda J. Sax. 1997. *The American Freshman: Thirty-Year Trends.* Los Angeles: Higher Education Research Institute, UCLA.

Baldi, Stephanie, Ying Jin, Melanie Skemer, Patricia J. Green, and Deborah Herget. 2007. *Highlights from PISA 2006: Performance of U.S. 15-Year-Old Students in Science and Mathematics Literacy in an International Context.* NCES 2008–016. Washington, DC: U.S. Department of Education, Institute of Education Sciences, National Center for Education Statistics.

Ballou, Dale. 1996. "The Condition of Urban School Finance: Efficient Resource Allocation in Urban Schools." *Selected Papers in School Finance 1996.* NCES 2008-016. Washington, DC: U.S. Department of Education, Institute of Education Sciences, National Center for Education Statistics.

Ballou, Dale, and Michael J. Podgursky. 1997. "Teacher Pay and Teacher Quality." Kalamazoo, MI: W. E. Upjohn Institute for Employment Research.

Barber, Michael, and Mona Mourshed. 2007. *How the World's Best-Performing School Systems Come Out on Top.* McKinsey and Company.

Belcheir, Marcia. 1998. "Assessing Readiness for Employment in the Field of Education." Research Report 98-06. Boise, ID: Office of Institutional Assessment, Boise State University. http://www.boisestate.edu/iassess/reports/1998/RR98-06.pdf.

Betts, Julian. 1995. "Does School Quality Matter? Evidence from the National Longitudinal Survey of Youth." *Review of Economics and Statistics* 77(2): 231–47.

Boe, Erling E., and Dorothy M. Gilford, eds. 1992. *Teacher Supply, Demand and Quality.* Washington, DC: National Academy Press.

Boyd, Donald J., Pamela L. Grossman, Hamilton Lankford, Susanna Loeb, and James H. Wyckoff. 2008. "Teacher Preparation and Student Achievement." Working Paper 20. Washington, DC: National Center for Analysis of Longitudinal Data in Education Research, The Urban Institute.

Cochran-Smith, Marilyn. 2005. "Taking Stock in 2005: Getting Beyond the Horse Race." *Journal of Teacher Education* 56(1): 3–7.

Corcoran, Sean P., William N. Evans, and Robert M. Schwab. 2004. "Women, the Labor Market, and the Declining Relative Quality of Teachers." *Journal of Policy Analysis and Management* 23(3): 449–70.

Darling-Hammond, Linda. 2000. "How Teacher Education Matters." *Journal of Teacher Education* 51(3): 166–73.

Figlio, David N. 1997. "Teacher Salaries and Teacher Quality." *Economics Letters* 55: 267–71.

Gitomer, Drew H. 2007. "Teacher Quality in a Changing Policy Landscape: Improvements in the Teacher Pool." Policy information report. Princeton, NJ: Educational Testing Service.

Goldhaber, Dan. 2004. "Why Do We License Teachers?" In *A Qualified Teacher in Every Classroom? Appraising Old Answers and New Ideas,* edited by Frederick Hess, Andrew J. Rotherham, and Kate Walsh (81–100). Cambridge, MA: Harvard Education Press.

———. 2006. *Teacher Pay Reforms: The Political Implications of Recent Research.* Washington, DC: Center for American Progress.

———. 2007. "Everyone's Doing It, but What Does Teacher Testing Tell Us about Teacher Effectiveness?" *Journal of Human Resources* 42(4): 765–94.

———. 2008. "Addressing the Teacher Qualification Gap: Exploring the Use and Efficacy of Incentives to Reward Teachers for Tough Assignments." Washington, DC: Center for American Progress.

———. Forthcoming. "Licensure Tests: Their Use and Value for Increasing the Quality of the Teacher Workforce." In *A Handbook on Teacher Assessment and Teacher Quality,* edited by Mary Kennedy. New York: Jossey-Bass.

Goldhaber, Dan, and Albert Liu. 2003. "Occupational Choices and the Academic Proficiency of the Teacher Workforce." In *Developments in School Finance 2001–02,* edited by William Fowler (53–75). Washington, DC: U.S. Department of Education, Institute of Education Sciences, National Center for Education Statistics.

Gonzales, Patrick, Juan Carlos Guzmán, Lisette Partelow, Erin Pahlke, Leslie Jocelyn, David Kastberg, and Trevor Williams. 2004. "Highlights from the Trends in International Mathematics and Science Study (TIMSS) 2003." NCES 2005-005. Washington, DC: U.S. Department of Education, Institute of Education Sciences, National Center for Education Statistics.

Goyder, John, and Kristyn Frank. 2007. "A Scale of Occupational Prestige in Canada, Based on NOC Major Groups." *Canadian Journal of Sociology* 32(1): 63–83.

Grogger, Jeff. 1996. "School Expenditures and Post-Schooling Earnings: Evidence from High School and Beyond." *Review of Economics and Statistics* 78(4): 628–37.

Guthrie, James W., and Richard Rothstein. 1999. "Enabling 'Adequacy' to Achieve Reality: Translating Adequacy into State School Finance Distribution Arrangements." In *Equity and Adequacy in Education Finance: Issues and Perspectives,* edited by Helen F. Ladd, Rosemary Chalk, and Janet S. Hansen (209–59). Washington, DC: National Academy Press.

Hanushek, Eric A. 1997. "Assessing the Effects of School Resources on Student Performance: An Update." *Educational Evaluation and Policy Analysis* 19(2): 141–64.

Hanushek, Eric A., and Richard R. Pace. 1995. "Who Chooses to Teach (and Why)?" *Economics of Education Review* 14(2): 101–17.

Hanushek, Eric A., and Steven G. Rivkin. 1997. "Understanding the 20th Century Growth in U.S. School Spending." *Journal of Human Resources* 32(1): 35–68.

———. 2006. "Teacher Quality." In *Handbook of the Economics of Education, Volume 2,* edited by Eric Hanushek and Finis Welch (1051–78). Amsterdam: Elsevier.

Hanushek, Eric, A., Dean T. Jamison, Eliot A. Jamison, and Ludger Woessmann. 2008. "Education and Economic Growth: It's Not Just Going to School but Learning Something While There That Matters." *Education Next* 8(2): 62–70.

Huling, Leslie. 1998. "Early Field Experience in Teacher Education." Washington, DC: ERIC Clearinghouse on Teaching and Teacher Education. http://www.eric digests.org/1999-4/early.htm.

Ingersoll, Richard M. 2003. "Is There Really a Teacher Shortage?" R-03-4. Seattle: Center for the Study of Teaching and Policy, University of Washington. http://depts.washington.edu/ctpmail/PDFs/Shortage-RI-09-2003.pdf.

Johnson, Susan Moore, Sarah E. Birkeland, and Heather G. Peske. 2005. "A Difficult Balance: Incentives and Quality Control in Alternative Certification Programs." Cambridge, MA: Project on the Next Generation of Teachers, Harvard Graduate School of Education.

Ladd, Helen F. 2007. "Teacher Labor Markets in Developed Countries." *The Future of Children* 17(1): 201–17.

Leigh, Andrew. 2009. "Teacher Pay and Teacher Aptitude." Working paper. Canberra: Australian National University.

Loeb, Susanna, and David N. Plank. 2008. "Learning What Works: Continuous Improvement in California's Education System." Policy Brief 08-4. Berkeley: Policy Analysis for California Education.

Maxie, Andrea. 2001. "Developing Early Field Experiences in a Blended Teacher Education Program: From Policy to Practice." *Teacher Education Quarterly* 28(1): 115–31.

Monk, David H., John C. Pijanowski, and Samid Hussain. 1997. "How and Where the Education Dollar Is Spent." *The Future of Children* 7(3): 51–62.

Murnane, Richard J., and Jennifer L. Steele. 2007. "What Is the Problem? The Challenge of Providing Effective Teachers for All Children." *The Future of Children* 17(1): 15–44.

Nakao, Keiko, and Judith Treas. 1994. "Updating Occupational Prestige and Socioeconomic Scores: How the New Measures Measure Up." *Sociological Methodology* 24:1–72.

OECD. See Organisation for Economic Co-operation and Development.

Organisation for Economic Co-operation and Development (OECD). 2004. "The Quality of the Teaching Workforce." Policy brief. Paris: OECD

———. 2005. "Teachers Matter: Attracting, Developing, and Retaining Effective Teachers." Paris: OECD.

———. 2008. "Education at a Glance 2008: OECD Indicators." Paris: OECD.

Rotherham, Andrew J. 2008. *Achieving Teacher and Principal Excellence: A Guidebook for Donors.* Washington, DC: Philanthropy Roundtable.

Schmidt, William H. 2008. "What We Know About Teacher Preparation in Other Countries." Paper prepared for the Human Capital Project. Washington, DC: The Urban Institute.

Schmidt, William H., Maria Teresa Tatto, Kiril Bankov, Sigrid Blömeke, Tenoch Cedillo, Leland Cogan, Shin Il Han, Richard Houang, et al. 2007. *The Preparation Gap: Teacher Education for Middle-School Mathematics in Six Countries.* East Lansing, MI: MSU Center for Research in Mathematics and Science Education.

Sclafani, Susan. 2008. "Singapore as a Model for Teacher Development." Aspen, CO: The Aspen Institute.

Snyder, Thomas D., Sally A. Dillow, and Charlene M. Hoffman. 2008. *Digest of Education Statistics 2007*. NCES 2008-022. Washington, DC: U.S. Department of Education, Institute of Education Sciences, National Center for Education Statistics.

Twombly, Susan, and Howard Ebmeier. 1989. "Educational Administration Programs: The Cash Cow of the University." Charlottesville, VA: National Policy Board for Educational Administration.

Walsh, Kate, and Sandi Jacobs. 2007. *Alternative Certification Isn't Alternative*. Washington, DC: National Council on Teacher Quality and Thomas B. Fordham Institute.

Wang, Aubrey H., Ashaki B. Coleman, Richard J. Coley, and Richard P. Phelps. 2003. "Preparing Teachers around the World." Policy information report. Princeton, NJ: Educational Testing Service.

Weaver, Charles N. 1977. "Relationships among Pay, Race, Sex, Occupational Prestige, Supervision, Work Autonomy, and Job Satisfaction in a National Sample." *Personnel Psychology* 30(3): 437–45.

Wilson, Suzanne M., Robert E. Floden, and Joan Ferrini-Mundy. 2001. "Teacher Preparation Research: Current Knowledge, Gaps, and Recommendations." Seattle: Center for the Study of Teaching and Policy, University of Washington.

Zarkin, Gary. 1985. "Occupational Choice—An Application to the Market for Public School Teachers." *Quarterly Journal of Economics* 100(2): 409–46.

Zeichner, Ken. 2002. "Beyond Traditional Structures of Student Teaching." *Teacher Education Quarterly* 29(2): 59–64.

PART II
Reform Ideas

6

The Human Capital Challenge

Toward a 21st-Century Teaching Profession

Frederick M. Hess

M y charge here is to explore avenues for rethinking the teaching profession. If we permit ourselves to cast off traditional ideas, traditions, and practices that have governed most efforts to boost "teacher quality," where might it lead us? I discuss seven anachronistic assumptions about the teaching profession that hamper forward-looking responses to the human capital challenge. In turn, I offer some thoughts about efforts to recruit, train, deploy, reward, and retain high-quality teachers and alternative directions for moving forward. In each case, even if one accepts my diagnosis, there are multiple ways to address the challenges at hand.[1]

I have been asked to provide a quick and thought-provoking sketch of these issues, rather than an intensive piece of research. Consequently, the strokes here are broad, and I frequently employ constructions like "many" and "potentially" in lieu of more precise language, because much of what I discuss does not exist as more than possibility. Generating even proximate predictions would require time and resources beyond those available for this thought piece, though such examinations would be the natural next step for parties interested in exploring such possibilities more fully.

An Anachronistic Model

The existing human capital pipeline in education is the result of more than a century of compromises, incremental adjustments, and calculated moves designed in response to the exigencies of another era. During the late 19th and early 20th centuries, the teaching profession was designed to match the rapid expansion of schooling. It relied on a captive pool of female labor, treated workers as largely interchangeable, and counted on mostly male principals and superintendents to micromanage the predominantly female teaching workforce. Later, in the mid-20th century, collective bargaining agreements, more-expansive licensure systems, and local and state statutes and regulations were layered atop these arrangements. Today, would-be reformers must recognize that machinery and assumptions that may have been sensible in the past are ill-suited given existing opportunities and challenges—and that merely tweaking familiar models is unlikely to deliver satisfying results.

To clarify, it may be useful to quickly note a few ways in which existing arrangements hamper efforts to tackle the human capital challenge; each is discussed at more length later. First, teacher preparation programs are constructed in the expectation that most aspiring teachers will decide on a lifelong teaching career while they are enrolled in college. This made sense 40 years ago, when the typical college graduate would hold five jobs in their career and most teachers were college-educated women with few career choices. Today, however, the average college graduate holds four jobs by the age of 30—making it hard to be confident that new hires can be retained for an extended period, much less for two decades. In short, teaching has clung to its industrial rhythms while recruitment, professional norms, and careers in other knowledge-based fields have significantly evolved.

Second, hiring systems, compensation systems, and benefits are designed for teachers who will remain in the same district or state for the entirety of their career. Again, this made sense when individuals were less mobile. Indeed, these systems were in some cases the fruit of hard-fought union victories intended to provide teachers with familiar protections and to boost sometimes anemic compensation. These systems worked well enough when schools were competing against an industrial model that promised security, stability, and seniority-based compensation. Today, though, pension plans that punish teachers who leave after five or ten years, salary ladders that reward continuous service, and state-specific credentialing are features that hinder efforts to attract talent (for more on this issue, see chapter 10).

Third, the job of "teacher" has remained remarkably undifferentiated over much of the past century. The vast majority of teachers within a given subject area (in grades 7–12) or grade level (in K–6) are treated as largely interchangeable, with beginning teachers given essentially the same responsibilities as their most experienced peers. All 4th-grade teachers in a district are expected to cover the same subjects, instruct the same number of students, and take on roughly the same number of ancillary duties. This may have made sense when little data were available with which to track teacher strengths or student needs. Today, however, it often results in a less-than-optimal use of talented educators.

Even many of today's "cutting-edge" efforts to reform school staffing, teacher recruitment, and teacher preparation represent nothing more than repackaging outmoded assumptions in the hopes of seeing dramatically different results. For instance, in perhaps the most widely discussed "critique" of teacher preparation of the past decade, the 2006 study *Educating School Teachers* ceded that teacher recruitment ought to be entirely geared toward new college graduates and that aspiring teachers should complete five years of additional training before being cleared to teach (Levine 2006). Missing from this equation was any question as to whether students ready to commit to a career in teaching at age 22 are the optimal population for recruits, any effort to grapple with the dearth of evidence that modal teacher preparation makes a consistent difference in performance, or that requiring up-front teacher preparation may dissuade potentially effective entrants into the teacher labor market.[2]

If we begin from the assumption that we need to unshackle ourselves from the legacy of once-reasonable arrangements that now constrain the teaching profession, what new set of ideas might direct a truly forward-looking approach to human capital? Below, I briefly outline seven assumptions (usually treated as sacrosanct) that need to be challenged if we are to construct a teaching profession more attuned to the challenges and opportunities of the 21st century.

1. Today's Professional Teaching Structure Rests on the Notion That the Modal Entrant Ought to Be a Recent College Graduate Intent on Making a Career in the Classroom; a 21st-Century Approach Would Abandon, or Even Reverse, That Assumption

In the early and mid-20th century, when most other professions were closed to women, schools enjoyed a captive pool of talented female applicants. Teaching offered modest opportunity for career growth or merit-based promotion, yet this did not pose a significant hurdle to attracting talent given that classrooms were primarily filled by women who enjoyed few viable alternatives. These realities, in turn, did much to influence teacher training, recruitment, compensation, work arrangements, benefits, and the entire shape of the teaching force. Districts developed seniority-driven systems compensation and benefits that were constructed on the presumption that teachers would stay in a given school district for decades. Given conditions of that era, this was a reasonable approach for both teachers and school districts desiring stability.

In recent years, however, broader economic trends have challenged these arrangements. By the 1970s, professional barriers for women began to crumble and schools could no longer depend on a steady influx of talented young women to fill the teaching ranks. The same women who once entered teaching began aspiring to jobs in engineering, law, medicine, and business. As Sean P. Corcoran describes in chapter 3, this has resulted in the teaching profession losing out on the top tier of high school graduates. Workers also became increasingly mobile during this period, rendering teacher licensing requirements more onerous and blue-collar benefit plans less attractive to those with options in other sectors and other geographic regions. With the well of ready teachers running dry, two possible avenues emerged. One was to find ways to continue attracting young women graduating from college and the other was to seek out an alternative pool of talent. Policymakers have, for the most part, adopted the default approach of hoping that the old model would keep working while eventually, starting in the late 1980s, moving to adopt some piecemeal efforts related to alternative licensure and mid-career recruitment. (Partly because professional development, compensation, and career opportunities were never reconfigured as part of those efforts, their impact has tended to be marginal.) These alternative programs have provided clear evidence that perhaps half of those who enter teaching after the age of 30 or from other professional occupations would not do so if forced to navigate traditional teacher preparation and licensure.[3]

Today, we should abandon the mindset that presumes a certain kind of "modal entrant," and especially from the expectation that these individuals will or should be recent college graduates. Indeed, the population of college-educated workers already well into their first or second career, made comfortable by early success, and now open to more rewarding, meaningful, and engaging work appears to be substantial (Gergen and Vanourek 2008). While estimating the size of this population requires surveys and ancillary efforts beyond those currently available, one can safely estimate this population almost certainly numbers in the millions. One question that emerges is what preparation individuals should be required to have before applying for teaching positions and what kinds of support and training ought to be available on an ongoing basis. These are large questions that I have addressed previously[4] and will touch upon a bit later. Here, I shall simply note that a 21st-century mindset would dictate that the costs and benefits of various licensure arrangements and the configuration of professional development ought be considered with an eye to the new labor market and not with a focus on the conventional, modal entrant.

A supply of mature college-educated workers interested in migrating to fields like teaching suggests the value of abandoning the presumption that the modal teaching entrant ought to be fresh out of college. Given current life spans and career trajectories, and with appropriate opportunities and support, it is eminently reasonable to imagine that a typical 35- or 45-year-old lateral entrant might teach effectively for 20 years or more. Even for those intent on building a teaching corps in which decade-plus stints of service are the norm, it is not at all clear that a 22-year-old entrant into the profession is more likely to remain for two or three decades than a 35-year-old entering the teaching ranks from a career in insurance, journalism, law, or sales. (I will touch on whether the decades-long career ought to be the assumed standard.)

It is not immediately clear why we would expect young entrants to be the most attractive pool of new teachers, given that effective teaching today generally entails not only the application of precise research-based instructional methods but also leadership, mentoring, guidance, life experience, organization, commitment, and knowledge. In principle, one can identify a list of qualities that contribute to effective teaching, including content knowledge, pedagogical and instructional expertise, life experience, wisdom, applied knowledge (including a practical sense of how schooling can be put to use), energy and enthusiasm, and "relate-ability" (e.g., the ability to empathize and connect with students). On balance, save for energy and relateability, the median working adult who transfers laterally into teaching generally has likely enjoyed more oppor-tunities to develop these qualities and skills than has the median new graduate. Moreover, as Alan S. Blinder notes in chapter 2, there is likely to be an increasing premium placed on creativity and the ability to work in teams, and one can make a strong case that lateral transfers into teach-ing would be far more likely to have a set of experiences that would allow them to teach these skills.

Now, I do not mean to suggest that we should discourage young entrants or discount the notion that some 22-year-olds are ready to play a valuable role in schools, either for a limited period (e.g., the private-school or Teach For America model) or by committing to a career of effective classroom teaching. Such recruits, when promising, should be courted and welcomed. I am suggesting that there are good reasons to not presume that the just-out-of-college-teacher should be the *modal* recruit. Such a shift need not require that we envision a profession dominated by educators who work in schools for just three or four years; it is entirely plausible that a strategy more attuned to the new labor market, more tightly linked to a professional vision of teaching, and which seeks to attract a much larger percentage of mature entrants making an informed career choice may well result in reduced rates of attrition.

Rethinking these assumptions, of course, yields different needs and expectations on the part of teachers when it comes to recruitment, prepa-ration, salaries, benefits, and career trajectories. If the ideal new teacher is a recent college graduate who intends to remain in the profession for decades, there are logical reasons for front-loading preparation in college and relying heavily on seniority to allocate salary and positional perks. If, however, the ideal entrant is someone age 30 to 55, who has worked for several years in another field, and accumulated experience and skills, this paradigm is needlessly constraining. Benefit systems that penalize shorter terms of service are a stumbling block for second-career teachers; compa-rable salaries and a defined 401(k) contribution will make a lateral move more attractive.

One note of caution here: to the extent that some professionals are seeking security and stability it does make sense to take that into account when crafting salary, work conditions, and benefits.[5] I am not seeking to map out or justify some new "one best system," but to suggest how we might rethink recruitment and the shape of the profession to recognize the opportunities and challenges of today's labor force. In some cases, in some locales, and for certain pools of potential recruits, this may well entail deliberately giving added weight to stability and security. The key, however, is that this be a deliberate design decision rather than a vague endorsement of an outmoded status quo.

In all this, it is vital to recognize the pivotal role that teaching colleges and education departments play as trainers and gatekeepers, since entrants from other sectors will not go through standard steps. Although 10 to 15 percent of teachers enter the profession through alternative routes today, three-quarters of the alternative programs are still run by traditional teacher preparation institutions (Walsh and Jacobs 2007). Most such programs still accept the premise that teachers should be expected to "complete" their training within the first two years of entering a classroom. They do not ask whether it is possible to devise more-targeted training to help teachers master the specific skills they need, when to use them, or how to do so with an eye toward the context and students in question.

2. Today's Structure Assumes That Most Professional Development Should Precede Teacher Employment and Be Coordinated through Institutions of Higher Education; a 21st-Century Approach Would Abandon, or Even Reverse, That Assumption

In the previous section, we briefly touched upon the contentious issue of teacher preparation. In the course of the 19th and 20th centuries, states made schools of education and teacher training programs at colleges and universities the de facto gatekeepers for the teaching profession. Except in unusual circumstances, aspiring teachers were required to graduate from a state-approved teacher training program. Initially intended to ensure quality, the arrangement proved problematic because it gave education professors a chokehold over who entered the teaching profession and isolated schools of education from outside competition. In many respects, these programs embodied a "one-size-fits-all" approach that presumed that a teacher certified by any program was ready to teach at any school. Today, this notion is reflected in the No Child Left Behind Act's "highly qualified teacher" provision, with its implicit assumption that a highly qualified teacher can be readily inserted into any classroom in any school and deliver results. The frailty of this mindset is especially salient at a time when school models like the Knowledge Is Power Program (KIPP), High Tech High, and the Big Picture Company seek teachers with substantially different skills and training. Providers can vary dramatically in their preferred approaches to instruction, pedagogy, and assessment.

Historically, we have thought about schooling and teacher training in terms of local geographies. When transportation and communication presented substantial barriers, it was logical to think about localized, dispersed teacher education in each community. With 15,000 school districts across the nation, the emergence of 1,300 geographically scattered, discrete teacher training programs was a natural response, and institutions of higher education already possessed the expertise, intellectual resources, organizational capacity, and facilities to manage that kind of preparation.

Those conditions no longer hold. Advances in communications and transportation make it possible to provide professional training and support over substantial distances; many other kinds of institutions already do so outside of the education sector and in K–12 schooling. CaseNET, developed at the University of Virginia and offering scenario-based courses to educators online, is one example of how this might work.[6] There is no reason for teacher preparation programs to confine their services to a particular locale or, as a result, commit themselves to providing teachers with the various skill sets that a given locale might require.

Today, a variety of professional development arrangements might constitute attractive substitutes—ranging from schools or school systems providing their own training to preparation offered by intermediaries and recruiting-cum-training operations. One promising effort to challenge the conventional approach is for K–12 schools to offer on-site training. The High Tech High School Graduate School of Education, for instance, offers a master's in education. Through coursework and by designing and implementing an action research project, graduate students pursue essential questions relevant to their practice and apply what they have learned in their own classrooms and schools. This model allows them to learn on site, receive context-specific feedback, and assess the quality of their work in terms of concrete student outcomes.[7] An important consideration here is that the larger system of employment, advancement, and compensation are largely unresponsive to the quality of preparation that an educator has received. Salary schedules and the lack of opportunities for professional advancement mean that there are few rewards for training at a highly regarded rather than a marginal institution. As Jennifer King Rice notes in chapter 11, there are some changes to the way we think about professional development that might make it far more meaningful.

In addition, with the emergence of national or statewide chains like KIPP, Aspire, and Achievement First, providers that run schools in multiple locales would likely benefit from training delivered in multiple locales and crafted to particular needs. With a mobile workforce in which educators need preparation specific to a school or school system environment, individual teachers gain the most from training that is portable—that they can continue when they move, and that is responsive to their many professional needs. The Hunter College partnership with KIPP, Uncommon Schools, and Achievement First is a promising step in this direction, but its geographic limitations and reliance on Hunter College's resources means that it is more of an incremental advance rather than a full-blown remodeling. While some institutes of higher education will inevitably prove sensible hubs for some of this (given their resources and expertise) and while it is inevitable that some faculty from these institutes would play an integral role in designing and delivering training, it is time to reconsider the centrality of the role they currently play in teacher training and professional development.

A shift away from the modal assumption of university-based, pre-service preparation will also require (and permit) a reallocation of professional development dollars. Today, traditionally prepared teachers are expected to bear the opportunity cost of additional schooling to pursue employment. Meanwhile, individual teachers, school districts, and state dollars finance university teacher preparation programs. Decoupling professional training from institutes of higher education will allow these dollars to be utilized differently, and funding such a shift is not possible unless policymakers and district officials alter licensure rules, hiring practices, and the credit-counting element of compensation systems so that new approaches have the opportunity to prove their mettle.

3. Today's Model Assumes That the Modal Teacher Will Work Full Time and Work as a Teacher for His or Her Entire Career; a 21st-Century Approach Would Abandon, or Even Reverse, That Assumption

An assumption deserving particular scrutiny is the notion that the vast majority of educational employees should be full-time workers or careerists. If specialized skills are concentrated in a smaller, more gifted and intensively trained body of professionals—medical doctors or attorneys, for example—then it is clearly desirable that these employees work full time and long term. Such employees would be difficult to replace. However, the role of attendants, clerks, paralegals, and secretaries can be approached rather differently. Because these jobs typically require far less training and expertise, employee turnover is less problematic. Meanwhile, arrangements that employ these personnel on a part-time or even volunteer basis (e.g., candy stripers) can attract employees uninterested in full-time work (e.g., graduate students, stay-at-home-parents) and permit employers to avoid paying full-time salary and benefits for part-time responsibilities.

These distinctions tend to be lost in education, where discussion of teacher "retention" makes no distinctions among teachers—treating the loss of high-skilled and less-skilled educators as equally problematic. State laws, district staffing models, and collective bargaining agreements all take for granted the premise that the vast preponderance of personnel will be full time. An established body of research suggests that the gross benefits of classroom experience taper off within the first decade of working. And, as discussed earlier, the assumption of long-term careers in teaching ignores the opportunities offered by the contemporary labor market. Yet, the default staffing model continues to presume the value of indiscriminately encouraging 25 years of service.

K–12 schooling employs a large number of school-based personnel who are not teachers, with the total number of school-based support staff (including aides, librarians, guidance counselors, and so forth) accounting for about 30 percent of school employees. One would be hard put, however, to make the argument that these employees, who have constituted a static percentage of employees over four decades, have facilitated specialization or increased teacher productivity.

Moreover, these roles have been peripheral to discussions about efforts to reform teaching, which have almost universally presumed that the teacher's job must include a densely woven web of duties. That is unduly limiting. An alternative approach might recognize elementary reading instruction as a distinct role parsed out from the other tasks of elementary instruction, with research-based preparation for diagnosing, instructing, and supporting early readers taught in highly specialized programs (perhaps analogous to accelerated programs that train many nurse practitioners). Or, scrutinizing teacher roles and responsibilities might suggest that tutoring in remedial math in grades 7–12 draws on a limited knowledge base and set of skills that may be readily mastered by a wealth of candidates. In such cases, adopting the private school model featuring a core of professional, veteran staff augmented by colleagues who teach for just a few years might permit expert and highly compensated educators to make full use of their skills while permitting support and ancillary work to be handled by less costly employees.

One approach to staffing could entail drawing more directly on community resources to augment or supplement school staff. Boston-based Citizen Schools, for example, provides highly regarded after-school instruction and career-based learning by arranging for local volunteers to work with students regularly. This approach effectively leverages local professionals part time and is designed to maximize the value of their contribution. Rather than having adults simply mentor or tutor students, Citizen Schools arranges weekly modules that permit adults to teach skills and tackle complex projects with interested students. Slimming the ranks of generic "teachers" can free up money to support and expand efforts like Citizen Schools, as well as compensate coordinators and participants. Such innovations point to the need to entertain solutions that are not wholly reliant on full-time, career-long staffing and to recognize how compensation approaches can facilitate or stifle these efforts.

4. Today's Model Assumes That Teachers Are a Generic Commodity and That No Costs Are Incurred When They Serve in Administrative and General Service Capacities; a 21st-Century Approach Would Abandon, or Even Reverse, That Assumption

Today, there are approximately 3.3 million K–12 teachers in the United States, representing nearly 10 percent of the college-educated workforce. It should be no great surprise that only a certain proportion of these educators are gifted at explaining concepts, communicating content, delivering lessons, teaching reading, connecting with troubled

children, and so forth. Yet, schools require all teachers—those with particular gifts and those without—in roughly equal measure, to devote time and
energy to bureaucratic duties, patrolling hallways and cafeterias, taking
attendance, grading homework, and compiling report cards. The problem
here is one of opportunity cost, whereby district officials are conscious of
costs related to salary and materials, but fail to account for the opportunity
costs of not taking full advantage of expertise and ability.

Other professions arrange work patterns much differently. In the best-
run law practices, for instance, even junior attorneys are not expected to
file their own paperwork, compile their billing reports, or type letters to
clients—these tasks are performed by paralegals and secretaries, less highly
trained (and less expensive) individuals who permit the lawyers to focus
on making use of their particular training and skills. In a well-run medical
practice, surgeons do not spend time filling out patient charts or negotiating with insurance companies—these responsibilities are left to nurses or
other support staff. In education, however, not an afterthought is given
about asking a gifted teacher of calculus or remedial reading to cavalierly
spend 25 percent of their workday taking on bus duty, study hall, or an
out-of-field class to accommodate scheduling constraints.

In schooling, two decades of surveys by the National Center for Education Statistics suggest that the typical teacher spends only about 68 percent of his or her classroom time on instruction related to core academic
subjects, with the remainder consumed by activities like administrative
tasks, fundraising, assemblies, socialization, and celebrating holidays.[8]
Unions have demanded large numbers of sick days as well as uniform
limits governing the number of classes and students that can be assigned
to teachers. Meanwhile, management negotiations have frequently resulted
in the universal imposition of duties and noninstructional responsibilities.[9] As a result, labor agreements routinely limit teacher interaction
with students to no more than 70 percent of a workday. Moreover, the
National Center for Education Statistics reports that there are more than
600,000 "instructional aides" in K–12 schools. Without going into detail,
I'll simply note that the scant evidence available leaves me skeptical that
these employees are used in a fashion that maximizes teacher effectiveness or alleviates teacher responsibilities. Indeed, rather than substituting cheaper instructional aides for more-expensive teachers, the two
populations have grown in tandem in recent decades.[10]

For instance, every year, tens of thousands of teachers give variations of
the same lectures on the Civil War, right triangles, the digestive system, and

countless other discrete topics. At the same time, every teacher is asked to be a master of both content knowledge and developmental psychology, as well as to pitch in on a heap of mundane tasks. Even schools that tout their commitment to professional development and data-driven instruction are pressing teachers to operate as generalists who have little opportunity to leverage their particular skills or focus on particular student needs. The challenge, in short, is to ensure that effective educators are devoting more of their time to educating. If teachers are devoting just 68 percent of their time to instruction, sensible strategies could reduce the need for classroom teachers by one-third without sacrificing instructional time and delegate many ancillary tasks to support personnel or systems.

There are two possible approaches. One, discussed more thoroughly by Paul T. Hill in chapter 7, would be to substitute technology for tasks where teachers are able to add limited value. For instance, employing a variety of tools or services might alleviate the need for teachers to devote substantial time to administering, grading, or data-entering formative assessments by allowing them to readily examine student achievement via convenient data tools. Tasks that once took hours per week can take just one-tenth that much time. Providing a stellar example of this is Wireless Generation's software, which permits K–2 teachers to use a Palm Pilot (a handheld wireless device) to conduct the diagnostics traditionally done on paper to assess early reading. Instead, teachers can enter the necessary data directly, speeding the process and making a wealth of easily manipulated information on student performance immediately available.

A second approach would entail hiring specialized support staff that do not require as much training and are relatively inexpensive. This would free up teachers with exceptional skills or extensive training to perform the work for which they are best suited.[11] It is this approach that I discuss next.

5. Today's Model Regards Most Teachers as Generalists, Not Specialists, and Expects Teachers to Juggle a Broad Array of Tasks and Responsibilities; a 21st-Century Approach Would Abandon, or Even Reverse, That Assumption

Historically, educators have been expected to perform a wide variety of responsibilities. Teachers run discussions, give lectures, grade essays, mentor their colleagues, supervise homeroom, patrol the cafeteria, and design lesson plans. As discussed previously, teachers not only handle a mix of instructional tasks, but schools and school systems operate on the implicit assumption that most teachers will be similarly facile at all these responsibilities. For instance, in a routine day, a 4th-grade teacher might be expected to help diagnose and coach a troubled reader, tutor an advanced science student, explain key math concepts, field a parental complaint, observe a peer, and work with children with special needs. In fact, widespread enthusiasm for mainstreaming of children with special needs, untracked classrooms, and "differentiated instruction" have increased the breadth of demands placed on a typical teacher in recent decades. Thus, while about 60 percent of today's K–12 teachers have diplomas or certificates that bear a master's or even a "specialist's" degree, these labels have a limited impact on work routines or responsibilities and ultimately amount to little more than honorifics.

Progress in medicine has charted a very different course. There, a century's worth of gains has been reaped by increasing specialization—with different doctors taking on more precisely defined roles and less expensive paraprofessionals like registered nurses and physical therapists taking on subordinate tasks. Medical specialties in the United States first sprouted about a century ago, between 1900 and 1920, in response to advances in research and technology. New developments made it harder for doctors to stay abreast of the latest medical treatments, creating pressures to specialize. Today, the American Medical Association officially recognizes 199 specialties within the medical profession.[12]

The first modern specialty to gain recognition was surgery, which used operative manual and instrumental techniques to care for bodily organs. A few years later, a second specialty emerged—the "internist," which entailed treating nonsurgical internal illnesses with physiological and other chemical-based methods. Soon after, the third (and final) "original" specialist role to arise was ophthalmology, which dealt with diseases of the visual pathways, including the eye and brain. Although it was initially unclear how "specialty status" would be conferred, guilds and other associations formed to self-regulate their professions (Stevens 1971). Over time, with advances in research, training, and knowledge, the number of specialists grew, from 17 percent of U.S. doctors in 1931, to 57 percent in 1960, to 93 percent in 1980, to 98 percent in 2000 (Stevens 1971, 181).[13]

Although specialization is the norm in medicine, such a mindset has been largely absent in schooling. Even in the most innovative and dynamic charter schools, teaching bundles together the roles of content deliverer, curriculum designer, diagnostician, disciplinarian, discussion leader, empathizer, clerk, secretary, and attendant—and asks teachers to fulfill these roles for a variety of students in a variety of content areas. Moreover, efforts to import specialization into schooling have often been halfhearted, with special education or English language learners "specialists" frequently spending one-third or more of their time on required paperwork, while assigning them to work with populations for whom their specialty is irrelevant. These arrangements mean that any benefits of teacher specialization or research-based preparation remain largely unexploited. Similarly, as noted in the previous section, the rapidly growing ranks of instructional aides have not been used to focus, narrow, or otherwise rearrange the work that teachers perform.

In schooling, there appear to be areas—including reading, special education, English language learning, and instruction in advanced subject matters—where it is not difficult to imagine identifying specialists in a meaningful fashion. The state of current research and development practice, teacher preparation, and working arrangements mean, however, that pedagogical and instructional specialization even in these areas may be more an aspiration than a reality. Identifying specialists in other realms will necessarily await advances in research. Cultivating the requisite knowledge would require an investment in research and development that dwarfs efforts made to date.[14]

Unfortunately, however, most efforts to import specialization into K–12 have done so in a reflexive manner that seeks to wedge the notion of specialization into the contemporary architecture of K–12 schooling. In particular, there is an implicit expectation that everyone can be a specialist, that schools can treat specialists the same as other workers, that there is no problem assigning specialists ancillary tasks, or that specialization can be embraced without fundamentally rethinking the organization and delivery of schooling. So long as we hold onto such assumptions, the transformative potential of specialization in education will remain limited.

6. Today, While the Step-and-Lane Contract Model Is Problematic, It Is Assumed That Even New Compensation Models Ought to Include Hierarchical Rankings of Educators or Be Based on Crude Value-Added Metrics; a 21st-Century Approach Would Abandon, or Even Reverse, That Assumption

Beginning in the 1920s, and accelerating in the 1950s, a push for professional solidarity among teachers fed efforts to equalize their pay regardless of position or grade. By the 1960s, compensation was rigidly based on a teacher's amount of classroom experience, formal education, and extra accumulated college credits. Today, veteran teachers are accustomed to these pay scales and fiercely resist to changing the rules now that they benefit from them. This pushback is readily understood, even by its critics, since it reflects the implicit understanding governing salaries, work conditions, and benefits that held sway when they entered the profession.

As a general rule, a useful way to attract, retain, motivate, and manage talented people is to reward them monetarily for their efforts. For too long, education has operated in accord with a manufacturing mindset that treats teaching as a standardized task and bases compensation on seniority and formal credentials. Such a pay system, however, makes it virtually impossible to reward teachers for raising student achievement, working hard, possessing rare skills or expertise, or taking on more challenging school or classroom assignments. For instance, school administrators report that it is "very difficult" to fill math or science positions more than 30 percent of the time but that they have the same difficulty filling elementary teaching positions just 6 percent of the time. Yet it is still the case that fewer than 10 percent of traditional public school districts use any incentives (such as cash bonuses, salary increases, or extra salary steps) to recruit and reward essential teachers (Kowal, Hassel, and Hassel 2007; Podgursky 2003).

The status quo undermines the quality of the teaching profession in two ways. Other things being equal, teaching is a less attractive profession for those who want to be recognized and rewarded on the basis of their accomplishments and hard work. Existing arrangements also have the unfortunate result of making teaching more appealing to those seeking security and the assurance that they need only work as hard as they choose to. U.S. workers judged to be performing in the highest quintile of employees received annual average raises of nearly 6 percent in 2007, whereas those in the bottom quintile received less than an additional 2 percent. Against this larger backdrop, treating employees uniformly puts K–12 schools at a decided disadvantage in competing for upper-echelon talent (Mercer 2007).

It would be an enormous mistake, however, to rely simply on assessments of student performance to gauge teacher quality, a topic Steven Rivkin focuses on in chapter 9. Teachers can contribute to student learning in a slew of ways that may not show up on standardized tests, including mentoring colleagues, counseling troubled students, helping maintain school discipline, and remediating students on material that will not be tested. Rather than trying to judge teachers with mechanical precision, it is better to formulate sensible instruments for evaluation and permit managers to make reasoned decisions. Public and private-sector ventures have made enormous progress on this front in the past 15 years, making available a wealth of potential models and relevant experience.

Even seemingly sophisticated proponents of reform have proposed relatively crude, test-based compensation reforms in such states as Arkansas, Florida, and Texas. Rather than seeking to retool the profession in light of new opportunities and challenges, too many of these proposals have adopted the blunt Pavlovian approach of paying more for higher test scores while neglecting questions of how this strategy might affect organizational incentives. Even the ProComp plan in Denver (with its various provisions on performance, skills, National Board Certification, and accompanying metrics) tends to take for granted the expectation that all teachers will perform similar functions and proceed up a linear hierarchy. Every teacher under a ProComp-style system still enters the Denver Public Schools at roughly the same salary and with roughly the same job description. Every teacher does the same general work, pursues the same bonuses, and seeks to claim the same career ladder. This would be akin to a law firm requiring every new law school graduate to start as a paralegal and then eventually become a lawyer, or hospitals requiring every new medical doctor to begin as a nurse, then become a general practitioner, and then a specialist. In schooling, it represents a waste of scarce talent and expertise.

It should not be presumed that specialization or differential compensation requires finely graded, new hierarchies. In place of "career ladders" that were all the rage in the 1980s or ProComp-style efforts that are popular today, the aim should be to create a profession with various roles and specializations. Just as a heart surgeon need not become a mentor or take on additional responsibilities to be highly compensated, a stellar reading or physics teacher ought to be able to reap large raises without becoming a department head or coach. Law and medicine have weakened or even severed the link between an employee's formal place in an organizational hierarchy and expected compensation. By allowing pay to reflect perceived value, rather than proceeding in lockstep with formal authority, these fields have fostered norms whereby it is normal for accomplished attorneys or doctors to spend their entire career making use of their skills and earn outsized compensation without ever moving into management or administration. That kind of a model in education would permit truly revolutionary approaches to recruiting and retaining quality educators.

Educators and educational policymakers frequently allude to the eye-popping compensation earned by lawyers and doctors yet rarely note that this is directly related to the role played by specialization and support staff. Many employees in law firms and medical practices are not especially well compensated. Clerical staff and paralegals in law firms routinely make one-third of what junior attorneys make and one-fifth or even one-tenth of what senior attorneys make. If doctors, lawyers, and all their ancillary and support staff were lumped together and paid the same, the enormous number of support staff included in any such calculation means that the overall pay of these generic professionals would look a lot more like that of teachers. Given the current dollars expended for salary, it would be no great feat to pay $150,000 a year to the top half-dozen teachers at the typical elementary or high school if roles and compensation were redesigned appropriately. The stumbling block is that merit pay or compensation reform attempt to erect new structures atop a foundation that accepts as a starting point current job descriptions, compensation levels, and numbers of employees.

7. Today's Model Assumes That the Modal Form of Content Delivery and Coaching Ought to Be Face-to-Face Instruction Carried Out by Legions of Teachers with Their Own Students; a 21st-Century Approach Would Abandon, or Even Reverse, That Assumption

Today's default educational model requires schools with many classrooms, each featuring a teacher working with a particular group of students. This "people-everywhere" strategy is expensive, limits the available talent pool (as some potentially effective educators may be unwilling to relocate to the communities where they are needed), and saddles schools with the challenge of attracting enough educators willing to relocate. Thus far this has not been a burdensome challenge for the premier schools districts, such as Westchester County, New York; Montgomery County, Maryland; or Fairfax County, Virginia, or for charter school operators like KIPP or Uncommon School, but it does impose a ceiling on the number of schools and districts that can rely on the people and strategies that drive success in these organizations today.

The people-everywhere approach also creates a reliance entirely on the domestic workforce, limiting schools' ability to take advantage of a wealth of highly educated, English-speaking people around the globe who may be willing to tutor our children at relatively inexpensive rates through web-based delivery systems. In accepting the assumption that each classroom should include a generic "teacher" and as small of a group of children as possible, even today's most effective charter schools are entirely dependent on their ability to attract talented, high-energy staff willing and able to work long hours at a high degree of intensity. Because of this, there is good reason to be skeptical about the scale at which these organizations can operate effectively and the likelihood that other districts can emulate their practices and success. To best make use of the skills of the teaching workforce, it is necessary to revisit the assumption that the modal form of content delivery and coaching ought to be face-to-face interaction between teacher and student.

Perhaps the most significant impact of education technology is its ability to eliminate barriers posed by geography—thus relaxing the constraints of the people-everywhere model. When experts who are not physically present use technology to tutor or facilitate instructional delivery, it creates opportunities for classrooms with large numbers of children (e.g., as in South Korea or Singapore) or where the "teacher's" role is dramatically streamlined. In either case, the challenge of finding local personnel becomes more manageable, because the technology renders locale less relevant.

Technology makes it easier for schools in different locations to communicate or share staff and makes it possible for central administrators to deliver support to campuses hundreds of miles away. One approach is offered by a model that routinely uses a roster of approved, part-time tutors to provide students with extensive assistance and support. The most intriguing models would tap into inexpensive, offshore, highly educated workers in nations like India. Washington, D.C.-based SMARTHINKING Inc., for instance, uses American and international tutors to provide intensive tutoring to students whenever they need assistance. Students can log on to the company's web site 24 hours a day, seven days a week, and work in real time with experts in various academic subjects.

Some skeptics have suggested that technology cannot be substituted for and very likely cannot meaningfully augment the key work that teachers do. This argument reveals a dismal failure to use new technologies—from the television to the personal computer to the Internet—as labor-saving devices. The problem, however, is not that technology cannot play a labor-saving role in education, but that schools have floundered under a "supplement, not supplant" mindset in which there has been fierce resistance to fully using new technologies.

Too often, rather than considering how to employ technology as a tool for rethinking teachers' work, discussions about the use of computers, web-based delivery, and instructional software focus on the power of particular applications while paying short shrift to questions of what needs to be done in policy, school organization, or the shape of teaching to take full advantage of those tools. And, as Hill points out in chapter 7, there are good reasons technology's potential has not been fully exploited: it threatens well-entrenched interest groups.

Conclusion

Ultimately, the goal is to rethink how we confront the teacher challenges of the 21st century by seizing opportunities to recruit the most promising talent and then fostering a more flexible, rewarding, and performance-focused profession. We are feeling our way toward a new and hopefully more fruitful era of teaching and learning. In getting there, we have been slowed by habits of mind, culture, and institutional inertia that imagine a future for schools and school districts that embodies today's familiar assumptions and romanticizes the most promising of today's successes. We should recognize that institutions change slowly and celebrate incremental advances—we should not allow that recognition to obscure the goal. We might wish for a simpler or neater path, but ultimately, our choice is between trusting the authorities to fix aged and troubled bureaucracies in deliberate and incremental steps or trusting in the ability of a rising generation to seize new tools, new opportunities, and human ingenuity to answer new challenges in unforeseen ways. If history teaches us anything, it is that this is really no choice at all.

NOTES

The author thanks Thomas Gift and Juliet Squire for their invaluable research and editorial assistance.

1. Per my understanding of the assigned topic, and with an eye to length, I do not address the complementary issue of leadership.

2. Just to be clear, "modal" is used here to denote cases where a vastly disproportionate group of people or programs share a particular set of characteristics.

3. For instance, a 2005 survey of those entering teaching via nontraditional routes reported that 59 percent of those older than age 50, 50 percent of those older than 40, and 46 percent of those older than 30 indicated that they would not have become teachers if an alternative route had not been available. Among those entering teaching from a professional occupation, 54 percent said they would not have done so if not for the availability of an alternative route. See National Center for Education Information (2005).

4. See, for instance, Hess (2001).

5. In a 2007 report, *Attracting the Next Generation,* the U.S. Merit Systems Protection Board, which conducts studies of the civil service for the White House and Congress, found that the average age of a new federal employee is 33. According to the survey, 28 percent of new hires claimed that the top reason they chose jobs in the federal government was "job security," trumping all other motivations. This suggests that "the old employment contract is not yet dead," the report said, and that younger generations still share a concern for traditional job benefits such as career stability, annual pay raises, vacation time, and health insurance (Steven Barr, "Entry-Level Hires Are Starting Later, Value Old-Fashioned Perks," *Washington Post,* February 13, 2008, D04).

6. With CaseNET, participants across the United States, Canada, and Norway meet in person with their local instructor each week. They access case materials on the web and then discuss these cases with colleagues at other sites using online discussion groups, videoconferencing, chat programs, electronic journals, and e-mail.

7. High Tech High, Graduate School of Education, "About HTH GSE," http://gse.hightechhigh.org/about_HTH-GSE.php; and "Programs," http://gse.high techhigh.org/programs.php.

8. See, for instance, Meek (2003).

9. See, for example, Hess and West (2006).

10. For details, see the Digest of Education Statistics at http://nces.ed.gov/programs/digest/.

11. For observers who are concerned about these distinctions introducing (or aggravating) wage-based "inequities" in K–12 schooling, I would encourage them to keep two things in mind. First, the importance and difficulty of work is a key measure, as is performance. Some exceptional paralegals do, in fact, make more than some attorneys. Second, and more broadly, compensation also relates to forgone earnings and investment in human capital. Highly trained professionals earn more, in part, because they have forgone earnings (and frequently paid tuition) in the course of their professional preparation and training. Not rewarding those investments introduces a separate set of inequities.

12. See American Medical Association (2008), 15–19.

13. Originally from American Medical Association, *Distribution of Physicians in the U.S. 1963*, vol. 1, table A; ibid., 1969, tables 1,10. For 1980 and later, see American Medical Association (2008), 404–6.

14. For a consideration of what this might look like, see Bryk and Gomez (2008).

REFERENCES

American Medical Association. 2008. *Physician Characteristics and Distribution in the U.S., 2008.* Chicago, IL: American Medical Association.

Bryk, Anthony S., and Louis M. Gomez. 2008. "Reinventing a Research and Development Capacity." In *The Future of Educational Entrepreneurship,* edited by Frederick M. Hess (181–206). Cambridge, MA: Harvard Education Press.

Gergen, Christopher, and Gregg Vanourek. 2008. "Talent Development: Looking Outside the Education Sector." In *The Future of Educational Entrepreneurship,* edited by Frederick M. Hess (23–44). Cambridge, MA: Harvard Education Press.

Hess, Frederick M. 2001. *Tear Down This Wall: The Case for a Radical Overhaul of Teacher Certification.* Washington, DC: Progressive Policy Institute.

Hess, Frederick M., and Martin R. West. 2006. "A Better Bargain: Overhauling Teacher Collective Bargaining for the 21st Century." Cambridge, MA: Program on Education Policy and Governance, Harvard University.

Kowal, Julie, Emily Ayscue Hassel, and Bryan C. Hassel. 2007. "Teacher Compensation in Charter and Public Schools: Snapshots and Lessons for District Public Schools." Washington, DC: Center for American Progress.

Levine, Arthur. 2006. *Educating School Teachers.* Washington, DC: The Education Schools Project.

Meek, Claudia. 2003. "Classroom Crisis: It's About Time." *Phi Delta Kappan* 84(8): 592–95.

Mercer Human Resource Consulting. 2007. "2007/2008 U.S. Compensation Planning Report." Louisville, KY: Mercer Consulting.

National Center for Education Information. 2005. "Profile of Alternate Route Teachers." Washington, DC: National Center for Education Information.

Podgursky, Michael J. 2003. "Personnel Policy in Traditional Public, Charter, and Private Schools." *NCSC Review* 1(1): 10–13.

Stevens, Rosemary. 1971. *American Medicine and the Public Interest.* New Haven, CT: Yale University Press.

U.S. Merit Systems Protection Board. 2007. *Attracting the Next Generation: A Look at Federal Entry-Level New Hires.* Washington, DC: U.S. Merit Systems Protection Board.

Walsh, Kate, and Sandi Jacobs. 2007. *Alternative Certification Isn't Alternative.* Washington, DC: National Council on Teacher Quality and Thomas B. Fordham Institute.

7

Consequences of Instructional Technology for Human Resource Needs in Education

Paul T. Hill

Technology is changing the way children learn, via programmed teaching toys, video games, and access to web sites. Children who have access to computers and programmed toys learn with the assistance of technology long before they enter school and continue doing so in their leisure hours throughout their lives. Homeschoolers use online materials extensively to supplement parents' teaching and for testing.

Technology is also increasingly used in formal education. Thousands of classroom teachers search the Internet for pictures, stories, and other enrichment materials as they make lesson plans, and they guide students to online resources including chat groups.[1]

Most uses of technology are supplementary. Classroom instruction, with teachers supervising defined groups of children, goes on as before. Standard brick-and-mortar schools, which the vast majority of American students attend, use technology, but in ways that reinforce rather than change traditional student and teacher roles. Though many neighborhood and charter schools use technology for testing, skills practice, enrichment, and online discussions, the vast majority of schools keep technology on the margins, as supplements to student and teacher work.

There are, however, schools that have used technology to create dramatically different teacher roles. Virtual or cyber schools offer whole courses, and in some cases entire high school curricula, online (see Tucker 2007).

K^{12}, an online, for-profit school, offers individual courses to paying students but also acts as a vendor to states and localities that want to offer online instruction for students who cannot or do not want to attend their neighborhood schools.[2]

Some district-run cyber schools, like the one in Federal Way, Washington, offer complete coursework online but also require students to meet in a brick-and-mortar facility once each week for discussions, testing, and, when necessary, remedial work. Homeschoolers rely on online resources to present key materials, leaving the parent/teacher to play supplementary roles (e.g., testing, assessment, and tutoring).

All these developments have potential implications for the human resource needs of K–12 education. New jobs are created as entrepreneurs develop new online instructional packages, homeschoolers find ways to share course materials, and cyber schools offer increasingly detailed and complete secondary school curricula. Online instruction requires materials developers, school leaders who manage enrollments and evaluate course quality, and teachers who stay in touch with students online.

Technology could also change human resource use in neighborhood schools, creating demands for administrators and teachers with different skills (and in different numbers) than such schools now use.

However, it is not yet clear how deeply or how soon technology will change custodial schools—those in which teachers lead instruction and supervise pupils in person. To date, virtual schools have attracted marginal groups of students (dropouts, students in remote areas, students who have become parents, homeschoolers). Moreover, there are important sources of resistance to any but marginal use of technology in custodial schools. This resistance will hamper the introduction of an efficient use of existing and new technologies in K–12 schools.

Teachers, their unions, and colleges and universities that now dominate teacher and administrator training face incentives that would incline them not to want technology to reduce the numbers of people employed in schools, or change teaching in ways that would render current skills obsolete. Not necessarily meaning to prevent technical innovation, state governments have created barriers to human resource change, including certification requirements, school staffing mandates, and class-size controls. State funding rules can also make it difficult for technical entrepreneurs to recover their development costs.

Despite the growing array of technology-based instructional options, changing custodial schools will take more than technology push. Nor is it likely that, by themselves, grants encouraging schools and districts to purchase software and equipment can reverse the marginalization of technology.

The barriers to full technology use—state laws and policies, shortages of people with necessary skills, and skepticism about whether the disruption associated with adoption of radically different approaches to instruction will pay off in benefits to students—will not fall by themselves. Intensive technology use could, at least for the foreseeable future, be limited to connoisseur teachers[3] and a relatively small number of cyber schools that serve specialized populations (e.g., homeschoolers, dropouts, older students, alternative school populations, children in remote areas).

Foundation and government leaders who hope technology will transform all of K–12 education need to do more than wait for change. In addition to supporting technology purchases, these leaders will need to identify human resource needs, stimulate creation of recruitment and training programs that can supply people with the skills needed to manage innovative schools, support the search for compelling evidence of the value of technology-rich instruction in custodial schools, and work for changes in key state and local policies that inhibit the adoption of technologies that enhance the efficiency (and hence may threaten incumbent employees) of public schools.

In this chapter I will do the following:

- Explore uses of instructional technology evident today in cyber schools and possible in the near future in custodial schools.
- Identify the human resource requirements of cyber schools and custodial schools that fully exploit the potential of technology.
- Suggest ways foundation and state leaders can support an expanded role for productive technologies in K–12 education via investments in human resources and research and development (R&D).
- Argue that investments in equipment, software, and human resources, though necessary, are not sufficient to ensure that district-run public schools take full use of technology. Foundations and elected officials must also work to remove deeply embedded policy barriers.

Current and Future Technology Uses

Informal uses of technology—by teachers to find enrichment materials and by students to do assignments, find materials for papers, pursue personal interests, and keep in contact with other young people—are by far the most common in education. There are no documented counts of the numbers of teachers who use the Internet to find enrichment materials, but there are some interesting examples of how it can be used. Curriki, for example, is a Wikipedia-style online sharing community for instructional materials that offers free access to materials, from single lessons to entire courses, contributed by teachers.[4] Curriki counts the numbers of teachers who download their materials but does not know how they are used.

Informal use of technology, like Curriki, will change the ways teachers and students use their time and will surely play a greater role in all forms of instruction over time. But such changes are likely to grow only gradually, as computer-literate young teachers replace older teachers for whom computers are an occasional tool and not something integral to their work.

Although these informal uses could lead to dramatic changes in the organization and human resource demands of K–12 education, they are unlikely to on their own. For example, teachers using materials from Curriki still expect to meet students every day and to work with groups of children in ways similar to their less–computer literate predecessors.

A few examples of more dramatic uses of technology, however, offer a peek into its potential to reshape K–12 schooling, both human resource demands and students' experiences. These examples include cyber schools and custodial schools with new instructional systems that use technology to reduce the demand for teachers and dramatically change teacher skill requirements.

Cyber Schools

A cyber school relies on online resources to present material, assess students' progress, and direct students toward enrichment materials. Teachers in cyber schools assess students' overall progress and individualize assignments for further online work. Teachers can also arrange to meet with a student online for individualized mentoring. But in cyber schools (and in many homeschooling situations where students spend a great deal of time online), teacher roles are the mirror image of those in conventional schools. Most instruction is delivered online or via other technical means, and teachers supplement and direct adaptations to individual needs.

It is clear that cyber schools create new roles for educators and administrators. Statewide cyber schools like those in Florida and Utah employ large numbers of teachers who check students' work and communicate with them online. (Utah's electronic high school, the nation's largest, enrolls nearly 50,000 students, one-third of the total enrolled in virtual schools nationally, and employs 100 teachers who design and oversee 150 different courses.) Other statewide cyber schools also employ teachers as developers and testers of online instructional materials. Some district-run online schools also bring students into a brick-and-mortar facility one day each week for assessment, project work, tutoring, and social interaction.

Teachers in these schools, often members of their local district's teaching corps, work very differently than their colleagues in brick-and-mortar schools. They work one on one with students via e-mail, checking in from time to time during their waking hours. Some teachers might also monitor online discussion groups, which function 24 hours a day. In Utah, cyber teachers develop their own courses, which are usually derived from courses the same teachers previously taught in conventional schools.

Teachers working for the large online vendor K[12] supervise students taking courses designed by others. Like the distance-learning modules available in higher education, cyber schools employ teachers as course designers and assessors of course deficits in light of student learning results. In some cases teachers are linked to students via e-mail or group discussion web pages. They can intervene by critiquing student statements and suggesting supplementary work, but programmed and online materials carry the burden of regular instruction. Teachers do not need classroom management skills or the ability to design daily lesson plans, but they need to understand what is available to students and how to diagnose and respond to student misunderstanding of material.

Though cyber schools have grown dramatically, they are still a niche phenomenon, providing options for children who live in remote areas, have dropped out of or refuse to attend conventional schools, or have special needs or responsibilities that make it impossible for them to attend a conventional custodial school.

Utah's cyber school serves an additional niche. Forty percent of its students are enrolled full time in conventional high schools but want to take one or more required courses online so they can attend Latter-Day Saint seminary or arts programs during the regular school day. This fact, and the low population density in all areas except the Wasatch Front, probably explains the scale of cyber schooling in Utah. The Utah Electronic High School provides something everyone—including school district leaders—wants. Because its courses are provided free, this arrangement does not cost the student or the regular school anything.[5]

Custodial Schools

The vast majority of children attend custodial schools where they must be present every day and are taught in groups by adults whose role is to impart knowledge, structure time, and provide supervision. This structure arose long ago and still makes sense for many students. Parents of younger children want schools to provide safe custody and a caring, motivating environment. Though on average secondary school students might not require as much supervision as elementary-age pupils, parents are rarely willing to dispense with adult oversight entirely. For these reasons it is unlikely that the pure cyber school model is likely to replace custodial schools that act *in loco parentis*.

However, there are many ways technology could strengthen instruction and increase student and teacher productivity in custodial schools. As Christensen (2008) notes, technology's greatest advantages are personalization and adaptability. Personalization happens in a relationship among three activities that define the instructional process:

- Primary instruction—organized presentation of materials that students are expected to learn, including examples, elaborations, and exercises intended to deepen understanding, skills, and the ability to make connections.
- Assessment—measurement of student learning, linked to primary instruction so that it is possible to assess the degree to which students have learned and understood key items of information, relationships, and skills.
- Supplementation—extra instruction, exploration, and practice intended to help students learn what they might not have mastered as a result of primary instruction.

Figure 7.1 shows the connections and feedback loops among these activities.[6] Ideally, each activity is closely coupled to every other and open to constant amendment in light of what students learn and fail to learn.

Technology can play roles in all three processes. At the maximum, all could be handled as in cyber schools by computer-based routines that assign material, make assessments, and follow decision trees to issue supplementary work. However, teachers could also do all this and provide instruction, assign projects, make available enrichment materials, lead discussions, assess student learning, and assign supplementary materials when necessary.

Figure 7.1. Connections and Feedback Loops among the Activities That Define Instruction

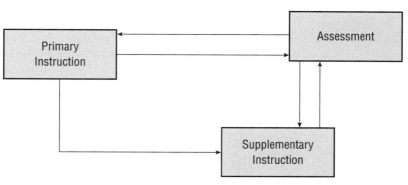

The potential for technology in mainstream custodial schools is to occupy midpoints at which teachers and technology play complementary roles. Such midpoints are being developed in individual classrooms as teachers use the Internet to find enrichment materials, and as schools adopt computer-adaptive testing that provides instant feedback on students' progress. However, in conventional schools these uses are generally limited to individual classrooms rather than used in an integrated way schoolwide. Individual teachers make their own idiosyncratic uses of technology but do not seek to innovate their way out of a job or to threaten others' jobs by finding uses of technology that might replace others' work.

Full exploitation of technology in custodial schools will require *new integrated instructional systems* that combine teacher work and technology to cover whole subjects or entire school curricula. Integrated instructional systems would fully integrate online individually paced presentation of material with teacher work (i.e., diagnosis, enrichment, and leadership of group interactions). Most material would be presented individually to students via technical means, but teachers would track students' work and intervene when needed. Consistent with the design of the instructional system, teachers could also suggest enrichment work, assign projects, lead discussions, and present materials not covered by technical means.

Fully integrated instructional systems would also combine technology with teacher work on assessment and supplementation. Teachers would need to interpret assessments, know what technology-based supplementary resources were available and what they were good for, and decide when to use supplementary resources and when to provide personal tutoring or coaching. If students are to benefit from teacher use of supplementary technologies, teachers must be clear about their instructional objectives and understand what resources are most useful as remedies to particular student performance problems. Teachers without these skills are likely to misuse technical supplements, thus wasting students' time and possibly creating confusion, or to miss opportunities for students to gain other help. In effect, effective use of supplements requires that teachers both be very good at providing conventional instruction and know how to use technology.

Integrated instructional systems would take full advantage of both technology-based delivery and in-person teacher–student and student–student interaction. Because they would transform the use of student and teacher work and reduce some teacher roles and enhance others, fully integrated instructional systems would be complex and challenging to develop and implement.

Such systems would redefine teaching. The teacher would use technical means whenever possible, reserving his own time and attention for intervention for things only he could do, such as explain an idea in a way not provided by the text or digital materials, intervene with an individual student, frame group work, or call attention to productive differences in the ways different students approach a task.

Human Resource Implications of Technology

Use of technology by individual teachers will build those teachers' repertoires of methods as well as the range of materials they can use. Collaborations among similarly disposed teachers, either within a given school or among teachers in different schools, could lead to new approaches to teaching particular subjects or even to formation of new kinds of schools. Over time, changes in individual teachers' practice could transform the pool of skills available for use in schools and lead to changes in the values and culture of the teaching profession.

Human resource changes will only go so far, however, if elected officials and district leaders avoid challenging current arrangements governing teacher employment, class size, and use of funds. Salaries, administrative expenses, and facilities use up the vast majority of dollars available for schools. Unless teachers are willing to press for changes in such arrangements, there will be strict limits to the amounts of money available for technology.

Technology use and transformation of human resource use are likely to be much more extensive in cyber schools and custodial schools based on new, fully integrated instructional systems.

Human Resources in Cyber Schools

Cyber school teachers track student progress online, use e-mail to answer queries and prod students who have become inactive, assign supplementary work to students who need or request it, monitor online student discussion groups, and administer tests via interactive online connections. Because students can log on to instructional web sites or send e-mail any time of the day or night, teachers' time at work is not limited by an 8:00-to-4:00 schedule. Teachers can "deliver" multiple courses simultaneously and need not work for eight consecutive hours each day. Some teachers keep conventional day jobs and catch up with student work at night.

Today, many cyber school instructors have been trained to work as conventional classroom teachers but have adapted their skills and methods to the online context. Utah Electronic High School teachers are all conventionally certified and have extensive classroom experience. They are selected by cyber school administrators on the basis of positive reputations for clarity and student-centeredness and are encouraged to adapt their conventional courses to online presentations. Cyber school leaders put new teachers in touch with others who have greater online experience, so there is a significant transfer of ideas and lore. But there is no formal training program. The principal has encouraged the state university from which she gained her own credentials to create training programs for cyber teachers, without success.[7] To date there are no online certification programs for cyber school teachers or administrators. Based on the experience of other sectors, these are likely to emerge if the demand for trained people grows.

Better-funded cyber schools than Utah's (e.g., K^{12}) can develop new courseware that presents materials in multiple ways and allows students to pursue issues that would, in conventional courses, be considered out of sequence. These materials can be developed by teams of teachers and software experts; unlike in Utah, where teachers develop the courses they teach, course development and teaching are often separate functions in commercial cyber schools. Teachers in commercial cyber schools are often not certified for classroom instruction. Whatever their backgrounds, cyber teachers need to be trained to pose questions for discussion groups, probe student knowledge via e-mail, interpret assessment results, and intervene to help individual students. Recruitment and training for such functions is done entirely by the cyber school operators. There is no formal training or recognizable career track.

Leaders. Cyber schools pose unique leadership challenges. Cyber school leaders are not so much principals as CEOs who raise investment capital for development of technology-based instruction, oversee R&D, and create capacities to maintain the technology and assess students online.

Kathy Webb, principal of the Utah Electronic High School, reports spending a great deal of her time finding certified teachers who want to try working online and analyzing course enrollment and withdrawal patterns. Students' failure to complete courses—for despite its huge enrollment, the school generates only as many credits as a medium size (about 700 students) high school—is a major performance problem that demands a great deal of her attention. Webb thinks her role should evolve toward that of a continuous improvement process manager, featuring constant analysis of student- and teacher-based data to assess course effectiveness, and rigorous development and testing of new courses. However, the Utah school is not funded to support these functions, and its outdated software architecture prevents access to the necessary student-, teacher-, and course-specific data.

Commercial cyber school heads provide instructional leadership via hiring and training the teachers, often numbering in the hundreds, who respond to students' e-mail, read student's papers, arrange online discussions, and analyze assessment results to determine whether a student needs special intervention. These "instructional leadership" functions are very different from ones performed in brick-and-mortar schools. Aside from recruitment and training, instructional leadership consists of sampling online teachers' transactions with students and identifying teachers who need to be further trained or replaced. To date, this knowledge is acquired on the fly or via networking and not imparted by formal training.

Signals are mixed about whether there is a shortage of individuals who can serve effectively as cyber school leaders or teachers. Proprietary cyber schools, and those that charge fees to serve homeschoolers, can make their own investments in recruitment and training. Their expansion to meet demand does not appear constrained by human resource deficits. However, district- and state-run cyber schools are much less flexibly financed and often are forced to live within certification and pay constraints set for conventional schools. These schools have little money to invest in recruitment and training, so conventional educators who work on cyber schools are forced to learn on the job. Though national and regional associations of cyber school leaders[8] are providing opportunities for information sharing, government-run cyber school leaders still struggle to master their own roles and to find appropriate teachers.

The fact that cyber schools can serve large numbers of students, and that enrollments can be scaled up without fully proportionate increases in staffing, suggests that successful cyber school leaders could draw large salaries and, in the case of proprietary schools, gain from stock ownership. These factors could attract the multiskilled leaders necessary.

In theory, cyber schools could greatly increase the student–teacher ratio and reduce costs relative to custodial schools. Good numbers are difficult to find, but it appears that Utah's cyber school operates at less than two-thirds the full-time per-pupil costs of the state's custodial schools. However, these results might reflect savings on facilities and ancillary services; many of the latter are provided by school districts and are not charged to the cyber school budget. If Utah's costs are counted on a per-credit basis, they are not particularly low, because online teachers spend a good deal of time on the large number of students who ultimately do not complete their courses

Human Resources in Technology-Rich Custodial Schools

Teachers. In custodial schools built around fully integrated instructional systems, teachers would become like physicians or other heavy users of technology. These professionals adapt their own practice as the tools improve yet retain responsibility for the student's (or the patient's) overall condition. Physicians now use imaging to observe phenomena whose existence they once could only infer and robotic devices for some surgical tasks where the human hand is less precise. These tasks allow doctors to focus on what only humans can do—assess a patient's overall health and progress, decide what interventions and medicines are needed, and judge whether standard therapies are working in a particular case. Moreover, some tasks can be accomplished far away from a patient, allowing greater expertise to be spread across a greater geographic area and greater specialization. Similarly, teachers would have to become very good diagnosticians and prescribers but avoid the temptation to "do it all," and focus on what they do best.

Like medical devices, technology-based instructional methods would need to be designed with specific teacher roles in mind and with routines for diagnosing effectiveness and identifying needs for further intervention. Teachers would need to regard themselves as users of tools and, like physicians, expect that the tools, and therefore their own complementary roles, would continue evolving.

These changes may be unappealing to some traditional teachers accustomed to providing all instruction directly. To make optimal use of technology a teacher must not only know how to combine her own work with that of digital tools but have an incentive to do it. Existing incentives—to keep everything under the teacher's control and to maximize the number of teachers employed—all work against optimal use of technology. So does the fact that use of technology requires skills unfamiliar to many teachers.

There is a boundary case between cyber- and technology-rich custodial schools. Students could spend most of their time online but meet in person periodically, either singly or in a group, with a teacher. Teachers would meet with a different group of students every day. This case would lead to new teacher roles. Aside from assessing students' work and analyzing test scores, teachers would devise enrichment activities in light of the needs of each group. Though teachers might specialize in a particular age group, so all their face-to-face groups might be studying the same material, they would be required to differentiate group needs, know what technology-based resources to use in different cases, and design remedial and enrichment activities. These roles require a great deal more breadth and adaptability than is expected of conventional classroom teachers.

Fully integrated instructional systems would bring major changes in teacher human resource use and would likely require a rethinking of the traditional teacher role in a school. Students would spend large parts of the day working through computers. The need to purchase access to technology-based materials would force schools to take advantage of the opportunity to trade in some teacher salaries for other purchases and thus employ fewer teachers. Schools would need teachers who were highly adaptive and able to identify student learning problems quickly and fashion effective remedies. Individuals who could only follow routines would not be effective in such situations, and creativity would be an important skill. Schools would be forced to compete in the labor market for individuals who could take initiative, adapt to the unexpected, and learn continuously from the effects of prior choices. These individuals are currently scarce and highly paid; schools would be forced to compete for them. But competing for these teachers would be very challenging given the way teachers are typically paid (discussed more extensively in chapters 3, 9, and 10) according to a salary schedule.

Teachers would have to prove themselves able to fill these demanding roles. Schools might hire new teachers conditionally until they demonstrated all the needed skills, and offer much lower pay at first. However, technology could allow highly skilled teachers to work with larger numbers of students and to focus their effort on tasks only they could perform. People with these skills could produce a great deal and be paid accordingly. Just as technology has proven to be a "physician extender" and allowed the most skilled and specialized surgeons to serve more people and potentially make more money, so too could technology lead to higher incomes for the most-productive teachers. School teaching forces would then be layered in ways common in private education: one layer of proven, high-ability teachers paid very well, and another layer of novice teachers, some of whom would prove themselves and become permanent.

Teacher pre-service training would be very different than it is today. Teachers would have to learn what technology-based instructional systems provide, how to assess students' progress, and how to determine whether learning deficiencies can be remedied by resources available via technology or whether direct teacher intervention is necessary. Training might be specific to particular instructional systems, so that aspiring teachers might choose whether to learn how to work in the context of an instructional system developed by a particular university, network of schools, or vendor.

In technology-rich custodial schools, as now, teachers would be socialized into their roles, both technical and social. Teachers would need to learn to value making the fullest possible use of the online assets available but, on the other hand, would need to be prepared to intervene when students failed to learn as expected. They would have to learn that unnecessarily expanding their roles might deprive students of important skills and information that the technology-based part of instruction could offer. Teachers would also need to learn (as few do now) about stimulating and motivating students and helping them see the advantage of alert use of the instructional resources available.

How much pre-service training is needed, and who should provide it, will depend on the nature of instructional systems that become available. It is hard to imagine that highly capable young college graduates would require more than a few months' intensive training before going to work as apprentice teachers.

Teacher in-service training would be focused on learning how to use new technology resources and how to diagnose and prescribe for student needs. Keeping current would become a precondition for employment, and highly paid teachers would be expected to invest in their own continuing education. Schools that wanted to adopt new technology packages or experiment with new options would have to invest in teacher training for these purposes.

To be able to afford the higher salaries of teachers able to use technology effectively, schools would probably need to pay lower salaries to teachers of subjects that did not require such a high degree of initiative and mental flexibility (e.g., physical education). Schools might also reduce the total amount of time teachers are in contact with students, expecting students to spend significant amounts of their time on computer-based individual and group work.

Leaders. School leaders' jobs are not likely to be much affected by marginal increases in use of technical add-ons for assessment and enrichment. Currently, school principals assemble resources, assess teacher interactions with students, and try to coordinate teacher work. These essential functions would not change in schools that used technology as merely a supplement to traditional teacher work.

However, for brick-and-mortar schools that fully integrate technology and teacher work, leaders will need to mix conventional and unconventional roles. Leaders must understand the instructional systems used by their schools and be able to identify teachers who are properly trained and motivated to make full use of the technology resources available. They must also keep current on R&D so they know when more effective instructional systems become available, what these cost, whether they have been demonstrated to work with students like those the school serves, and what changes in teacher training and roles they require. Leaders must constantly assess their own schools' instructional systems in light of what is available and what level of investments would be required to adopt new approaches.

School heads might face a constant burden of fundraising to make new investments in computers and software. These costs, which traditional low-tech schools face to a much lesser degree (for occasional purchases of new books and related teacher training), will be a special burden for leaders of technology-rich schools. Successful school leaders will probably need to find ways to operate at a surplus and save money for major investments whenever equipment and methods become obsolete.

Large enrollments and large pupil–teacher ratios will probably be necessary to allow technology-rich schools to maintain significant annual surpluses. Thus, a locality with large numbers of schools built around integrated instructional systems might need slightly fewer school leaders than a locality with mainly traditional schools.

At the same time, like conventional school heads, leaders of schools employing integrated instructional systems must be able to judge whether teachers are connecting with their students and helping them learn to the standard the school expects. Making such judgments will require more than the traditional classroom visits. Leaders will also need skills and tools to analyze teachers' and students' uses of technology. Leaders must also be able to identify problems in the design or implementation of the technology-based parts of instruction. Though principals in such schools will need help from the network or vendor that developed the instructional system, they will also need to know how to find and fix problems and recognize the need to adapt the instructional system to the particular needs of a group of students.

Leaders will also need entrepreneurial and political skills that will vary, as they do now, depending on whether their school is district-run or holds a charter. Leaders of these schools will need to combine the R&D and technology management skills of other cyber school leaders with the political and business management skills of charter school leaders. Such leadership jobs probably are not for neophytes or "cause" people who have great moral fervor but little technical expertise.

Thus, in schools with fully integrated instructional systems, principals will need a mixture of entrepreneurship and political skills, conventional teacher and student relationship skills, specific technical knowledge about the instructional system being used, the ability to monitor student and teacher work online, and skills in working with (and in some cases selecting) the developer of the school's instructional system.

It seems unlikely that individuals with the skills and motives necessary to run schools based on integrated instructional systems will come directly from the colleges of education that train conventional school leaders. Nor is it easy to see how standard certification or licensing can apply to leaders of such schools. In the near future, training will be a byproduct of the development of online and other technology-based

instructional methods and will need to come from developers and vendors. As such technology applications become more common, it might
be possible to evaluate alternative models and identify key traits and
sources of leadership. For the time being, however, prescriptive licensing
and certification can only interfere with innovation and performance.

Table 7.1 summarizes the likely consequences of widespread adoption
of integrated instructional systems on the skills needed by teachers and

Table 7.1. Human Resource Effects of Technology

	Demand	Salaries	Training
Cyber schools			
Teachers	Lower numbers per thousand students, different skills	Could be lower on average	Specific to cyber school model; might need to be provided by cyber school managers
Leaders	Lower numbers per thousand students, very different skill mix	Unclear on salaries, opportunities for profits, and benefits	Not yet clear
Custodial schools			
Teachers	Lower numbers, higher skills	Much greater differentiation, much higher top salaries	Profound changes in pre-service training, socialization, in-service learning
Leaders	Lower numbers, higher skills, combining school and business management, technology use	Higher salaries reflecting greater productivity	Recruits from schools, business, R&D sectors; all will require significant additional pre-service and continuing training on skills to complement those they enter with

school leaders, salary levels, and training and career structures. Whether these consequences become evident depends on how common schools using integrated instructional systems become. If technology remains a marginal factor in the work of a majority of teachers, human resource requirements will not change dramatically. The next sections ask what it will take to accelerate and deepen the use of instructional technology in custodial schools.

Table 7.1, though accurate, hides major uncertainties of two kinds. First, beneath broad generalizations, it is not clear exactly what school leaders will have to be able to do, or how difficult it will be to find people who have all the needed skills in the right combinations. Second, the numbers of people needed with particular skills depend heavily on whether the political and policy environment encourages or interferes with more widespread use of technology.

I next identify human resource unknowns and suggest how philanthropies and government leaders might anticipate them. Finally, I identify policy barriers to optimal use of technology and suggest how philanthropies and government leaders might remove them.

Resolving Unknowns about Human Resources

Aside from a few interviews with cyber school leaders, there is very little information about how heads of cyber schools use their time, what skills they must have personally, and what skills they can easily buy on the open market. We can speculate that people who develop and test purpose-built online courses need different skills than people who develop courses for conventional classrooms, but we can only speculate about what those differences are.

Similarly, we have only anecdotal information about the necessary attributes of cyber school teachers, and how teacher work and skill demands vary between commercial versus district- or state-run cyber schools.

Finally, we do not know how or where incumbent cyber school leaders and teachers acquired the skills they need, or whether those same sources could produce dramatically larger numbers of trained people.

However little we know about cyber school human resource needs, it is actually more than we know about the needs of technology-rich custodial schools. The examples that exist (e.g., San Diego's High Tech High) have not been closely studied. We know that school leaders have backgrounds in law, business, and education, but not what those leaders must do. We also know that schools like High Tech High draw teachers from combinations of traditional and nontraditional sources and that they do a good deal of training on site. But, despite the existence of some exemplars in the United States and elsewhere, we cannot readily describe the skills needed or say what recruitment or training programs would be needed.

At the current low level of technology use in schools serving mainstream students, human resource constraints are not crippling. Individual schools might struggle to find the people they need (as do poorly funded cyber schools like Utah's), but demand for skills of the kinds described above is not extreme. However, if policy and funding environments were more open to technology innovation, human resources could quickly prove a constraint to progress.

In a situation where public funding mechanisms do not support technology-based innovation, entrepreneurs have little money to invest in training. People with ideas about new instructional systems can find the costs of staff training a barrier to market entry, and (as is now the case) higher education institutions will consider big investments too risky.

Because both policy and human capital are barriers to innovation, it makes sense to attack both at the same time. Just as investments in R&D and human resources make innovative programs easier to create, implement, and prove, so too can better policies free up funds needed for R&D and human resource investments.

Attacking Human Resource Constraints

In today's policy environment philanthropic investments in human resource development are clearly needed. I would suggest seven foundation initiatives:

1. Research to identify skills used by school leaders and teachers in cyber schools and custodial schools making extensive uses of technology. This would entail surveys and job shadowing with entrepreneurs leading cyber and other technology schools, to discover roles played, skills in shortage, current sources of people, and needs for in-service training—skills that are most scarce and hardest to develop.
2. Close examination of the costs of technology-based instruction, including managerial oversight, course development and revision, and teaching, all denominated on credits awarded, not students enrolled.

3. In light of the first two initiatives, analysis of existing training sources to determine whether any could be a promising provider (e.g., colleges of education, technical training institutions, other higher education institutions, specialized educator training institutions like New Leaders for New Schools).
4. A design initiative to write performance specifications and estimate operating costs of a prototype training institution for leaders and teachers in technology-rich schools.
5. Investments in creation and testing of two to three such institutions, possibly as additions to the programs of the New Teacher Project and New Leaders for New Schools.
6. An experimental scholarship program to support training of classroom teachers, technology entrepreneurs, and persons experienced in business.
7. Continuous assessment of the performance of newly trained leaders and feedback of lessons into the design of training programs.

This investment strategy, especially the testing of alternative training institutions, will provide a reality-based grounding for the discussion of technology-based instruction. To date, it is difficult to validate anyone's claims on costs, human resource use, or results. As in other fields, it is likely that technology-based instruction works better in particular forms and circumstances than others, and that the necessary human resources and technical capacities are more available in some localities than in others. At the moment the discussion for and against this strategy is largely driven by generalized hopes and fears. A rigorous investment strategy can change this.

Foundation investments of the kind described above could prepare the way for a broader use of productive instructional technology in mainstream public and private schools. Today, despite growth of cyber schools and rapid improvements in technology applications, many political and economic factors prevent full exploitation of technology. The losers, aside from innovators who seek financial rewards, are the children in poorly staffed urban and rural schools who could benefit most from technology-based instruction in subjects that their teachers have not mastered. These potential benefits are not enough to overcome all the barriers by themselves. Government and philanthropic investments are needed in research and development to assemble, test, and press for use of new integrated instructional systems; for development of complementary human resources; and to then change the allocation and use of public funds.

Policy Barriers

Table 7.1's predictions about the number of teachers and leaders needed in custodial schools are valid only if large numbers of custodial schools adopt technology-based integrated instructional systems. However, dramatic changes in custodial schools are by no means certain.

Unlike other sectors of the economy, in which technology has increased productivity by reducing the numbers of people employed and taking fuller advantage of what only trained professionals can do, conventional schools have changed little. In fact, public schools now employ more teachers than ever before, and teacher roles have changed little. Past investments in technology have had little effect on the everyday work of public school teachers and administrators. Moreover, state funding schemes, school staffing laws, and teacher certification rules present major barriers to more integrated use of technology. Technology makes changes in teaching and learning possible, but transformation of mainstream education is by no means certain.

Use of online assessments and technical supplementation of teacher-led instruction are unlikely to change the numbers of teachers schools want to employ. Nor is teacher preparation likely to change if custodial schools keep technology at the margins. As is now the case, teachers' training will be focused on face-to-face instruction. Additional training on use of online test results (e.g., from computer adaptive tests) and supplementary materials might be added to education school curricula. In light of the small changes implied in teacher roles, it is unlikely that schools or districts will want to experiment with new ways of paying teachers; moreover, parents and teachers are likely to continue pressing for small class sizes, so the overall demand for teachers is likely to change significantly.

Why Technology Might Not "Just Spread"

An argument is just starting to develop between "inevitabilists," who think conventional schools won't be able to resist new technology applications as they become available, and "conditionalists," who think technology push alone will not be able to change conventional schools.

The most prominent inevitabilist is Clayton Christensen (2008), who argues that brick-and-mortar schools will not be able to resist increasingly ambitious uses of technology, which will ultimately create new capital–labor trade-offs that will reduce the numbers of teachers needed and reward new kinds of teaching skill. Charter and contract schools will adopt productive uses of technology, and district-run schools will be forced to follow suit.

Christensen argues by analogy from business competition. Disruptive technologies—products and processes that undermine the demand for an established brand by offering a simpler, cheaper approach that meets the needs of all but the highest-end customers—start by appealing only to customers that the established brand does not serve at all. As the disruptive technology improves, it draws more and more customers away from the established brand, thus driving its costs so high that it can no longer compete. Over time, the disruptive technology itself becomes the established brand.

To Christensen, cyber schooling fits the image of a disruptive technology. It substitutes expensive labor for less-expensive technology, and it appeals to populations that the conventional public school system neglects—homeschoolers, dropouts, students in remote areas, and so on.

This parallel between cyber schools and disruptive business products is impressive, but it misses an important point. In businesses, customers are free to switch from one product to another whenever they like and to redirect the money they have been spending immediately. This is not the case in K–12 public education. Even when students enroll in cyber schools, some or all of the money available for their instruction stays behind in the conventional schools they left. Cyber schools like Utah's receive their budgets through an entirely different process than regular public schools—they receive a direct state appropriation that is not calibrated as enrollment changes; the conventional schools pay nothing for the cyber school's services. District-run cyber schools cost less than regular district schools, but they generate the same amount of income for the district as do students in conventional schools. Thus, a district with a cyber school has more, not less, money to devote to its conventional schools. Much the same is true in most states when a cyber charter school competes for district students. The cyber school receives less than the full per-pupil amount received by the district. In effect, a district that loses students to a charter school can lose some dollars, but its average per-pupil expenditure can rise.

The conditionalists, among whom I count myself, are skeptical about tipping points and other transition models based on sectors of the economy that enjoy customer choice and free movement of funds. These conditions do not apply in public education. Public schools are insulated from the competitive financial pressures that are the active ingredient of Christensen's theory.

Though some districts make competitive responses to charter and voucher schools, none has been forced to change its basic operating model. Moreover, districts have proven highly insensitive to loss of enrollment. As Goldhaber (2008) has shown, school districts can cope with steady enrollment losses as long as normal teacher attrition is fast enough to make firings unnecessary. Threatened districts can also leverage extra funding out of their state legislatures. City school districts like Denver, San Francisco, Oakland, Seattle, Dayton, Cleveland, Salt Lake City, and Cincinnati have resisted changing their human resource strategies, labor contracts, and technology uses despite these losses.

Conditionalists think technology push is important but not enough by itself to cause fundamental change in methods used in custodial schools. Competition among cyber schools will lead to continuous improvement in their course work and other student services. But that does not mean that custodial schools that serve the majority of students will automatically use what cyber schools develop.

In public school districts, budgetary and interest group politics ensure that technology, no matter how much is purchased, will be used as a supplement to traditional teacher-delivered instruction, not as an alternative to it. School districts use computers and link students to online instruction, but usually as a supplement to traditional course work. In the vast majority of custodial schools today, technology does little to change teaching and has few implications for teacher roles, numbers, or skills. These "bolted on" technology uses often happen because legislatures or foundations provide extra funds to purchase computers, software, and Internet connections. But they have little effect on students' core in-school instructional experience or on teachers' practice.

The attraction of "bolted on" technologies for conventional public schools is precisely that they do not force change in teacher roles or staffing patterns. Technology uses do not compete for existing funds and do not affect the numbers of teachers required or the demands made on them. From the perspective of technology vendors, specially funded "bolted on" uses are perfectly acceptable. They create some demand for technology products, enough to create good businesses for some vendors, whether or not the products are used to any effect.

Given the political power of teachers' unions and teacher training institutions, and parents' skepticism about unfamiliar forms of education, it is unlikely that conventional schools will make trade-offs between teacher salaries and technology purchases unless they are forced by competition to do so.

Conventional schools are also protected from technology competition by state legislatures' insistence on segregating expenditures for current services from investments in R&D. Charters and cyber schools are already under attack because they use money for R&D and for salaries of people whom students never see—uses that opponents claim constitute waste or profiteering.

Public policy and funding mechanisms favor stasis, not innovation. State and local funding for K–12 education is now attached to particular programs, buildings, administrative structures, and teachers. Pupils are assigned to particular schools, and even if their parents decide to take them elsewhere, the sending school and the teachers it employs are protected from financial losses. Even if school leaders would like to innovate, they are not free to cash in teacher salaries or other mandated expenditures in favor of new kinds of purchases. Thus, public funding is not neutral about supporting technical innovations, but biased against them.

Conditionalists would argue that today's cyber schools are a potentially important source of innovation, but they cannot become serious competition for regular brick-and-mortar schools unless three things happen: (1) they are able to demonstrate equivalent or superior performance measured on student learning; (2) they receive public funding in ways that allow significant spending on research, development, and technical infrastructure; and (3) students are free to transfer from conventional to cyber schools for all or part of their instruction and to take with them as much money as public school districts would receive for the same instruction.

Under those circumstances,

- cyber schools could develop a track record of superior performance, at least for some children and in some subjects, drawing significant numbers of students away from conventional schools.
- custodial charter or private schools might find ways to provide quality instruction with fewer teachers, thus saving money that could be used for new courses or other experiences that students and parents value.
- parents whose children learn better via technology (having worked with computers virtually since birth) could threaten to transfer

children to cyber or charter schools, putting political pressure on school boards and state legislatures.
- parents who want children to attend custodial schools most of the time might insist that children be able to gain some credits by taking online courses at district expense.

If these conditions could be met, conventional public schools would feel the pressure of competition and be forced either to accommodate to having fewer students or transform their course offerings to draw back departing students. These changes would have human resource implications: the number of teachers employed managing instruction online would increase, and the numbers of teachers employed in conventional classroom roles would decrease.

Whether the inevitabilists or the conditionalists are right depends on more than simply whether potentially productive technology applications are available. Despite the dramatic growth in possible instructional technologies, it is still necessary to ask whether and at what rate technology developments are likely to penetrate mainstream public and private schools. In the foreseeable future (i.e., the next 10 or 15 years), will technology-based instruction remain a niche phenomenon limited to cyber schools serving marginal populations, with only marginal uses in mainstream schools? Or can competition force innovative technology-based forms of instruction into mainstream schools?

Technology-driven changes in the numbers and skills of teachers needed could be particularly attractive in localities that can no longer afford to pay large teacher corps or that cannot find people capable of providing coherent instruction in key subjects. Many rural and inner-city schools face both these problems. Charter schools, which must compete with better-funded conventional public schools, also need more cost-effective ways of providing instruction. Charter schools seeking to serve disadvantaged city students might be the point of the wedge for creative new uses of technology and teacher work.

None of these sources of pressure is particularly strong enough today, and all face significant challenges. Though in the very long run technology is likely to infiltrate all forms of education, we might be many years from the sort of the technology revolution heralded by Perelman (1993) and Christensen. In the late 20th century, other innovations—for example, filmstrips—were expected to revolutionize K–12 education. But they did not, for reasons similar to those discussed above.

Removing Policy Barriers

The potential benefits of technology are unlikely to be realized without changes in policy that allow money and pupils to migrate from conventional public schools to schools making much greater and more systematic use of digital resources.

Vouchers for all or part of a student's schooling, or even automatic transfer of funds on an equal per-credit basis from conventional to technology-based schools, would both guarantee funding for attractive technology-using schools and force conventional schools to compete by incorporating technology into their own programs.

Aside from letting money follow students, the most important thing government can do to encourage technology innovation in schools is to pay for results (e.g., courses completed or student credits generated) rather than for the costs of service delivery. Technology-based instruction should be cheaper to deliver than more conventional teacher-intensive instruction, but it requires significant expenditures in research, development, and testing. Government must pay for instruction in ways that support investment. To be as effective as it can be, technology-based instruction must be subject to continuous improvement, including occasional abandonment of methods and equipment that were once state of the art. Entities that develop truly superior modes of instruction must also be able to make profits and use them as the basis for raising investment capital or selling stock.

If government paid for education in the ways described, an active marketplace for technology-based instruction would surely arise, generating significant spending on research and development.

As I have argued elsewhere,[9] in the absence of dramatic changes in the ways government pays for education, technology development will require major government or philanthropic investments in R&D, to subsidize development and proof of highly effective new technology-based instructional systems. Under current government funding polices, school districts and groups of independent schools lack the funds to support the needed search for technology options and development and testing of prototype systems. But government, particularly the U.S. Department of Education, and foundations could sponsor it.

More flexible government funding for education could also generate private human resource investments needed to create a supply of teachers and school leaders with the requisite skills. Profitable firms know what human resources they need and can pay to find and train the right people. Colleges and universities (particularly entrepreneurial institutions like the University of Phoenix and entrepreneurial community colleges) will also fill unmet demand for training.

Conclusion

Online instruction, instant student assessment and feedback, diagnostics leading to remedial assignments, and other technology applications could transform public education. The first beneficiaries could be children in remote areas and children in disadvantaged communities where few strong teachers are available. But all students, including the elite, could benefit from technologies that carry the burden of delivering routine didactic and remedial instruction, and let human teachers do what only they can do well. Teachers and school leaders could benefit as physicians and others have done, by using technology to make their work more productive.

However, as this chapter has shown, America could soon have a two-sided education system, one that makes heavy use of technology to educate marginal students online, and another that provides conventional education for "mainstream" students and keeps technology at the margin.

Whether the benefits of technology are widespread or isolated will depend on the actions of philanthropists and government leaders, who can decide whether to wait however long it takes for the technology push to work, or to accelerate use of technology by targeted investments in human resources, R&D, and policy change.

NOTES

1. As but one example, schools throughout Idaho routinely use computer-adaptive testing, which gives teachers instant feedback on what children have learned recently and where they are falling behind.

2. For more information, see http://www.k12.com.

3. On connoisseurship, see Elmore (1996).

4. Curriki is available at http://www.curriki.org.

5. Utah's cyber high school is funded by the state separately from conventional schools, and no money is transferred when students take online courses.

6. For a more elaborate typology of potential technology uses, see Zucker (2008).

7. Personal communication with the author.

8. See, for example, the National Network of Digital schools, http://nndsonline.org.

9. See Hill (2008). See also Bryk (2007).

REFERENCES

Bryk, Anthony S. 2007. "Ruminations on Reinventing an R&D Capacity for Educational Improvement." Paper presented at the American Enterprise Institute conference "The Supply Side of School Reform and the Future of Educational Entrepreneurship," Washington, D.C., October 25.

Christensen, Clayton M. 2008. *Disrupting Class: How Disruptive Innovation Will Change the Way the World Learns.* New York: McGraw Hill.

Elmore, Richard F. 1996. "Getting to Scale with Good Educational Practice." *Harvard Educational Review* 66(1): 1–26.

Goldhaber, Dan. 2008. "Does One Size Fit All? A Framework for Thinking Through the 'Right' Size for Educational Vouchers." In *Handbook of Research on School Choice,* edited by Mark Berends, Matthew J. Springer, Dale Ballou, and Herbert J. Walberg (309–19). New York: Routledge.

Hill, Paul T. 2008. "Spending Money When It Is Not Clear What Works." *Peabody Journal of Education* 83(2): 238–58.

Perelman, Lewis J. 1993. *School's Out: A Radical New Formula for the Revitalization of America's Educational System.* New York: Avon.

Tucker, Bill. 2007. *Laboratories of Reform: Virtual High Schools and Innovation in Public Education.* Washington, DC: Education Sector.

Zucker, Andrew A. 2008. *Transforming Schools with Technology: How Smart Use of Digital Tools Helps Achieve Six Key Educational Goals.* Cambridge, MA: Harvard Education Press.

8

Teacher Deselection

Eric A. Hanushek

The national educational challenge was most forcefully articulated by the nation's governors in 1989. As they met in Charlottesville, Virginia, they felt the need of the nation to improve the performance of students—a need articulated a half decade previously in *A Nation at Risk* (National Commission on Excellence in Education 1983). And they declared that the United States should be first in the world in mathematics and science by the turn of the century (National Education Goals Panel 1991). The problem was that we had no experience to draw upon that would indicate how this could be done. In the intervening two decades we have come to recognize that improving teacher effectiveness is perhaps the only viable way to accomplish the governors' goals, but even there the policies and mechanisms are far from obvious.

This discussion provides a quantitative statement of one approach to achieving the governors' (and the nation's) goals—teacher deselection. Specifically, how much progress in student achievement could be accomplished by instituting a program of removing, or deselecting, the least-effective teachers? A variety of policies for hiring and retraining teachers have been proposed, but they have not been very successful in the aggregate, as student performance has not improved. At the same time, it is widely recognized that some teachers do a very poor job, and few people believe that the worst teachers can be transformed into good teachers. What would happen if we simply adopted policies of systematically removing the most ineffective teachers?

Motivation

At the time of *A Nation at Risk,* the United States was not performing very well on international tests, but its school attainment far exceeded that in other countries. For example, 88 percent of U.S. students had finished high school, but only 72 percent of similarly aged students in Organisation for Economic Co-operation and Development (OECD) countries had done so.[1] Further, central features of the U.S. economic system—such as openness to trade, secure property rights and a well-developed legal system, and highly adaptable labor and product markets—insulated the economy from any flaws in the development of its labor force.

The world has changed dramatically since then. Other countries, intent on emulating the successes of the U.S. economy, have dramatically increased the school attainment of their populations. Figure 8.1 shows the expected school attainment in 2003. The United States falls noticeably below the average of 17.3 years for OECD countries, a remarkable shift in two decades. On other fronts, competitors have also been moving rapidly to improve their economic conditions to match those of the United States. As a result, other nations are currently much more competitive than at the time of *A Nation at Risk*—when the nation was told in unequivocal terms that the education system was not preparing our students to be competitive in the world.

The 1989 governors' meeting called for moving U.S. students up to the top of international rankings. But they did not attempt to describe what that would mean for the United States economy. We are now able to do that.

Start by considering how far behind the leader countries U.S. students are. Figure 8.2 shows the ranking of countries based on average mathematics score on the Program for International Student Assessment (PISA) tests in 2003.[2] U.S. students perform significantly below the OECD average. The top scorer on this assessment, Hong Kong, is two-thirds of a standard deviation (sd) ahead of the average U.S. student.

An improvement of 0.5 sd would move U.S. students close to the top—roughly where Canadian students fall and slightly behind such countries as Japan and the Netherlands.

Figure 8.1. Education Expectancy, 2003

Number of years

Years	Countries
22	
	Australia (21.1)
21	
	Sweden (20.1), United Kingdom (20.4)
20	
	Iceland (19.2), Belgium and Finland (19.7)
19	
	Norway (18.2), Denmark (18.3), New Zealand (18.6)
18	
	Germany, Hungary, and Poland (17.2); Netherlands (17.3)
17	Spain (17.0)
	Ireland and Switzerland (16.7); France, Italy, and United States (16.8); Portugal (16.9)
16	Austria (16.1), Korea (16.4), Greece (16.5), Czech Republic (16.6)
	Slovak Republic (15.3)
15	
	Luxembourg (14.8)
14	
	Mexico (13.2)
13	
12	Turkey (12.0)

Source: OECD (2005), table C.1.1.

Note: Number of years includes all levels of education from primary education to adult life, under current conditions, excluding education for children under the age of 5.

Explanation: In Portugal, a 5-year-old child can expect to be enrolled during 16.9 years over his or her lifetime.

What would a 0.5 sd improvement mean for the U.S. economy? Recent analysis of how economic growth is affected by having a better-educated population shows that the implications would be dramatic (Hanushek et al. 2008). Figure 8.3, reproduced from that paper, shows how meeting the 1989 governors' pledge through improving student performance by 0.5 sd (making U.S. students perform like Canadians) would have affected current and future gross domestic product (GDP).

Figure 8.2. Mathematics Performance on PISA, 2003

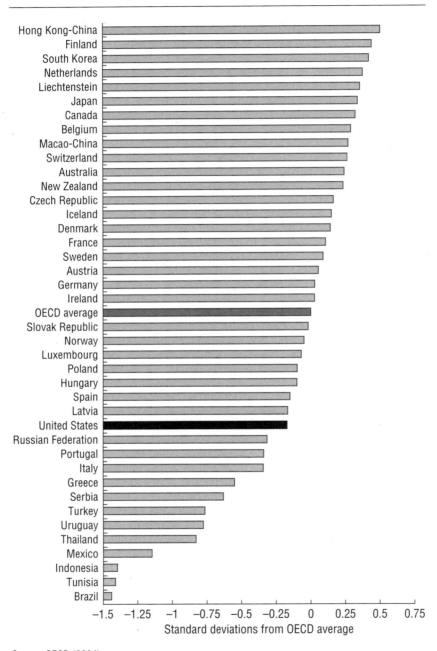

Source: OECD (2004).

Figure 8.3. Increases in GDP from Improving Student Learning
by 0.5 Standard Deviation

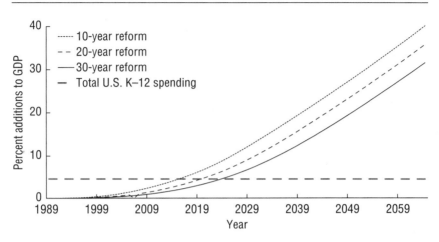

Source: Hanushek et al. (2008).

The governors' pledge of achieving dramatic improvements by 2000
is equivalent to the curve for a 10-year reform plan in figure 8.3.[3] This
curve shows that by 2015 we could have expected GDP to be more than
4.5 percent higher than will be obtained without student improvement.
(U.S. student performance according to the National Assessment of Educational Progress is essentially similar today to what it was at the time of
the governors' summit meeting.) *This addition to GDP is equivalent to the
proportionate expenditure for our 2008 national spending levels on K–12
education.* Or, seen differently, GDP in 2008 was more than $14 trillion;
that makes the 2 percent increase in 2008 GDP predicted by the 10-year
reform plan curve equivalent to about $300 billion.

If the reforms had been begun at the time of the governors' meeting
but had stretched out for a longer period before they obtained their
results, the improvements in GDP would take commensurately longer
but would still have powerful implications for the U.S. economy. For
example, a reform plan that took 30 years to bring students up to the
level of Canada's students would cover K–12 expenditures with the
added economic outcome by 2024.

The final motivating element for this chapter is that so little was
accomplished by the policies that followed the governors' meeting or the

previous call to action from *A Nation at Risk.* A variety of approaches have been pursued (Peterson 2003). These have involved expanding resources in many directions, including increasing real per-pupil spending by more than 50 percent since 1983. Yet U.S. performance has remained unchanged since 1970, when we started obtaining evidence from the National Assessment of Educational Progress (figure 8.4).

The aggregate picture is consistent with a variety of other studies indicating that resources alone have not yielded any systematic returns in student performance (Hanushek 2003). The character of reform efforts—at least until recently—can largely be described as "same operations with greater intensity." Thus, pupil–teacher ratios and class size have fallen dramatically, teacher experience has increased, and teacher graduate degrees have grown steadily, but these have not translated into higher student achievement. On top of these resources, a variety of programs have been introduced with limited aggregate success. The experience of the past several decades vividly illustrates the importance of true reform—that is, reform that actually improves student achievement.

The recent movement to a standards- and accountability-based reform may change this picture, but the evidence is yet to be clear. In any event, the discussion below is consistent with accountability and with the No

Figure 8.4. National Assessment of Educational Progress Scores for U.S. 17-Year-Olds, 1969–99

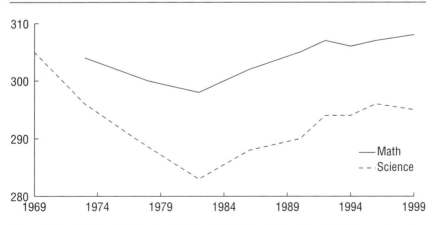

Source: National Center for Education Statistics, "The Nation's Report Card," http://nces.ed.gov/NATIONSREPORTCARD/.

Child Left Behind Act in the sense that it describes a set of teacher policies that could lead to the results sought under the accountability systems.

The implication of the discussion is that improvements in student outcomes—if they occur—would be expected to have powerful effects. At the same time, doing more of the policies we have been pursuing is unlikely to lead to the performance improvements we seek.

The Power of Effective Teachers

A first question—given the previous section—is whether or not achieving such gains could be feasible with realistic reform strategies. Recent research suggests that it is feasible but that it will take redirection of efforts.

One explanation for past failure is simply that we have not directed sufficient attention to teacher quality and teacher effectiveness. By many accounts, the quality of teachers is the key element to improving student performance. But the research evidence suggests that many of the policies that have been pursued have not been very productive. Specifically, although the policies may have led to changes in measured aspects of teachers, they have not improved the quality of teachers as measured by student performance.[4]

Rivkin, Hanushek, and Kain (2005) estimated differences in teacher quality on an output basis. Specifically, the concern is identifying good and bad teachers on the basis of their performance in obtaining gains in student achievement. An important element of that work is distinguishing the effects of teachers from the selection of schools by teachers and students, and the matching of teachers and students in the classroom. In particular, highly motivated parents search out schools that they think are good, and they attempt to place their children in classrooms where they think the teacher is particularly able (Hanushek, Kain, and Rivkin 2004a). Teachers follow a similar selection process (Hanushek, Kain, and Rivkin 2004b, 2004c). Thus, from an analytical viewpoint, it is difficult to sort out the quality of the teacher from the quality of the students in her classroom. The analysis of teacher performance in Rivkin and colleagues (2005) goes to great lengths to avoid contamination from any such selection and matching of kids and teachers.[5] In the end, that analysis estimates that the differences in annual achievement growth between an average and a good teacher in math are at least 0.11 sd of student achievement.[6]

Before going on, it is useful to put this lower-bound estimate of the variation in quality into perspective. By this quality estimate, if a student had a good teacher as opposed to an average teacher for four or five years in a row, the increased learning would be sufficient to close entirely the average gap between a typical low-income student receiving a free or reduced-price lunch and the average student who is not receiving free or reduced-price lunches.

Reasonable estimates of annual achievement growth (which are used throughout the following calculations) are actually higher than this lower bound—specifically, 0.20 to 0.30 sd. These larger estimates reflect likely differences in teacher quality among schools; the fact that the similarly conservative estimates for reading as opposed to math are 0.15 sd instead of 0.11 sd; and a series of other factors that bias the previously discussed estimate downwards (Rivkin et al. 2005).

The implications of these differences are dramatic. Let us consider the impact of low-quality, or ineffective, teachers on student achievement. If the average learning growth each academic year is one grade-level equivalent, the estimates of variations in teacher quality indicate that the least effective 5 percent of teachers see gains that are at best two-thirds of a grade-level equivalent. The bottom 1 percent of teachers achieve no more than one-half of a grade-level equivalent in annual gains. (These calculations assume that 1.0 sd of teacher quality—moving from the center of the distribution to the 84th percentile—is 0.20 sd of student achievement; using a calculation of 0.30 sd makes these conclusions even more grim.)

External validation of these estimates comes from Hanushek (1992). The calculations of the low end of the distribution developed here are similar to the effects I previously calculated, but those estimates also suggest that the most conservative estimates may be too optimistic. The prior analysis of the range in performance in Gary, Indiana, schools suggests that the bottom 5 percent are no better than one-half grade-level equivalent in growth per academic year. These direct estimates of teacher differences are actually close to the higher estimates of teacher quality (0.30 sd of student achievement).

Clearly, the students with ineffective teachers are harmed. Students can probably recover from a single year of having a bottom 5 percent teacher, but a few years might lead to lasting problems—ones that dog students for a lifetime.

Let's look at the aggregate impact of the bottommost teachers. Figure 8.5 plots the impact on overall student learning of "deselecting"

Figure 8.5. Alternative Estimates of How Removing Ineffective Teachers Affects Student Achievement

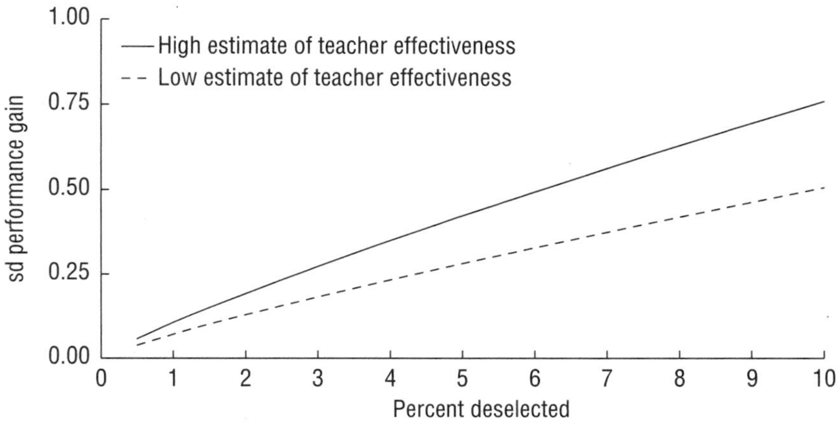

Source: Author's calculations.

(i.e., moving out of the classroom) varying proportions of ineffective teachers. As an example, consider what would happen to average student performance if we could eliminate the least effective 5 percent of teachers from the distribution. The estimates of the impact of teachers on student achievement indicate that these students would on average gain 0.28–0.42 sd of performance.

These estimates of the importance of teacher quality permit some calculations of what would be required to yield the reforms discussed earlier. To begin with, consider what magnitude of teacher deselection might yield an improvement in student performance to the level of Canada (0.5 sd of student achievement). Figure 8.4 shows that eliminating the least effective 6–10 percent of teachers would bring student achievement up by 0.5 sd.

The estimates given here need to be put into the policy context. Consider a school with 30 typical teachers. These estimates suggest that eliminating the bottom two or three could boost student achievement up to the level of Canada's students.

This kind of policy is very consistent with the McKinsey evaluation of the policies found in high-performing school systems around the world (Barber and Mourshed 2007). Their evaluation suggests that the best school systems do not allow ineffective teachers to remain in the classroom for long.[7] These conclusions are also consistent with more-local evidence, such as that for New York City, in Kane, Rockoff, and Staiger (2006) and the related policy prescriptions in Gordon, Kane, and Staiger (2006).

Policies of making active decisions on retention and tenure are, of course, alien to the current school system. A number of states currently have laws and regulations that lead to tenure decisions as early as two years into a teacher's career, with the mode being just three years (National Association of State Boards of Education 1997; National Council on Teacher Quality 2007). On top of that, the teacher evaluation process as typically seen is very cursory (Toch and Rothman 2008). Nonetheless, these are inconsistent with providing a quality education to all students, because some students must necessarily be relegated to these ineffective, and damaging, teachers.

The idea is that policies be put in place to identify the most-ineffective teachers and to move them out of the classroom. Developing such policies, negotiating them with teachers, and implementing them in the schools clearly take time. Thus, the reform paths in figure 8.3 sketch alternative time patterns for implementation that are likely to be relevant. Moreover, the prior calculations of impacts on student performance assume that all students have the higher-quality teachers for their entire K–12 school career. Thus, even if implemented immediately, it would take more than 10 years for any cohort to go through all schooling at the higher level. On the other hand, as noted earlier, had these policies been put in place as called for by the governors in 1989, we would today be reaping the unmistakable gains from the improved working of our national economy. Had we actually started with effective reform in 1983 as called for in *A Nation at Risk,* the gains to GDP would be sufficient to cover all of our expenditure on K–12 schooling.

It should also be noted that obtaining the gains from this policy presumes that the bottom 5 to 10 percent of the current distribution of teachers is eliminated *permanently.* To eliminate them permanently, it is necessary either to have a continuing deselection process or to upgrade the overall level of teacher effectiveness in the future. In particular, if hiring follows the current pattern, the new hires would have the same 5 to 10 percent of ineffective teachers, who would have to be deselected on an ongoing basis.

In the long run, it would probably be superior, however, to develop systems that upgrade the overall effectiveness of teachers. The difficulty is that past approaches have not proved very successful, at least as judged from student outcomes. A variety of approaches have received widespread attention—induction programs, mentoring, professional development, and the like—and have been the focus of much policy interest. The interest in them has come substantially from the fact that they take current teachers and transform them into a more effective group. There has been little reason to believe that, at least as currently operated, these approaches are effective.[8] If they work, they could ensure that the pool of teachers is improved (and that continual deselection would not be needed). The key is "if they work."

The full impact of setting up a deselection process is difficult to project in the abstract. First, one might expect that a policy that selected and rewarded teachers on ability would alter who entered teaching. While more-risk-adverse people may shy away from teaching, a different group that wishes to be judged and evaluated by their contributions may come forward (see Hoxby and Leigh 2004). Moreover, there could be efficiency gains, for example, through improved professional development. (For more on the potential of using professional development to upgrade the quality of the teacher workforce, see chapter 11.) Today, when performance is not effectively evaluated, teachers and principals give little attention to the usefulness or quality of any professional development programs—and the result appears to be little average gains from the existing professional development. But, if classroom effectiveness mattered, teachers might be more engaged in selecting and participating in good professional development. Nonetheless, these ramifications are speculative, since we have little experience with how the market might operate with the introduction of true performance evaluation.

Cost Considerations

Policy initiatives on teacher deselection clearly alter the nature of the teaching contract. Today, few teachers are involuntarily separated from teaching, particularly after the probationary period. (In fact, some of the nation's worst performers—California and the District of Columbia—require decisions on tenure at the end of a two-year probationary period, making it very difficult to evaluate teachers.) As a result, the possibility of deselecting ineffective teachers increases the risk of employment as a teacher. Attempting to change the quality of the overall distribution may require increased compensation to attract new and more-effective teachers who are also willing to take the added employment risk.

Analyzing reform policies directly by cost is not feasible because we know very little about the supply function for teacher quality. While there has been some work on the cost of hiring teachers with different characteristics (such as experience or advanced degrees), these characteristics do not readily translate into teacher quality (Hanushek and Rivkin 2004).

There are alternative ways to consider the costs of any policies aimed at improving the teaching force. Perhaps the simplest is to use the prior calculations of the benefits to provide an estimate of the upper bound on the feasible expenditure for new policies (based on the simple idea that costs must be less than benefits in order for the policy to be efficient).

Much of the current discussion of teacher quality is centered on statements about the overall level of salaries. It seems clear that teacher salaries have slipped relative to alternative earnings of college-educated workers, particularly for women (Hanushek and Rivkin 1997, 2004, 2006).[9] For various reasons, however, this does not give much policy guidance for the current discussions. In simplest terms, we do not know how teacher quality responds to different levels of salaries (Hanushek and Rivkin 2004). Moreover, policies that simply raised salaries across the board (even if advanced as a way to increase the attractiveness of the profession) would almost certainly slow any reform adjustments, because they would lower teacher turnover and make it more difficult to improve quality through new hiring.

Nonetheless, the aggregate growth numbers suggest that the annual growth dividend from an effective reform plan would cover most conceivable program costs over a relatively short period. Figure 8.3 shows an increase in GDP from improved student performance with varying implementation periods. Consider what real reform does. The "Canadian" improvement plan previously described that reached its goal in 20 years would already yield GDP that was 1.6 percent higher at the end of the 20-year implementation period. In other words, a 20-year reform plan begun in 2010 would yield this higher 1.6 percent level of GDP in 2030. In the U.S. economy in 2005, 1.6 percent amounted to $200 billion. That year, total spending on instructional salaries and benefits was just $233 billion (Snyder, Dillow, and Hoffman 2008, table 169). In other words, the increased GDP through improved student achievement would almost immediately cover current teacher salaries and benefits fully—suggesting considerable room to pay for better teachers and to compensate for the higher risk of entering teaching.

The conclusion of the cost considerations is simple. The benefits from quality improvements are very large. Thus, they can support large and expansive incentive programs *if the programs work.* U.S. schools have, in fact, expanded in a variety of ways over the past four decades—real expenditures per pupil in 2000 are more than three times those in 1960. It is just that these past programs have not led to significant improvements in student performance. Put another way, the benefits do not justify all types of expenditure. They do justify many conceivable programs if they can be shown to be effective.

Conclusion

Many discussions of teacher policies concentrate almost entirely on upgrading the effectiveness of current teachers. This involves special induction programs, mentoring, ongoing professional development, and the like. Past approaches have not proved to be generally effective. Good programs have been difficult to implement on a broad scale, as seen through the results in student achievement.

This analysis points to the large cost of allowing the most-ineffective teachers to remain in the classroom. The bottom end of the teacher force is harming students. Allowing ineffective teachers to remain in the classroom is dragging down the nation.

If the bottom end of the teacher distribution cannot be improved through various remediation efforts, the alternative is more active deselection policies that trim off the least effective teachers. What stands out from an analysis of the impact of teachers on achievement is that relatively modest changes in the bottom end of the distribution have enormous implications for the nation.

It is unclear why we permit a small group of teachers to do such large damage. The majority of teachers are effective. They are able to compete with teachers virtually anywhere else in the world. Yet these effective teachers are lumped in with a small group of completely ineffective teachers, who are permitted to continue damaging students' educational experiences.

The problem does not seem to be with identifying these ineffective teachers. Some evidence shows that principals are able to identify these bottom performers.[10] It is almost certainly true that there is even broader recognition of the bottom teachers—by principals, other teachers, and parents. Instead, it seems simply to be a lack of will to act on readily available information.

NOTES

1. These numbers reflect comparisons for the population born from 1961 to 1970; see OECD (2007), table A1.2a. These statistics, however, overstate the U.S. situation because they include GED completion in the calculation of high school success. This problem, along with other measurement issues, is discussed in Heckman and LaFontaine (forthcoming).

2. PISA is testing conducted by the OECD on international students for all OECD countries and a selection of other countries that voluntarily participate. PISA tests a random sample of 15-year-olds in each country. These tests, now on a three-year cycle, assess math, science, and reading skills. Alternative assessments at different ages are provided by TIMSS (Trends in International Mathematics and Science Study). The TIMSS shows some different comparative results, with U.S. 4th-graders doing relatively well, U.S. middle-school students in the middle, and U.S. 12th-graders in the bottom rankings.

3. For a description of how these calculations are accomplished, see Hanushek and Woessmann (2008, 2009).

4. For a review of existing literature, see Hanushek and Rivkin (2004, 2006). They describe various attempts to estimate the impact of teacher quality on student achievement.

5. To do this, they concentrate entirely on differences among teachers within a given school to avoid the potential impact of parental choice of schools. Moreover, they employ a strategy that compares grade-level performance across different cohorts of students, so the matching of students to specific teachers in a grade can be circumvented. As such, it is very much a lower-bound estimate on differences in teacher quality.

6. For this calculation, a teacher at the mean of the quality distribution is compared to a teacher 1.0 sd higher in the quality distribution (84th percentile), labeled a "good teacher." The estimate of 0.11 comes from the mathematics estimates. The comparable estimates for reading are 0.15 (revised estimates). These results relate specifically to grades 4–7. It is plausible that the distribution of teacher quality at high school is even more dispersed than shown here.

7. The method of ensuring good teachers, according to this study, does depend on the country. Some of the highest performing countries do this largely at entry by selecting from the very top of the pool of college graduates. Others have particularly effective professional development programs. For the United States, moving to selection of teachers from the top of the new graduate distribution appears infeasible. See Hanushek and Rivkin (2004).

8. Recent high-quality studies cast doubt on arguments about professional judgment and about various teacher induction and mentoring programs. See Garet et al. (2008) and Isenberg et al. (2009).

9. There is a current debate about how salaries of teachers compare to those in different professions; see Podgursky (2003) and Allegretto, Corcoran, and Mishel (2004).

10. See, for example, Armor et al. (1976), Jacob and Lefgren (2006), or Murnane (1975).

REFERENCES

Allegretto, Sylvia A., Sean P. Corcoran, and Lawrence Mishel. 2004. *How Does Teacher Pay Compare? Methodological Challenges and Answers.* Washington, DC: Economic Policy Institute.

Armor, David J., Patricia Conry-Oseguera, Millicent Cox, Niceima King, Lorraine McDonnell, Anthony Pascal, Edward Pauly, and Gail Zellman. 1976. *Analysis of the School Preferred Reading Program in Selected Los Angeles Minority Schools.* Santa Monica, CA: RAND Corporation.

Barber, Michael, and Mona Mourshed. 2007. *How the World's Best-Performing School Systems Come Out on Top.* McKinsey and Company.

Garet, Michael S., Stephanie Cronen, Marian Eaton, Anja Kurki, Meredith Ludwig, Wehmah Jones, Kazuaki Uekawa, et al. 2008. *The Impact of Two Professional Development Interventions on Early Reading Instruction and Achievement.* NCEE 2008-4030. Washington, DC: U.S. Department of Education, Institute of Education Sciences, National Center for Education Evaluation and Regional Assistance.

Gordon, Robert, Thomas J. Kane, and Douglas O. Staiger. 2006. "Identifying Effective Teachers Using Performance on the Job." Hamilton Project discussion paper. Washington, DC: The Brookings Institution.

Hanushek, Eric A. 1992. "The Trade-Off between Child Quantity and Quality." *Journal of Political Economy* 100(1): 84–117.

———. 2003. "The Importance of School Quality." In *Our Schools and Our Future: Are We Still at Risk?* edited by Paul E. Peterson (141–73). Stanford, CA: Hoover Institution Press.

Hanushek, Eric A., and Steven G. Rivkin. 1997. "Understanding the Twentieth-Century Growth in U.S. School Spending." *Journal of Human Resources* 32(1): 35–68.

———. 2004. "How to Improve the Supply of High-Quality Teachers." In *Brookings Papers on Education Policy 2004,* edited by Diane Ravitch (7–25). Washington, DC: Brookings Institution Press.

———. 2006. "Teacher Quality." In *Handbook of the Economics of Education,* edited by Eric Hanushek and Finis Welch (1051–78). Amsterdam: Elsevier.

Hanushek, Eric A., and Ludger Woessmann. 2008. "The Role of Cognitive Skills in Economic Development." *Journal of Economic Literature* 46(3): 607–68.

———. 2009. "Do Better Schools Lead to More Growth? Cognitive Skills, Economic Outcomes, and Causation." Working Paper 14633. Cambridge, MA: National Bureau of Economic Research.

Hanushek, Eric A., John F. Kain, and Steve G. Rivkin. 2004a. "Disruption versus Tiebout Improvement: The Costs and Benefits of Switching Schools." *Journal of Public Economics* 88(9/10): 1721–46.

———. 2004b. "The Revolving Door." *Education Next* 4(1): 77–82.

———. 2004c. "Why Public Schools Lose Teachers." *Journal of Human Resources* 39(2): 326–54.

Hanushek, Eric A., Dean T. Jamison, Eliot A. Jamison, and Ludger Woessmann. 2008. "Education and Economic Growth: It's Not Just Going to School but Learning Something While There That Matters." *Education Next* 8(2): 62–70.

Heckman, James J., and Paul A. LaFontaine. Forthcoming. "The American High School Graduation Rate: Trends and Levels." *Review of Economics and Statistics.*

Hoxby, Caroline M., and Andrew Leigh. 2004. "Pulled Away or Pushed Out? Explaining the Decline of Teacher Aptitude in the United States." *American Economic Review* 94(2): 236–40.

Isenberg, Eric, Steven Glazerman, Martha Bleeker, Amy Johnson, Julieta Lugo-Gil, Mary Grider, Sarah Dolfin, and Edward Britton. 2009. *Impacts of Comprehensive Teacher Induction: Results From the Second Year of a Randomized Controlled Study.* NCEE 2009-4072. Washington, DC: U.S. Department of Education, Institute of Education Sciences, National Center for Education Evaluation and Regional Assistance.

Jacob, Brian A., and Lars Lefgren. 2006. "When Principals Rate Teachers." *Education Next* 6(2): 59–69.

Kane, Thomas J., Jonah E. Rockoff, and Douglas O. Staiger. 2006. "What Does Certification Tell Us about Teacher Effectiveness? Evidence from New York City." Working Paper 12155. Cambridge, MA: National Bureau of Economic Research.

Murnane, Richard J. 1975. *The Impact of School Resources on the Learning of Inner-City Children.* Cambridge, MA: Ballinger Publishing Company.

National Association of State Boards of Education. 1997. "Teacher Tenure." *Policy Updates* 5(3): 1.

National Commission on Excellence in Education. 1983. *A Nation at Risk: The Imperative for Educational Reform.* Washington, DC: U.S. Government Printing Office.

National Council on Teacher Quality. 2007. *State Teacher Policy Yearbook, 2007.* Washington, DC: National Council on Teacher Quality.

National Education Goals Panel. 1991. *Building a Nation of Learners, 1991.* Washington, DC: National Education Goals Panel.

OECD. See Organisation for Economic Co-operation and Development.

Organisation for Economic Co-operation and Development (OECD). 2004. *Learning for Tomorrow's World: First Results from PISA 2003.* Paris: OECD.

———. 2005. *Education at a Glance: OECD Indicators 2005.* Paris: OECD.

———. 2007. *Education at a Glance: OECD Indicators 2007.* Paris: OECD.

Peterson, Paul E., ed. 2003. *Our Schools and Our Future: Are We Still at Risk?* Stanford, CA: Hoover Institution Press.

Podgursky, Michael J. 2003. "Fringe Benefits." *Education Next* 3(3): 71–76.

Rivkin, Steven G., Eric A. Hanushek, and John F. Kain. 2005. "Teachers, Schools, and Academic Achievement." *Econometrica* 73(2): 417–58.

Snyder, Thomas D., Sally A. Dillow, and Charlene M. Hoffman. 2008. *Digest of Education Statistics 2007.* NCES 2008-022. Washington, DC: U.S. Department of Education, Institute of Education Sciences, National Center for Education Statistics.

Toch, Thomas, and Robert Rothman. 2008. "Rush to Judgment: Teacher Evaluation in Public Education." Washington, DC: Education Sector.

9

The Estimation of Teacher Value Added as a Determinant of Performance Pay

Steven G. Rivkin

Lagging test scores in comparison to the rest of the world, large and persistent racial and income achievement gaps, and a widespread need for remedial coursework at the postsecondary level provide evidence that the traditional public school structure fails to give many students a high quality of education. Although some argue that inadequate resources are the primary source of low performance—and resources are limited in many schools—both the empirical evidence and evaluations of parents and community leaders indicate that problems extend far beyond resource deficiencies.

Recent emphasis on accountability and incentives in public education as tools to improve the quality of instruction has led to the adoption of new outcome-based policies designed to raise achievement and reward effective teaching. No clear consensus has emerged on the effects of accountability and pay-for-performance reforms, though work by Lavy (2002, 2004) suggests that performance-based bonuses induce greater effort and higher student achievement. Over the long run, the success of such reforms hinges on a number of factors, but the validity of the teacher effectiveness (a term I use interchangeably with quality) measures is one of the most important. Unless the quality estimates are accepted as informative and fair, opposition will remain strong. Moreover, inaccurate or inadequate quality measures and poorly designed pay-for-performance programs will introduce adverse incentives to teach narrowly to test content, concentrate on only a fraction of the students, forgo important non-tested outcomes, or elicit frustration and distrust in response to reward structures with systemic flaws.[1]

As the research literature discusses in great detail, the determinants of both student and teacher choices and the allocation of students among classrooms complicate efforts to estimate the contributions of teachers to learning that can be used in a pay-for-performance program. The imprecision of tests as measures of achievement, failure of some examinations to measure differences in skills, and limited focus of the tests on a few subjects further complicate efforts to rank teachers and schools on the basis of the quality of instruction.

The availability of longitudinal data with repeated test score observations for individual students potentially makes possible statistical methods that mitigate many impediments to the implementation of a pay-for-performance program based on precise and consistent estimation of teacher value added. This chapter discusses the benefits of longitudinal data in the context of a cumulative model of learning. It highlights both the ways in which panel data methods can lessen problems introduced by student, teacher, and principal choices and remaining issues that threaten the validity of pay-for-performance programs based on estimates of teacher value added.

The next section discusses estimating teacher quality in the context of a cumulative framework of learning similar to that developed by Todd and Wolpin (2003). Emphasis is placed on difficulties introduced by the purposeful sorting of students and teachers among communities, schools, and classrooms and by test measurement error. Such sorting may serve the educational goals of schools, and parents certainly have the freedom to pursue family objectives, but these numerous decisions complicate efforts to measure the contributions of teachers and schools. I then highlight the benefits of longitudinal data in trying to mitigate biases introduced by test error and confounding factors, and the advantages and disadvantages of specific empirical approaches to the estimation of teacher fixed effects. Finally, I discuss the plusses and minuses of specific pay-for-performance structures in the context of the previous discussion.

Cumulative Model of Learning

Estimating teacher quality is complicated by the fact that the sum of teacher, peer, family, and community influences affects achievement. This section begins by describing a model of learning that highlights some key statistical problems (referred to as specification issues) that arise from the nonrandom sorting of students and teachers into classrooms and schools.[2] Then it describes some potentially troubling test measurement issues that may introduce problems in pay-for-performance systems.

Model of Learning

The estimation of teacher value added to achievement requires a framework for separating the contribution of the current teacher from the contributions of families, schools, and peers and the cumulative influences of all previous influences. Administrative data typically contain limited student information, including special needs, subsidized lunch status, Title I eligibility, race, ethnicity, and gender, as well as information about school programs and resources. Such information can control for differences among students, peers, and schools in statistical efforts to identify the quality of teachers as measured by their value added to student achievement. However, the limited information available in virtually all data systems—in combination with the fact that important family influences and determinants of school quality are difficult to quantify—raises concerns that these simple methods that control only for differences in recorded, easily quantifiable variables may produce misleading estimates of teacher quality.

If students and teachers were randomly assigned to schools, such data limitations would have less serious consequences, but this is not the way students and teachers are matched to one another in classrooms. For example, it is likely that families with greater commitment to schooling tend to select higher-quality schools with more-effective teachers. One can account for this, in part, with readily observable differences in family income and other characteristics, but families differ in more subtle ways that are also important to the learning process and may not be entirely captured by the types of variables that statisticians have at hand (e.g., turning off the television when it is time to do homework). Similarly, evidence has shown that, on average, teachers tend to favor schools with higher-achieving students. As a result, there is a match between certain types of students and teachers that makes it difficult from a statistical standpoint to disentangle differences in teacher quality from both differences in school quality and differences in student skills.

Administrator decisions about school and classroom placement generate additional complications. Principals may systematically place higher-achieving students with higher-quality teachers, potentially leading to overestimates of the true variation in quality. Alternatively, principals may place more-difficult-to-educate students with the better teachers, producing the opposite effect.

Finally, estimates of teacher quality will be sensitive to test measurement error, particularly the type that is common within a classroom or school. There is certainly some randomness in how well a teacher covers the specific vocabulary words or mathematics problems that happen to appear on a test in a given year and in the number of children who miss lessons leading up to the test. The precision of estimates of teacher value added also tends to be higher the larger the number of students taught, as there is substantial student-specific test error caused by errors filling out forms, familiarity with specific questions, mental and physical condition on test day, and other factors.

Given the possible inadequacy of available controls for student, family, school, and peer differences and influences of test measurement error, analyses must use more-advanced statistical methods to produce fair measures of teacher value added. Fortunately, the availability of longitudinal data that provide repeated test score observations as students progress through school make possible a number of methods that can mitigate the influences of confounding factors.

Benefits of Longitudinal Data

The proliferation of state administrative education data, largely in response to the requirements of the No Child Left Behind Act, facilitates the use of value added and other panel data methods to isolate the contributions of teachers and schools to achievement. Of particular value is the availability of pre-test scores (e.g., a test score from the immediate prior grade), which enable researchers to control for initial achievement differences. Much research applies such a value-added approach to large survey datasets or smaller school- or state-level data, and the pre-test scores almost certainly mitigate the aforementioned selection-induced problems. Concerns remain, however, that unobserved student and school differences can still confound estimates of program effects or other school and teacher parameters even given the use of models that estimate growth from pre- to post-test.

The availability of three or more observations per student and multiple teachers per grade in state administrative datasets enables the use of student or school fixed effects to account for unobserved differences in both students and schools that remain following the inclusion of prior-year test scores.[3] These fixed effects account for all time-invariant differences because the comparisons that are made are either within student (in the case of student fixed effects) or within school (in the case of school fixed effects). One can think about the student fixed effects models as identifying the impact of teachers based on whether students who have certain teachers tend to deviate from their longitudinal trajectory of performance. The inclusion of school fixed effects alters the nature of the teacher comparisons, because teacher quality is estimated relative to the performance of colleagues in the same school rather than relative to all other teachers in the sample. This has substantial implications for the distribution of any pay-for-performance rewards.

Accounting for Student Skills

A key issue is the appropriate method for controlling for differences in student skills. Families, communities, teachers, and schools exert cumulative effects that establish the knowledge base at the start of a grade and therefore affect the level of achievement at the end of the grade. One would expect these effects to depreciate over time (i.e., the effects of a good 3rd-grade teacher on 3rd-grade test scores are larger than the effects of a good 3rd-grade teacher on 5th-grade test scores).

The availability of repeated test scores facilitates the use of value-added models that explicitly control for skill differences at the start of a grade by including test scores for the prior grade or grades into the statistical model. Those scores are assumed to capture skill differences resulting from the sum of prior influences up through and including experiences in the previous grade (grade $g-1$).

Such models also control at least partially for achievement differences due to differences in student "ability," that is, student differences caused by the panoply of early childhood influences, prenatal care, heredity, and other factors—factors often jointly referred to simply as innate ability—that have a continuing influence on learning. As ability affects the quantity of skills and knowledge acquired at each grade, the effects of ability on achievement may increase with age. The exact formulation and interpretation depend, however, on the measurement of achievement. If measured with vertically integrated tests (i.e., those explicitly designed for cross-grade comparisons), differences in ability would contribute to a widening of the skill distribution over time.[4] On the other hand, if skills were measured by location in the distribution, as is the case with standardized or percentile scores, ability-induced differences in relative achievement would remain constant over time.[5]

Only the contemporaneous effect of "ability" is not directly accounted for by lagged achievement. There is little reason to believe that, conditional on prior score, schools or parents act to alter teacher characteristics in ways that are related systematically to this unobserved ability. Nonetheless, the lagged score may fail to account for *all* potentially confounding factors.

If the lagged score does not adequately control for ability differences, it is possible to make use of the multiple observations per student and add a student fixed effect to the model, which essentially estimates teacher value by comparing a student's performance with different teachers. As I will discuss, this approach means that teachers are ranked through comparisons with other teachers of the same students, a different type of ranking than that produced by specifications without student fixed effects. This may be inappropriate in an annual pay-for-performance scheme designed to produce teacher rankings for that year alone. Nonetheless, the student fixed effects can mitigate problems introduced by unobserved student differences not accounted for by prior achievement measures.

Accounting for School Quality Differences

A second key issue in estimating teacher value added is the separation of the effects of teacher quality from the effects of other school factors on achievement. Smaller classes, better facilities, better-run schools, and more paraprofessionals can lead to higher test scores, and it is important that the effects of these and other variables do not confound the estimates of teacher value added. Although such characteristics as class size can be included in a statistical model, it is often difficult to account for all relevant school factors with available data.

Fortunately, the panel data make possible the use of statistical methods that account for fixed differences in schools in much the same way that student fixed effects account for differences in student ability. As long as there are test score observations for multiple teachers in a school, school fixed effects can be included in a model. In this case, teacher quality would be estimated relative to other teachers in the same school. An additional advantage of this approach is that it eliminates potential biases introduced by the purposeful sorting of students among schools without having to include student fixed effects.

The inclusion of school fixed effects would alter the nature of the teacher comparisons by eliminating any average differences in teacher quality among schools along with any other differences in school factors. If there is extensive sorting by quality, some high-quality teachers would receive modest or even negative value-added estimates if they happen to teach in a school with other high-quality teachers. On the other hand, some ineffective teachers would receive positive estimates if their peers tended to be even less effective.

Because school quality may vary over time and by grade, it is important to account for any such systematic differences. As long as there are multiple teachers in a grade, one can include school-by-grade-by-year fixed effects and account for all factors specific to a school, grade, and year, including curriculum, facilities, professional development, and leadership. In this case, teachers would be compared only with other teachers in the same grade and school.

Accounting for Differences in Peers

As is the case with student, family, and school influences, the available information is unlikely to account for all differences in peers that affect achievement. A variable such as peer average achievement on prior year tests will not capture all aspects of students that can affect classroom environment. Prior achievement is obviously not a perfect predictor of behavior, parental support for students, or other factors.

Unlike the other factors, however, it is not possible to account for unobserved peer factors with classroom fixed effects, because this would make it impossible to estimate teacher value added. Consequently, it is necessary to rely on available information to control for the confounding influences of peer composition.

If students were randomly assigned to classes, unobserved variation in classroom composition would sometimes help some teachers and hurt others, thereby moving estimates of their value-added estimates away from their true values. But the randomness of the teacher–student match means that this movement would not be systematic, implying that we would not expect the teacher-effectiveness estimates for particular teachers (or types of teachers) to consistently over- or understate true teacher contributions to student learning. However, it is likely that the student and teacher characteristics are taken into consideration in the division of students among classrooms. For example, a principal who wishes to equalize school quality within a grade will tend to mix more-difficult-to-educate students with better teachers, whereas a principal who responds to the most persistent parents or who desires to please better teachers will tend to do the opposite. In the former situation, estimates of teacher value added will systematically understate the performance of better teachers and the differences in teacher quality, and in the latter case, the estimates will systematically overstate the effectiveness of better teachers and the variation in performance.

Test Measurement Issues

A crucial consideration in empirical analysis of student achievement is that achievement as measured by a given standardized test rarely, if ever, equates with the conceptual notion of achievement as the level of mastery of a particular academic area. First, all tests measure knowledge with error—that is, the score reflects a combination of knowledge, luck, and whether the test-taker had a good day. Second, tests inevitably emphasize some skills more than others.

Curricular differences among schools and districts influence subject-matter time allocation and therefore knowledge of particular material. Consequently, test coverage affects examination results, and even unbiased estimates of teacher value added in a specific subject do not necessarily index quality, in the sense that some teachers might take far more time than others to produce a given amount of learning. Moreover, the reward structure might induce a misallocation of resources away from other valued subjects. Finally, teachers may alter their classroom practices in ways that increase test scores but not the comprehension of important concepts (e.g., by devoting time to practicing tests).

Even ignoring issues of test coverage and teacher responses, the imprecision of tests leads to errors in the rankings of teachers. A particular striking example provided by Kane and Staiger (2001) is the much higher probability that quality estimates for schools or teachers with small numbers of students will fall in the tails of the distribution, meaning that reward or punishment systems that focus on those at the top or bottom are likely to disproportionately reward or punish low-enrollment schools or teachers. In general, it is important to recognize that such noise exists when using the tests in high-stakes situations, attempt to learn about the reliability of tests, and take steps to mitigate the magnitude of the error where possible.

Improvements in the test instrument can reduce the influence of measurement error, and the use of multiple years of teacher observations in longitudinal data can increase the signal-to-noise ratio of the value-added estimates. Bayesian shrinkage estimators of the type described by Kane and Staiger (2001), a focus on the persistent component of multiple years of value-added estimates for a teacher (see Hanushek et al. 2004), or other methods can mitigate the influence of this type of test error.

Estimating teacher value added from multiple years of job performance has drawbacks, which may offset the benefits of reducing the error variance. Two of the drawbacks seem particularly germane. First, new teachers have only one year of data. Second, teacher performance varies from year to year. Novice teachers learn on the job and tend to improve in their first few years. More generally, experimentation with new curricula; personal events, such as marriage, divorce, childbirth, and so on; and other factors contribute to differences over time in the quality of instruction. Having to carry along the failures of prior years would certainly dampen the incentive to excel provided by a performance pay scheme.

Value Added and Policy

The myriad factors that influence cognitive growth over extended periods, the purposeful sorting of families and teachers into schools and classrooms, and the imperfections of tests as measures of knowledge complicate efforts to estimate teacher fixed effects and rank teachers according to quality of instruction. Yet despite potential shortcomings, value-added analysis can provide valuable information for evaluating and compensating teachers. The availability of longitudinal data with repeated test scores for students enables the use of methods that overcome many of the impediments to the production of unbiased estimates of teacher effectiveness.

Here are three key questions for those designing pay-for-performance systems:

1. Should teachers be compared to all others in the district or just to those in the same school?

2. Should school average value added or teacher value added determine the amount of any performance pay?
3. Should multiple years of information be used if the data are available?

For the first question, there are clear trade-offs to consider in the
determination of the appropriate pool for teacher comparisons. Available data will not account for all differences in school quality that affect
achievement, meaning that estimated value-added differences among
teachers will conflate true differences in teacher quality with variation in
school factors. This will tend to favor better teachers to the extent that
better-run schools with higher resources attract more-effective teachers.
Yet the magnitude of any such school effects may not be large, given both
the available controls for school differences and measures of prior student achievement that account for persistent differences in school quality that span the grade spectrum.

Of course a sole focus on teacher performance differences within a
school circumvents this problem entirely. Lavy (2004) finds that pay for
performance raises academic achievement relative to achievement in
schools where teachers do not compete for bonuses. Notice that this result
is not driven by the fact that student performance is higher for teachers
who receive awards. Rather, average performance is higher in schools
where teachers compete for rewards.

By comparing teachers only with colleagues in the same school, some
teachers who do not receive rewards because of competition with very
effective colleagues will outperform some who do receive awards because
of weaker competition in their school. On one hand, this may generate
complaints that the system is unfair. On the other hand, it also provides
an incentive for effective teachers to work in schools with teaching staff
that is not particularly strong. Note that the inclusion of student fixed
effects also limits the comparisons in less transparent ways and is probably not appropriate in a pay-for-performance plan.

An important consideration is the impact of test coverage on estimates of teacher value added. Tests focused on basic skills or results
measured by passage rates may penalize teachers of high achievers, for
whom a majority of students could pass the exam on September 1 and
who focus class time on material not covered on the tests. As long as
the initial achievement levels were adequately accounted for, even
highly effective teachers of such students would appear to do little to
raise scores (a failure to account for such preexisting differences would

unfairly penalize teachers with less-well-prepared students and not iso-late the effectiveness of the current teacher). This may confer advan-tages on teachers with less-well-prepared students. A potential solution is to compare teachers with others teaching similar students on prior test score information contained in longitudinal data. One could even construct a measure such as that proposed by Hanushek and colleagues (2004) in which each student's gain would be compared with all others in the district or state with similar prior year achievement, and teacher estimates of value added would thus capture effectiveness given the initial distribution of students.

The second question is whether to focus on outcomes at the teacher or school level. On the one hand, rewarding individual teachers pro-vides very strong work incentives and does not benefit teachers who free ride on the efforts of others. On the other hand, individual rewards may discourage collaboration and teamwork and may conflict with other objectives of the schools. Of particular importance is the match-ing process used to assign students to classrooms, and the use of teacher test score results to assign grades or performance pay might compro-mise the ability of principals to balance the educational experience for students. It would be unfair to assign more-difficult students to the more-effective teachers if doing so would reduce the compensation of those teachers.

School average value added overall or in a single grade provides an alter-native approach for providing incentives to teachers and school adminis-trators. This does not impede principals from considering the strengths and weaknesses of teachers and students in the classroom allocation process. In addition, this provides a strong set of incentives for school lead-ers, who make the key personnel, spending, and curricular decisions and should be held accountable for their actions. Lavy (2002) finds that such incentives increase student achievement. A potential drawback of school-level incentives is the possibility that estimates of school value added com-bine the true effectiveness of schools with unobserved differences in student and family characteristics, thereby advantaging schools in higher-socioeconomic-status communities. In addition, the same test-coverage issues for the ranking of teachers also potentially influence the ranking of schools, meaning that it is important to account for both differences among students and the complications introduced by the test instruments.

Finally, the question of whether to use multiple years of data if they are available pits the desire to use as much information as possible to increase the precision of the estimates against the recognition that the quality of instruction varies from year to year for all teachers and that differences in data availability would require different measurement methods for different teachers. Perhaps most important, multiyear schemes weaken teacher incentives: low value added in prior years regardless of actual performance could almost rule out a reward in the current year regardless of effort, performance, and outcomes, and high measured value added in prior years may also dampen work incentives by conveying such an advantage to these teachers.

NOTES

1. Neal and Schanzenbach (2007) and Reback (2008) examine the effects of tests on the distribution of achievement. Kane and Staiger (2001) illustrate how poorly designed reward structures can introduce adverse incentives and raise serious concerns about the fairness of a pay-for-performance scheme.

2. This discussion draws from Hanushek and Rivkin (2008).

3. Models may also use school-by-grade-by-year fixed effects.

4. In testing terms, this implies having vertically scaled scores that indicate skills and knowledge over time and not just measurement relative to a grade-specific norm for learning.

5. Note that, more generally, this holds for all time-invariant factors. Consequently, if the distributions of school quality and family and community environments were fixed through grade g, current characteristics would fully describe schooling, family, and community histories. Of course, this would rule out the use of panel estimators and make it virtually impossible to identify the causal effects of specific factors. Moreover, the notion of constant school and teacher quality contradicts evidence of substantial student mobility and within-school variation over time in the quality of education.

REFERENCES

Hanushek, Eric A., and Steven G. Rivkin. 2008. "Harming the Best: How Schools Affect the Black–White Achievement Gap." Working Paper 14211. Cambridge, MA: National Bureau of Economic Research.

Hanushek, Eric A., John F. Kain, Daniel M. O'Brien, and Steven G. Rivkin. 2004. "The Market for Teacher Quality." Working Paper 11154. Cambridge, MA: National Bureau of Economic Research.

Kane, Thomas J., and Douglas O. Staiger. 2001. "Improving School Accountability Measures." Working Paper 8156. Cambridge, MA: National Bureau of Economic Research.

Lavy, Victor. 2002. "Evaluating the Effect of Teachers' Group Performance Incentives on Pupil Achievement." *Journal of Political Economy* 110(6): 1286–1317.

————. 2004. "Performance Pay and Teachers' Effort, Productivity, and Grading Ethics." Working Paper 10622. Cambridge, MA: National Bureau of Economic Research.

Neal, Derek, and Diane Whitmore Schanzenbach. 2007. "Left Behind by Design: Proficiency Counts and Test-Based Accountability." Working Paper 13293. Cambridge, MA: National Bureau of Economic Research.

Reback, Randall. 2008. "Teaching to the Rating: School Accountability and the Distribution of Student Achievement." *Journal of Public Economics* 92(5/6): 1394–1415.

Todd, Petra E., and Kenneth I. Wolpin. 2003. "On the Specification and Estimation of the Production Function for Cognitive Achievement." *Economic Journal* 113(485): F3–F33.

10

Modernizing Teacher Retirement Benefit Systems

Robert M. Costrell, Richard W. Johnson,
and Michael J. Podgursky

Retirement benefits have long been an important part of teacher pay. Traditionally, current compensation, received primarily as salaries, has been considered relatively low for teachers, but pension benefits have been relatively high. Almost every state in the nation offers its public school teachers traditional defined-benefit (DB) pension plans that provide lifetime payments beginning at retirement. Benefits increase with years of service and, in some states, long-tenured teachers can receive annual retirement payments that approach the salaries they earned while they were teaching.[1] Because many states allow teachers to retire as early as age 55, some retirees collect benefits for more than 30 years, sometimes longer than their careers. Additionally, many states and districts offer teachers retiree health benefits, providing stand-alone health insurance until retirees qualify for Medicare at age 65 and then supplementing Medicare benefits.

The structure of retirement systems in K–12 public schools may not serve all teachers, school districts, or taxpayers well. For young teachers, these pension systems can impose sharp penalties for mobility, because the benefits in teacher pension systems are heavily back-loaded (i.e., they accrue to teachers disproportionately in the last years of teaching). They also severely penalize teachers who remain in the profession for a full career but who change pension systems. A 55-year-old educator who taught for 30 years in Missouri, for example, would have at least twice the pension wealth of an otherwise identical educator who split her career equally between Missouri and another state. As workers change jobs more frequently, retirement plans that reward long tenures and punish mobility are becoming less attractive to mobile young professionals. In this respect, the retirement systems in education place the teacher labor market at a relative disadvantage when it comes to attracting new, but mobile, talent into the teaching profession.

In addition, many teacher pension plans create strong financial incentives for teachers to retire as soon as they qualify for benefits, often at relatively young ages (Costrell and Podgursky 2009b). The incentives pull teachers to certain retirement ages and push them out past those ages. However, in today's workforce, many professionals prefer to delay retirement as the average lifespan lengthens. In fact, many schools prefer to retain their most experienced teachers, especially as the supply of younger teachers shrinks. Thus, some districts hire back retired teachers, effectively paying some teachers salaries and pensions simultaneously (this is often referred to as "double dipping").

The private sector has largely abandoned the types of retirement benefits that public school teachers receive. Whereas nearly all public school districts participate in traditional DB pension plans, most private-sector employers have switched to defined-contribution (DC) retirement plans that function essentially as tax-advantaged retirement savings accounts and do not introduce strong incentives to retire at any particular age. Between 1980 and 2007, the share of private-sector workers participating in DB plans fell from 39 to 20 percent, while the share that participated in DC plans but not DB plans increased from 8 to 31 percent (Bureau of Labor Statistics 2007b; Pension and Welfare Benefits Administration 2001–2002). Many private-sector employers that maintain DB plans have converted to "cash balance" pension plans. These plans permit pension wealth to grow more smoothly over a worker's career and thus do not impose such strong penalties on worker mobility (Johnson and Uccello 2004). Additionally, most private-sector employers have stopped providing retiree health insurance (Johnson 2007).

This chapter examines teacher retirement systems. It describes how teacher pensions work and the unusual retirement incentives they create. It discusses some of the unintended consequences of the retirement system, including many districts' tendencies to rehire pensioners and the increased utilization of retiree health benefits. It also describes recent trends in private-sector retirement benefits and discusses how cash balance plans that combine features of DC plans and traditional DB plans might better meet the needs of teachers, school districts, and taxpayers. Finally, we consider whether higher education's experience with financial services company TIAA-CREF provides useful lessons.

Background

The "Standards Revolution" by states in the 1990s and the federal No Child Left Behind Act (NCLB) represent a commitment by states and the federal government to improve school performance and close achievement gaps. Several studies have found that teacher quality is the most important school-based determinant of student performance and that teacher effectiveness varies widely within school districts and even within schools (e.g., Aaronson, Barrow, and Sander 2007; Rivkin, Hanushek, and Kain 2004). This implies that consistent student exposure to high-quality teachers over several years could in principle significantly raise achievement and narrow gaps. Education policy discussions have thus increasingly begun to focus on ways to recruit, retain, and motivate the most effective teachers. This, in turn, has led some to critically examine the structure of teacher compensation.

A focus on teacher compensation is important for two reasons. First, and most obvious, most of the K–12 education dollars go to teacher compensation. During the 2005–06 school year, the most recent year for which national data are available, U.S. public schools spent $187 billion on salaries and $59 billion on benefits for instructional personnel, accounting for 55 percent of total current expenditures for K–12 and 90 percent of instructional expenditures.[2]

Retirement benefits figure prominently in this spending, and their share of education costs appears to be rising. Figure 10.1 presents quarterly data from the Bureau of Labor Statistics (BLS) on employer contributions for retirement as a percentage of salaries for public K–12 teachers and comparable data for private-sector "management, professional, and related" employees.[3] Note that benefits as a percentage of salary for teachers are currently more than twice that of the private-sector professionals.[4] While the contribution rate has been relatively flat for private-sector professionals, it has increased for public school teachers.

Differences in Social Security coverage explain part of the observed gap between employer retirement contributions for private professionals and

Figure 10.1. Employer Contributions for Retirement Benefits: Public School Teachers and Private-Sector Managers and Professionals, 2004–09

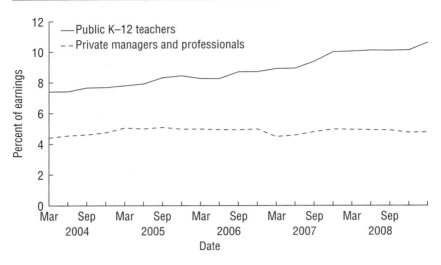

Sources: BLS (2009); Costrell and Podgursky (2009c, abridged).

public school teachers. Both employers and employees in covered jobs are subject to a 6.2 percent Social Security payroll tax on salaries up to a certain limit each year ($106,800 in 2009). These costs are not included in figure 10.1. However, only 73 percent of public school teachers are covered by Social Security, according to the BLS (2008, table 5). The BLS data provide information on employer contributions for Social Security for private-sector professionals but not for public K–12 teachers. We can estimate Social Security contributions for school teachers assuming that 73 percent of public school teacher compensation is subject to the full tax, and the remaining 27 percent is not subject to any tax. Figure 10.2 presents an estimate of the combined employer contributions to employer-sponsored retirement plans and Social Security for the two occupational groups. The gap is narrower under this broader measure of retirement contributions, but the pattern is similar to the one in figure 10.1. The employer contribution rate for private-sector professionals has been relatively flat over the past four years and well below that for teachers. The rate for public school teachers shows a clear upward trend.

Figure 10.2. Employer Contributions for Retirement Benefits and Social Security: Public School Teachers and Private-Sector Managers and Professionals, 2004–09

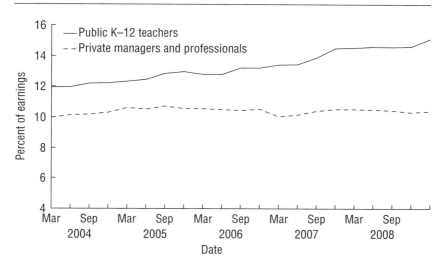

Sources: BLS (2009); authors' estimate of teacher Social Security; Costrell and Podgursky (2009c, abridged).

The reasons for this divergence cannot be determined from this data source, but the trend is consistent with known patterns of benefit enhancements for teacher pensions (at least until recently) and the private-sector shift toward less-costly defined-contribution plans. Looking forward, there is good reason to believe the divergence will continue to expand as the drop in DB pension fund values since 2007 and the corresponding rise in unfunded liabilities lead to an increase in states' required contributions to amortize those liabilities.

In addition to the size of these expenditures, a second reason for focusing on the structure of compensation is that a substantial labor economics literature, including studies of teachers, shows that employer compensation policies affect the behavior and composition of the workforce (Baron and Kreps 1999). Most teacher research has focused on current teacher compensation. However, a small but growing literature has begun to focus on the labor market effects of teacher retirement benefit systems (Brown 2009; Costrell and McGee 2009; Costrell and Podgursky

2009b; Furgeson, Strauss, and Vogt 2006; Hansen 2008, 2009; Hansen, Podgursky, and Costrell 2009; Ni, Podgursky, and Ehlert 2009).

How Teacher Pensions Work

Public school teachers are almost universally covered by traditional DB pension systems. We call these plans traditional because they were once the norm in both the public and private sectors. However, as noted above, the majority of private-sector employers have now moved to 401(k)-type systems or fundamentally restructured their DB plans. In the traditional DB plan that continues to dominate in the public sector, the employer agrees to provide a regular pension check to employees when they retire and to continue payments until they die.

Most DB teacher pension plans require both teachers and employers to contribute a portion of their salaries each year to a pension trust fund. On average, these contributions are smaller for teachers who are part of the Social Security system and larger for those who are not covered. In the systems covered by Social Security, teachers contribute an average of 4.5 percent to the pension fund and their employers contribute 9.0 percent, for a total of 13.5 percent. This is in addition to the 12.4 percent combined employer and employee contribution to the Social Security system. By contrast, in noncovered systems, teachers contribute an average of 7.8 percent and employers contribute 11.1 percent, for a total of 18.9 percent. The overall average for the joint contribution is 15.6 percent (Costrell and Podgursky 2009b).

Once a teacher is vested in the plan, which usually takes 5 or 10 years, she qualifies for a pension upon reaching a certain age or length of service. Eligibility rules vary, but they typically allow teachers to draw a pension before age 65 (often at age 55), especially if teachers have been working since their early or mid-20s. Teachers who leave the system before vesting do not receive any pension benefits, although the plan typically returns their contributions, with interest.

Benefits at retirement are determined by a formula of the following type:

$$\text{Annual Benefit} = (\text{years of service}) \times (\text{final average salary}) \times m.$$

"Final average salary" averages the highest few years (typically three) of salary, and m is a percentage known as the multiplier. In Missouri, for example, teachers earn 2.5 percent of final average salary for each year of teaching service. Thus, a teacher with 30 years of service would earn 75 percent of the final average salary. If the final average salary were $60,000, she would receive $45,000 per year, payable for life. Teachers who separate from service before reaching the plan's retirement age receive deferred benefits that begin once they reach retirement age. Their benefits are frozen until that time and are based on the salary they received when they left, unadjusted for inflation. Once the pension draw begins, it typically increases with inflation, although the exact adjustment varies from state to state.

Table 10.1 summarizes some of the key features of DB pension plans in six states. Although not randomly chosen, they are indicative of many teacher pension plans and cover roughly 29 percent of public school teachers. The National Education Association and other groups publish more complete tables, showing similar state variation in pension parameters (NEA 2004).[5] Although these comparative tables provide useful information about the individual parts of the pension system, they do not tell us about the overall incentive effects of the system on teacher behavior. To appreciate the powerful incentive effects of retirement systems and make informative comparisons across states, we use the data in table 10.1 to examine how teachers accumulate pension wealth with each year of employment.

Work and Retirement Incentives

The present value of the future stream of benefits that a teacher receives from a DB plan can be estimated with standard actuarial methods.[6] This pension wealth equals the 401(k) account balance that would generate the same stream of payments if it were converted into a life annuity. The changes in pension wealth over a teacher's career capture the incentives embedded in the pension system.

Figure 10.3 depicts pension wealth, in inflation-adjusted dollars, for a 25-year-old female entrant to the Ohio teaching force, at various separation ages. Clearly, the accumulation of pension wealth is not smooth and steady but rises with fits and starts after age 49, due to eligibility rules for early retirement and the like. During her first 24 years in the classroom, this teacher accumulates roughly $300,000 in pension wealth. Over the next six years, however, she accumulates more than $100,000 *each year,*

Table 10.1. Key Features of Selected State Defined-Benefit Teacher Pension Plans

	Ohio	Arkansas	California	Massachusetts	Missouri	Texas
In Social Security	No	Yes	No	No	No	Varies by district
Vesting (years)	5	5	5	10	5	5
Retirement eligibility (normal or early)	**Normal:** Age = 65 or YOS = 30 **Early:** Age = 60 or Age = 55 if YOS = 25	**Normal:** Age = 60 or YOS = 28 **Early:** YOS = 25	Age = 55 or Age = 50 if YOS = 30	Age = 55 or YOS = 20	**Normal:** Age = 60 or YOS = 30 or Age + YOS = 80 **Early:** Age = 55 or YOS = 25	**Normal:** Age = 65 or Age + YOS = 80 and Age = 60 **Early:** Age = 55 or YOS = 30 or Age + YOS = 80
Contribution rates	District 14%[a] Teacher 10%	Employer 14% Teacher 6%[b]	Employer 8.25% State 4.52%[c] Teacher 8%[d]	State 15.6%[e] Teacher 11%[f]	District 12.5% Teacher 12.5%	State 7.98%[g] Teacher 6.9%[h]
Multiplier (percent per year of service)	Years 1–30: 2.2% Year 31 only: 2.5%	2.15% + $900	Linear segments: 1.1% at age 50 1.4% at age 55	Linear: 0.1% at age 41 to 2.5% at age 65	**Normal, or Age = 55:** 2.5%, YOS ≤ 30, 2.55%, YOS > 30	2.3%

					Early, 25 ≤ YOS < 30:
	Year 32 only: 2.6% For YOS ≥ 35, add 9% to total		2.0% at age 60 2.4% at age 63 For YOS ≥ 30, add 0.2%, to max of 2.4%	For YOS ≥ 30, add 2% × (YOS − 24) Max replacement = 80%	2.2%, YOS = 25 rising linearly to 2.4%, YOS = 29
COLA formula	3%, simple	3%, simple	2%, simple, plus floor of 80% initial purchasing power	3%, simple, on first $12,000	Consumer price index, compound, up to 1.80 maximum factor	None in statute (periodic, retroactive)

Sources: National Association of State Retirement Administrators, "Public Fund Survey," http://www.publicfundsurvey.org/www/publicfundsurvey/actuarialfundinglevels.asp; individual state Comprehensive Annual Financial Reports and pension handbooks, and Costrell and Podgursky (2009b).

YOS = years of service; COLA = cost-of-living adjustment

a. Includes 1% for retiree health insurance.

b. Contributory members only. Average is 4.8%, including non-contributory.

c. Includes 2.5% for 80% floor on initial purchasing power (see the COLA formula row).

d. Includes 2% for a supplemental defined contribution plan.

e. Calculated from fiscal year 2007 state appropriation.

f. For all teachers hired since 2000.

g. Includes 1.4% for retiree health insurance.

h. Includes 0.5% for retiree health insurance.

Figure 10.3. Pension Wealth, Ohio

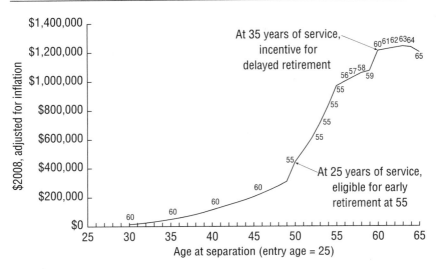

Sources: Costrell and Podgursky (2007, 2009b).

Notes: Age of first pension draw indicated. Assumptions: 2007–08 Columbus salary grid, inflating at 2.5%; interest rate = 5%; female 2004 CDC Mortality Table.

approaching the million-dollar mark by age 55. Pension wealth peaks in her early 60s and then declines.

This chart and related calculations clearly indicate the penalties for teacher mobility in a DB pension system. A teacher who separates after 15 years of teaching at age 40 has an annuity that she can begin collecting at age 60. The present value of this annuity is worth about 13 percent of her cumulative earnings—that is, the joint contribution that would be required to fund the annuity. By contrast, if she were to work for 30 years, she could begin collecting her annuity immediately at age 55, and the present value of that annuity would be worth about 38 percent of her cumulative earnings. Thus, the 15-year teacher's pension wealth is only one-third the magnitude of the 30-year teacher's, even controlling for cumulative earnings.[7]

The next set of charts provides a useful tool for analyzing retirement incentives. These charts show the change in pension wealth from an additional year of work, expressed as a percentage of salary, for Ohio and the five other states. They measure *deferred* income earned each year (net of interest earned on prior pension wealth and net of employee contributions), received on top of a teacher's *current* salary. Behind each of these spiky charts is a pension wealth accrual chart such as figure 10.3.

Consider Ohio, depicted in figure 10.4. A teacher who enters service at age 25 accrues virtually no pension wealth during her early years on the job, net of her own contribution. Her deferred income gradually rises to 23 percent of annual earnings in her 24th year (at age 49). Her 25th year of experience yields a sudden large increase in pension wealth, as it jumps by 164 percent of her annual earnings. Each of the next five years also yields deferred income that approaches or exceeds her current income. The growth in pension wealth drops off sharply over the next few years, turning negative for ages 56–59, followed by another sharp spike at age 60 (when she has accumulated 35 years of experience), equal to 132 percent of her salary that year. Beyond age 60, pension wealth shrinks once again, and at an accelerating rate.

Figure 10.4. Deferred Income per Year as a Percentage of Salary, Ohio: Net Addition to Pension Wealth from an Additional Year of Teaching

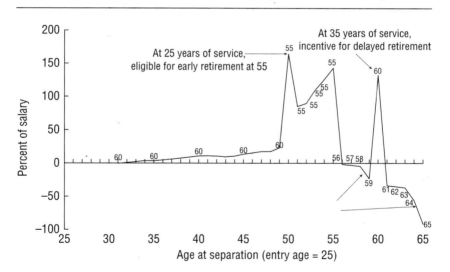

Sources: Costrell and Podgursky (2007, 2009b).

Notes: Age of first pension draw indicated. Assumptions: 2007–08 Columbus salary grid, inflating at 2.5%; interest rate = 5%; female 2004 CDC Mortality Table. Addition to pension wealth is net of interest on prior wealth and net of employee contribution.

Changes in pension wealth for our representative teachers in Arkansas, Missouri, California, Massachusetts, and Texas are depicted in figures 10.5 through 10.9. Note that four of these five states have spikes at age 50 or 55 (25 or 30 years of service), of varying magnitude. Arkansas's spike is unusually large (465 percent), indicating that a teacher in that state earns almost five times her salary in additional pension wealth during her 25th year of service. Missouri's spike at the 25th year of service is not as large, but there are large accruals for other years as well. The spikes in California and Massachusetts are smaller, and they were only created relatively recently by formula enhancements in 1999 and 2001. In the case of Texas, shown in figure 3.9, there used to be spikes at ages 45 and 52, but recent changes have eliminated them for new teachers.

What causes pension wealth to spike in certain years and then decline? At first blush one might expect pension wealth accrual to be fairly steady over time. After all, both the teacher and employer contribute the same percentage of pay year after year. But that is the wrong way to think

Figure 10.5. Deferred Income per Year as a Percentage of Salary, Arkansas: Net Addition to Pension Wealth from an Additional Year of Teaching

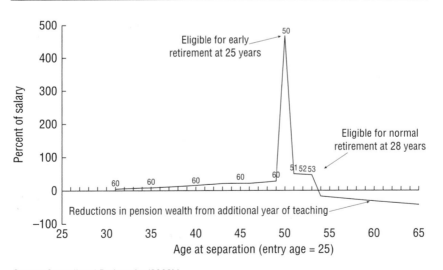

Source: Costrell and Podgursky (2009b).

Notes: Age of first pension draw indicated. Assumptions: 2007–08 Little Rock salary grid, inflating at 2.5%; interest rate = 5%; female 2004 CDC Mortality Table. Addition to pension wealth is net of interest on prior wealth and net of employee contribution.

Figure 10.6. Deferred Income per Year as a Percentage of Salary, Missouri: Net Addition to Pension Wealth from an Additional Year of Teaching

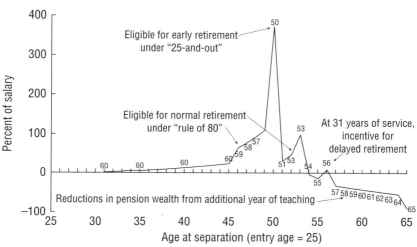

Source: Costrell and Podgursky (2009b).

Notes: Age of first pension draw indicated. Assumptions: 2007–08 Jefferson City salary grid, inflating at 2.5%; interest rate = 5%; female 2004 CDC Mortality Table. Addition to pension wealth is net of interest on prior wealth and net of employee contribution.

about teacher pension wealth, because it is only loosely tied to contributions. Fluctuations in pension wealth are driven primarily by changes in annual annuity payments (as determined by the benefit formula given above) and the number of years that teachers can expect to collect. The expected duration of benefit receipt is the wild card in these systems.[8] Once teachers pass the spike (or spikes), pension wealth accrual turns negative. This is not because the annual pension annuity falls; in fact, it is rising. Rather, pension wealth falls each year beyond the spike because the teacher collects the pension for one fewer year and the annual payment is not enhanced sufficiently to offset this loss.

Spikes in pension wealth accrual create two key incentives for teachers— a *pull* factor and a *push* factor. First, teachers have strong financial incentives to stay on the job until they reap the benefit of the spikes. Even if a teacher is no longer suited to the job, it may be worthwhile to "put in one's time" for a few more years to collect several hundred thousand dollars in pension wealth. Second, once a teacher is beyond the spike and into

Figure 10.7. Deferred Income per Year as a Percentage of Salary, California: Net Addition to Pension Wealth from an Additional Year of Teaching

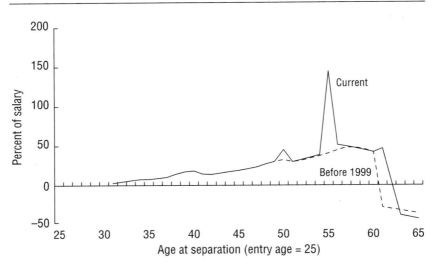

Source: Costrell and Podgursky (2009b).

Notes: Assumptions: 2007–08 Sacramento salary grid, inflating at 2.5%; interest rate = 5%; female 2004 CDC Mortality Table. Addition to pension wealth is net of interest on prior wealth and net of employee contribution.

the region of negative deferred compensation, the pension system creates a disincentive to stay on—a push out the door—even if she excels at her job.

There is ample evidence that such incentives affect behavior. Anecdotal evidence abounds of teachers (and others) timing their retirement decisions to maximize pension benefits. Pension plans routinely provide online calculators to help their members do so. Labor economists have developed more-systematic evidence of the behavioral impact of DB pensions in other fields, particularly in the private sector (Asch, Haider, and Zissimopoulos 2005; Friedberg and Turner 2009; Friedberg and Webb 2005; Lumsdaine, Stock, and Wise 1997; Samwick 1998; Stock and Wise 1990). There has been less research on teacher pensions, but the available evidence indicates strong effects on retirement timing (Brown 2009; Costrell and McGee 2009; Furgeson, Strauss, and Vogt 2006; Ni, Podgursky and Ehlert 2009; Podgursky and Ehlert 2007).[9] Existing teacher pensions appear to encourage early retirement, thus

Figure 10.8. Deferred Income per Year as a Percentage of Salary, Massachusetts: Net Addition to Pension Wealth from an Additional Year of Teaching

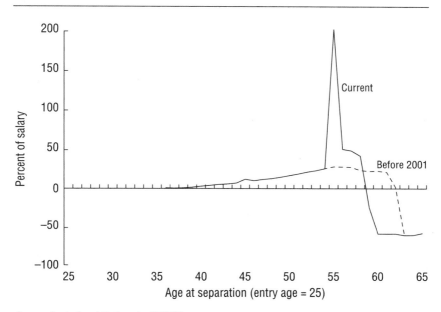

Source: Costrell and Podgursky (2009b).

Notes: Assumptions: 2007–08 Boston salary grid, inflating at 2.5%; interest rate = 5%; female 2004 CDC Mortality Table. Addition to pension wealth is net of interest on prior wealth and net of employee contribution.

shortening professional careers. For example, the median retirement age for teachers is just 58 (Podgursky and Ehlert 2007). Interestingly, the emphasis on deferred income in teachers' compensation packages was originally thought to serve the public interest by promoting long tenures (NEA 1995).[10]

Employing Retired Teachers

Although teacher pension systems often create strong financial incentives for teachers to retire at relatively young ages, many teachers, even those who nominally retire in their 50s, will continue to work into later life.

Figure 10.9. Deferred Income per Year as a Percentage of Salary, Texas: Net Addition to Pension Wealth from an Additional Year of Teaching

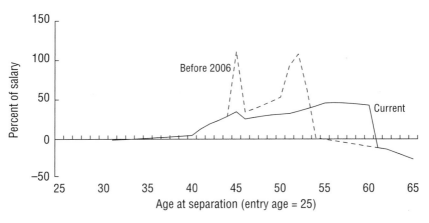

Source: Costrell and Podgursky (2009b).

Notes: Assumptions: 2007–08 Austin salary grid, inflating at 2.5%; interest rate = 5%; female 2004 CDC Mortality Table. Addition to pension wealth is net of interest on prior wealth and net of employee contribution.

Given concerns about teacher shortages and pressures from the No Child Left Behind Act to ensure that qualified teachers staff all classrooms, it makes little sense, on educational grounds, for districts to nudge effective teachers out the door at such early ages. Not surprisingly, all these teacher pension systems have provisions allowing educators to collect their pensions while continuing to teach.

This practice of postretirement reemployment seems to have gained in popularity (at least until recent funding difficulties created pressures to restrict this practice). Here are some examples.

- *Part-time employment.* All the pension systems considered here allow retired teachers to continue working part time in covered employment (without accruing additional benefits).
- *Employment in shortage areas.* Many states permit retired educators to teach full time for a specified period in certain fields that lack enough qualified teachers.
- *Breaks in employment.* Some states allow teachers to return to full-time employment and collect their pensions after a specified break

in service. California requires a break of 12 months. In Ohio, a teacher can return to work the day after she retires but must wait two months before receiving pension benefits.[11]

- *DROP plans.* Many states have implemented deferred retirement option plans (DROPs), which permit teachers to continue working full time for a specified period (1 to 10 years), during which all or most of their pension check goes into the equivalent of an individual retirement account.[12]

Of course, nothing prevents retirees from working in other fields or from continuing teaching in other states or districts that belong to different pension systems. For example, Missouri teachers in the state pension system can retire and teach full time in the St. Louis or Kansas City systems, or a Kansas City, Missouri, teacher can cross the border and teach in Kansas City, Kansas.

All these practices mean that the decision to "retire" (i.e., collect a retirement check) is not necessarily a decision to quit teaching in public schools. We are not aware of any comprehensive national data measuring the number of teachers who work while collecting pensions. Data for Missouri teachers indicate that 15 percent of those who retired between the 2001–02 and 2006–07 school years worked at least one year (part or full time) after retirement (Podgursky and Ehlert 2007).

The significance of these practices has not been fully examined. At a minimum, these practices blur the distinction between current and deferred compensation, since employed teachers are collecting a paycheck and a retirement check. This practice of double dipping may well be a rational response to an irrational system that pushes effective teachers into early retirement (along with ineffective teachers). However, the system as a whole does impose costs on taxpayers. As reemployment becomes easier, the incentive to "retire" at or near a pension spike becomes more pronounced—there is no downside to retirement if employment can continue—and this raises the cost to taxpayers. Allowing teachers to double dip may also be in a district's interest if pension costs are borne by the state, because new teachers cost the district less than older ones. This also raises taxpayers' cost, especially in cases where the entity that makes the employment decision (the district) does not incur the full cost of the decision.

This practice has no parallel in the private sector, because early retirement incentives there are always part of a downsizing effort, not one that offers reemployment. In higher education, where DC plans (overwhelmingly TIAA-CREF) predominate, some colleges have encouraged "phased retirement," moving professors to half-time employment status with a commensurate reduction in pay, but continuing to maintain contributions to the retirement plan based on full-time equivalent earnings. In general, partial retirement is easier to implement in a DC-type system. Also, in contrast to the typical teacher pension system, pension wealth in a DC (or cash balance) plan never falls simply because participants choose to continue working. Thus, there is no work penalty or tax to offset. The costs and benefits of phased retirement are far more transparent (Clark 2004).

Retiree Health Insurance

Another consequence of early teacher retirement is the increased demand for retiree health insurance coverage. Teachers who retire in their 50s must wait several years to qualify for Medicare at age 65. Because individual health insurance policies are quite expensive at older ages, many school districts and states have extended health insurance coverage to retirees. Unlike teacher pensions, retiree health benefits are typically funded on a pay-as-you-go basis. Instead of creating a fund to cover future liabilities, states pay for benefits out of current tax revenue as they are incurred. However, new government accounting rules (GASB 45) now require districts to estimate these liabilities in their financial statements.[13] Initial indications suggest that the figures are staggering. For example, the Los Angeles Unified School District, which provides complete health insurance coverage to all retirees, estimates its unfunded retiree health liability at about $10 billion (Standard and Poor's 2007). A recent report by the Cato Institute estimates that the unfunded liabilities of state and local governments under GASB 45 could total $1.4 trillion (Edwards and Gokhale 2006).[14]

Clark (2009) has gathered the available information on teachers' retiree health plans and liabilities from all states. In many states, the liabilities for teachers are not readily distinguished from those of other public employees. There is also wide variation across states in the magnitude of the liabilities, because some states heavily subsidize retiree health insurance and other states do not.

The consequences of early teacher retirements for publicly funded health liabilities have not yet been studied. However, it seems clear that taxpayer costs increase as early retirement boosts the total number of people—active and retired—who rely on the school system for health insurance.

Legacy Cost Burdens on Taxpayers and New Teachers

In addition to the powerful incentive effects on teacher retirements, the retirement benefit system's growing costs are absorbing a progressively larger share of current per-student educational spending. Whether this is the most effective way to structure teacher compensation to recruit and retain young teachers is open to question. Moreover, a significant component of employer contributions does not even go to future benefits for active teachers, but instead is a "legacy cost" for unfunded employer liabilities on behalf of previous cohorts of teachers.

When a retirement system is fully funded, benefits for each generation of teachers are fully financed by contributions (and the investment returns they earn) made over the career of the teacher by the school district, state legislature, and the teachers. Yet many teacher retirement systems have large unfunded liabilities. The most recent available estimates of unfunded liabilities (and funding ratios) for pension funds in the six states considered in this study are $1.8 billion (85.3 percent) for Arkansas (June 30, 2007), $18.7 billion (88.8 percent) for California (June 30, 2007), $9.3 billion (72.2 percent) for Massachusetts (including Boston, January 1, 2008), $5.7 billion (83.4 percent) for Missouri (June 30, 2008), $18.2 billion (79.1 percent) for Ohio (June 30, 2008), and $11.5 billion (90.5 percent) for Texas (August 31, 2008).[15] All these estimates predate the plunge in pension fund values from fall 2008 through early March 2009 (the date of current writing).

These unfunded liabilities mean that employer and teacher contributions must not only cover the currently accruing liabilities for the active teacher's future retirement (known as "normal costs"), but also be used to pay down the debt on retirement benefits for prior generations of teachers. These legacy costs are considered part of the employer's contribution (since employees can always recoup their contributions). Thus, they represent additional taxpayer burdens or expenditures that are not available to compensate new teachers.

For example, in the Missouri teacher pension system, normal cost— the percentage of payroll required to fund benefits accruing for current teachers—was 21.7 percent in fiscal year 2008. The combined employer and employee contribution, however, was 26 percent that year. Thus, an amount equal to 4.3 percent of payroll was diverted to pay legacy costs. The corresponding figures for employer contributions in other states to amortize the unfunded liabilities were 2.6 percent in Texas, 8.8 percent in Ohio, and 5.5 percent in Arkansas. California's actuaries calculate the amortization two different ways, reaching estimates of 0.5 percent and 4.1 percent. In Massachusetts, the state's contributions to amortize the unfunded liabilities totaled 14.3 percent of payroll in fiscal year 2008, making up the vast majority of the state's 16.3 percent contribution that year.[16] Again, these amortization rates predate the recent drop in pension fund values. Barring a rapid recovery in equities, we would expect these amortization rates to rise over the next several years.

Reform Lessons from the Private Sector and Higher Education

The private sector has faced similar, although not identical, issues, so developments there are instructive, especially because public K–12 education competes with the private sector for talent. As noted earlier, many private-sector employers have switched from DB to DC retirement plans, whereas nearly all public school districts continue to offer traditional DB pension plans. There is also some evidence that the private-sector DB plans that remain are less generous than teacher plans.[17] Although cost cutting is undoubtedly a major driver of developments in the private sector, the potential lessons for K–12 lie instead in the more rational structure of benefits and incentives that prevail in the private sector.

DC plans do not promise specific retirement benefits, conditioned on specified eligibility rules. Instead, employers offering 401(k)-type plans—the most common type of DC plan—set up retirement accounts in the employee's name and make regular contributions, usually as a percentage of salary. Employees can also contribute to their retirement accounts and defer taxes on their contributions until they withdraw funds from their accounts. Employer contributions sometimes depend on how much the participant contributes. Some employers, for example, match worker contributions up to a certain amount. Account balances grow over time with contributions and investment returns, and employees receive the funds in their accounts when they separate from their employer.[18]

Unlike defined-benefit plans, defined-contribution plans do not encourage early retirement or penalize workers who change jobs. Because the plan benefit is simply the account balance, DC plan benefits may continue to grow as long as the worker remains with the employer and contributes to the plan. Workers do not forfeit a monthly benefit check if they remain on the job for a month after the plan's retirement age. Instead, account balances grow smoothly with plan contributions, except for variations arising from fluctuating investment returns (discussed below). Consequently, DC plans do not create financial incentives for workers to retire at certain ages, by plan design. DC plan participants have been found to retire about two years later than their counterparts with traditional DB pensions (Friedberg and Webb 2005). As a result, DC plans are well suited to employers that wish to retain older workers as population aging limits the available pool of younger workers.

Additionally, DC plans do not penalize workers who frequently change jobs. Workers in DC plans who leave their jobs before retirement can take their accounts with them or keep them at their old employer. Either way, the balances will continue to earn investment returns until participants cash them out. Traditional DB plans, by contrast, penalize workers who leave their jobs at young ages, because they forfeit the sizable benefit increases that occur when the pension wealth accrual spikes at certain ages, and their benefits remain fixed at the level they attained at the time of separation, eroding over time with inflation.[19]

One drawback of DC plans is that they may expose workers to substantial investment risk, as we have recently seen. Bad luck or poor investment choices—either by investing in overly risky securities or by investing too conservatively—may leave participants with insufficient retirement benefits. This can also affect the timing of retirement decisions. The riskiness of DC plans may be especially worrisome to public-sector workers, including teachers, who appear to be more risk averse than private-sector workers (Munnell, Haverstick, and Soto 2007).

An increasingly popular alternative to DC plans and traditional DB plans is the cash balance plan, a hybrid that combines features of both plan types (Johnson and Uccello 2004). Employers with cash balance plans set aside a given percentage of salary for each employee and credit interest on these contributions. Interest rates are generally tied to some benchmark, such as the U.S. Treasury bill rate. Benefits are expressed as an account balance, as in DC plans, but these balances are only bookkeeping devices. Plans pay benefits, either as a lump sum or annuity, from commingled funds invested in a pension trust on behalf of all participants. Cash balance plans are considered DB plans for legal and regulatory purposes. In 2005, 25 percent of all private-sector workers in DB plans were covered by cash balance plans, not traditional DB plans (BLS 2007a).

The key advantage of cash balance plans is that they do not create retirement incentives at certain ages. The plans' neutrality on separation age may be simply depicted. In the pension wealth accrual graphs (figures 10.3–10.9), the lines with spikes would be replaced with flat lines, at a percentage given by the employer contribution. There are no spikes that induce teachers to stay until their mid-50s and then leave. Pension wealth never declines: If a teacher wants to work another year, the account grows by the contributions, plus the investment return, which can be converted to an annuity at retirement. (All private-sector cash balance plans must include an annuity option.) If a teacher works another year, the starting annuity is increased in an actuarially fair manner, because there is one less year of retirement to cover.

Such a retirement-neutral plan leaves the employee with much more latitude to arrive at an individually optimal separation decision, based on his or her lifestyle preferences. It also makes it much easier for schools to tailor their workforce to the educational needs of their students. In our view, this is preferable to the heavy-handed DB formulas, supplemented by makeshift DROP formulas or other reemployment provisions.

Another potentially relevant model for K–12 retirement reform may be found in higher education. TIAA-CREF, established in 1918, represents a popular and effective system that provides lifetime annuities and retirement security, as well as transparency and complete mobility of retirement benefits, to several million faculty and other employees in roughly 15,000 nonprofit institutions. Some private K–12 school teachers participate as well. Although nominally a DC plan, TIAA-CREF has avoided many problems associated with such plans. Administrative costs are very low, members have relatively few investment choices, and annuity payout options are the norm. By providing a guaranteed annual return combined with an annuity payout, TIAA-CREF more closely resembles a cash balance DB plan, in that downside market risk continues to be borne by the plan (Greenough 1990).

Finally, recent private-sector experience with retiree health benefits may be instructive for public school districts. Many private-sector employers have cut back or eliminated retiree health benefits as health care costs have increased. Between 1988 and 2006, the share of large private-sector employers (with 200 or more employees) that offered retiree health benefits fell from 66 to 35 percent (Kaiser Family Foundation and Health Research and Educational Trust 2006). In 2003, only 25 percent of private-sector workers were employed at firms that provided retiree health benefits (Buchmueller, Johnson, and LoSasso 2006). In addition, firms that continue to offer retiree health benefits have increasingly shifted costs to retirees. For example, between 1994 and 2004, the median monthly contribution for retiree health benefits by retirees age 55 to 63 increased from $25 to $111 (in inflation-adjusted 2004 dollars; Johnson 2007).

Unlike pensions of current public employees, which are protected by state law or constitutions, retiree health benefits for public employees are not generally protected by the state. Consequently, there are some indications that more public employees and their employers will face difficult choices of whether to continue retiree health benefits and at what cost. This scenario is particularly likely for teachers, to the extent that their early retirements make retiree health benefits more costly. For example, in 2007 the Ohio Teacher Retirement System proposed raising employer and employee contribution rates by 2.5 percent each, to continue to be able to offer subsidized retiree health insurance.[20] It was strongly implied at the time that if the proposal were to fail—and there was significant opposition from the school districts—benefits would be discontinued.[21]

Teacher Quality

We have discussed extensively the peculiar incentive structures built into teacher pension systems and some of their consequences for school staffing. In this section, we consider the consequences of these pension systems for teacher quality. Our discussion is brief and speculative because there is no experimental or quasi-experimental literature in teaching on which to draw. Thus, we must rely on findings from other sectors and analyze bits of available evidence within teaching.

First, limited evidence suggests that young teachers are not particularly well informed about their pension benefits. For example, DeArmond and Goldhaber (2009) find that only about one-third of Washington State teachers who were covered by a hybrid DB/DC plan knew that they were. A small sample of young teachers in a selective policy fellows program

found that 40 percent had "little or no understanding" of the Massachusetts teacher pension plan (Tran and Huang 2009). These limited data for
teachers seem credible since they are consistent with findings of poor
retirement benefits knowledge among young workers generally (Gustman
and Steinmeier 1999).

On its face, this lack of knowledge would suggest that changing the
level of benefits within a conventional DB system would have little effect
on recruitment of young teachers, since the latter are mostly unaware of
the benefit. Indeed, young teachers may be rationally ignorant of these
benefits since they occur far in the future, and a large percentage of these
teachers may never collect these benefits.[22]

The question for benefit reform is whether shifting to more-transparent
forms of pension benefits, such as DC or cash balance, would raise the
prospective value of those benefits to young teachers and potential recruits,
for the same overall cost. Unfortunately, there have been no policy studies
of the few cases where teachers have been able to choose DC plans.[23]

Vigdor (2008) has noted that, compared with other professions, teacher
salary gains are relatively back-loaded. In other professions, salaries rise
more rapidly at the beginning of a professional career. We have seen that
accrual of pension wealth is highly back-loaded as well. Teachers who leave
a plan before traditional retirement age, or who work a full career but
switch plans, face very sharp reductions in pension wealth relative to
teachers who work full careers in a single plan. Costrell and Podgursky
(2009a) analyze a sample of state teacher plans and find that about half an
entering teacher cohort's net pension wealth is redistributed to teachers
who separate in their 50s from those who separate earlier, compared with
a fiscally neutral cash balance plan. Similarly, they find that teachers who
split a 30-year career between two pension plans often lose more than half
their net pension wealth compared with teachers who complete a career in
a single system.

Once teachers are vested and have accumulated roughly 10 years of
experience, it is likely that these mobility penalties act to lower teacher
turnover. In a comparison of teacher turnover to that of nurses, social
workers, and accountants, Harris and Adams (2007) find that teacher
turnover rates fall below those of the other professions by the time a
teacher reaches age 40 (controlling for teacher demographics). From self-
reported data on pension coverage, Harris and Adams conclude that the
turnover reduction effect of teacher pension coverage is larger than in
those other professions. Evidence from other sectors, cited in Friedberg

and Turner (2009), also finds that average worker tenure rises when DB plans are in place. While DB plans may have the effect of lowering turnover of younger or mid-career teachers, it is unlikely that this produces much of a teacher quality gain, since most researchers find that the returns for experience are negligible beyond the first few years on the job (Hanushek 2003).

Unfortunately, from a policy point of view, no experiments compare the teacher quality effects of traditional pension plans with those of well-designed alternatives. The current system does not permit "regulatory space" for such experiments. Although school districts are free to experiment with other aspects of teacher compensation, such as performance pay (and many do), they lack the flexibility to experiment with teacher pension systems. Ideally, what we would want to see is a comparison of the labor market effect of identical compensation packages structured differently. Following Vigdor (2008), one package would front-load more salary and trim deferred benefits. Other packages might hold the overall mix of deferred and current compensation constant but provide teachers with retirement plans that are portable and have smoother wealth accrual over a teaching career, such as DB or DC. In all the experiments, the goal would be to assess the effect on teacher recruitment and workforce quality.

Conclusions and Reform Principles

Policy discussions about teacher recruitment, retention, and quality usually focus on salary, but retirement benefit systems can also have important consequences for the teaching workforce. Pension benefits may seem distant and uncertain to young teachers, especially because many young workers change jobs frequently. Pension costs, however, are incurred from the start as employers and employees make plan contributions that together average more than 15 percent of salary and sometimes exceed 20 percent. Many young teachers, who are paying off student loans, starting families, and buying homes, might prefer to receive more of their compensation up front rather than have it diverted into a system that may never benefit them. In addition, as some young teachers contemplate leaving teaching for another career—or taking a career break to start a family, perhaps returning to work in another state—the mobility penalties in a DB system may seem more salient.

A new or reworked retirement system could better serve the needs of teachers, school districts, and taxpayers. It should embody the following key features:

- *Neutrality.* Each additional year of work should add pension wealth in a fairly uniform way. There should be no spikes or cliffs in pension wealth at any particular year of service. Longevity decisions by individuals and their employers should be based on other grounds more directly connected to education needs and personal priorities.
- *Transparency.* The accrual of benefits should be simple and clear. Teachers should not have to rely on consultations with retirement counselors (typically late in one's career) to understand the implications of life choices. Entry-level teachers should be able to see what benefits they will be accruing from the beginning of their career.
- *Portability.* Many young professionals change jobs frequently, which has led many private-sector employers to move toward systems that do not penalize mobile young workers. The current DB systems offer few, if any, benefits to mobile young teachers and allocate the lion's share of benefits to high-seniority incumbents. Portability may help attract energetic, talented individuals who could add much to the teaching force. This might include mid-career switchers, such as engineers and other technical workers who could make valuable math and science teachers but are harmed by vesting rules. It might also assist in recruiting recent college graduates with math and science majors. A teacher who worked for 10 years in Missouri at a starting pay of $30,000 would amass $82,000 (adjusted for inflation) in a retirement account if she could take her employer and employee contributions with her when she left.[24]
- *Sustainability.* The pension system should be self-funding. It should not follow a pattern of benefit enhancements when the stock market is up, followed by funding shortfalls and contribution hikes when the market sours. Individual benefits should be tied to contributions by and for the individual teacher. The disconnect between contributions and benefits is the source of much legislative mischief, allowing costs to be shifted to future generations of taxpayers and teachers.

A DC system satisfies all these conditions far better than the traditional DB teacher pension systems, although it shifts market risk to the teacher. Cash balance systems also satisfy the conditions above, but without shifting risk. Alternately, TIAA-CREF, a DC system with some cash balance features, has for decades provided retirement benefits for mobile higher education faculty and researchers at thousands of colleges, universities, and nonprofit research institutions. To attract and retain a talented teaching workforce, particularly given the job mobility of educated workers in today's labor market, states need to consider such reforms to their retirement benefit systems.

Shifting to cash balance formats or DC plans, and thus eliminating the tilt in benefits against short-timers, will almost certainly reduce benefits for some while raising benefits for others and may also be more expensive overall, depending on how generous the new program is. The point here is not so much the generosity of current plans, but their idiosyncratic structure, resulting in very uneven distribution of benefits and strong incentives to time career decisions to arbitrary plan parameters. In our view, that is the most compelling reason for considering pension reform.

Education policymakers should at least consider experiments that provide alternatives to traditional DB plans for new teaching recruits and evaluate their utility in recruitment and retention of high-quality teachers. Indeed, if new recruits are provided with actuarially fair choices among alternative retirement plans, the incremental costs to states and districts should be modest. Even if many teachers continue to choose the traditional DB option, providing new recruits and career-changers (particularly in areas such as math and science) with choices may, at the margin, help attract some of the most mobile and academically gifted candidates who have the best nonteaching options.

NOTES

1. For some teachers, the combination of Social Security and pension benefits can exceed preretirement earnings.

2. National Center for Education Statistics, "Common Core of Data," http://nces.ed.gov/ccd/.

3. BLS data are from the *2009 Employer Costs for Employee Compensation* reports, available at http://www.bls.gov/schedule/archives/ecec_nr.htm. Data for public school-teachers are available beginning in March 2004. "Management, professional, and related" workers is the most disaggregated occupational grouping for private-sector employees that seems appropriate for comparison with public school teachers. For details, see Costrell and Podgursky (2009c, unabridged).

4. In dollar terms, the comparison of retirement costs depends on whether one considers hourly, weekly, or annual compensation. This mirrors the well-known (and

much debated) comparisons for total employer costs. See Costrell and Podgursky (2009c, unabridged, 10–12).

5. See also National Association of State Retirement Administrators, "Public Fund Survey," http://www.publicfundsurvey.org/www/publicfundsurvey/actuarial fundinglevels.asp.

6. The calculations depend on assumptions about interest rates, inflation, life expectancy, and future salary growth. See Costrell and Podgursky (2009b).

7. If we net out the employee's contribution (10 percent of earnings), the relative disparity is even greater: The 15-year teacher's net pension wealth is 3 percent of cumulative earnings, one-ninth of the 28 percent figure for the 30-year teacher. In fact, it takes 11 years for the teacher's net pension wealth to cross into positive territory at all, as compared with simply taking out the money that the employee has put in. For a more complete analysis of the costs of mobility, see Costrell and Podgursky (2009a), where it is estimated that the cost of mobility in Ohio for a teacher splitting a 30-year career is 74 percent of the pension wealth she would have attained by staying in the state. For the other states analyzed, the mobility cost ranged from 41 to 74 percent.

8. For a detailed analysis of how these formulas work, see Costrell and Podgursky (2009b).

9. Many studies examine how teachers' *current* compensation affects turnover (Hanushek, Kain, and Rivkin 2004; Murnane and Olsen 1990; Podgursky, Monroe, and Watson 2004; Stinebrickner 2001).

10. As the NEA report points out, however, this purpose has "been lost for many in the mists of time . . . Many pension administrators would be hard-pressed to give an account of why their systems are structured as is except to say that 'the legislature did it' or 'it is a result of bargaining' " (1995, 3).

11. The Federal Pension Protection Act of 2006 will require states to lengthen such breaks in employment by January 1, 2011, to continue receiving preferred tax treatment.

12. See Costrell and McGee (2009) for an analysis of Arkansas' T-DROP system, which is particularly important in that state for mitigating the sharp incentives to retire after 28 years of service, as depicted in figure 10.5.

13. In 2004, the Government Accounting Standards Board (GASB) finalized GASB 45, a new accounting standard requiring state and local governments, public colleges and universities, and school boards to report costs associated with retiree health benefits (and other nonpension post-employment benefits) over the service time of employees, rather than as the current year's cash outlay. The new rules went into effect in December 2006 for large entities and in December 2008 for smaller jurisdictions.

14. The Pew Center on the States (2008) estimates that unfunded retiree health liabilities for state employees alone reach $381 billion.

15. These data are from the comprehensive annual financial reports for each of these pension funds, downloaded from their web sites. These liabilities do not include unfunded retiree health benefits.

16. These figures are updated from those reported in Costrell and Podgursky (2009b). The calculation for Massachusetts is based on Commonwealth Actuarial Valuation Report, January 1, 2008, pp. 8 and 11.

17. The BLS reports that the average replacement factor is 1.59 percent for those private plans with constant multipliers, and that the median falls between 1.50 and 1.74 percent (BLS 2007a). For public school employees in such plans, the median replacement factor is 2.00 percent (BLS 2008). One caveat is that only 43 percent of privately covered employees belong to plans with constant multipliers (most of the others vary with service or earnings), compared with 85 percent of public school employees. Another caveat concerns Social Security. For teachers covered by Social Security—and thus comparable to private-sector employees—we roughly estimate that the average replacement factor is 1.86 percent; for those not covered, we estimate an average of about 2.36 percent, and 2.05 percent overall.

18. The Internal Revenue Service imposes a 10 percent penalty on most withdrawals before age 59 1/2.

19. See Costrell and Podgursky (2009a) for fuller analysis of the costs of mobility under teacher DB plans.

20. A portion of the increase was also slated to shore up the pension fund (Costrell and Podgursky 2007).

21. Two years later, as this book went to press, the Ohio Teacher Retirement System shifted its proposed contribution hike entirely to the pension fund because of the suddenly more urgent problem of pension underfunding.

22. Most states enhanced benefits significantly over the past decade, and the enhancement rate varied significantly between states (Clark and Craig 2009). Unfortunately, there has been no analysis to date of the teacher workforce quality effects of these changes.

23. New teachers in Ohio and Florida have the choice of a DB or DC plan. All teachers in Alaska are placed in a DC plan. Several other states have hybrid plans, in which teachers can choose to put their contributions into a DC plan. See Hansen (2009).

24. This estimate assumes starting pay growth of 3 percent per year and a 5 percent annual return on pension assets.

REFERENCES

Aaronson, Daniel, Lisa Barrow, and William Sander. 2007. "Teachers and Student Achievement in the Chicago Public High Schools." *Journal of Labor Economics* 25(1): 95–135.

Asch, Beth, Steven J. Haider, and Julie Zissimopoulos. 2005. "Financial Incentives and Retirement: Evidence from Federal Civil Service Workers." *Journal of Public Economics* 89(2/3): 427–40.

Baron, James N., and David M. Kreps. 1999. *Strategic Human Resources: Frameworks for General Managers.* New York: John Wiley & Sons.

BLS. See Bureau of Labor Statistics.

Brown, Kristine. 2009. "The Link between Pensions and Retirement Timing: Lessons from California Teachers." Conference Paper 2009-12. Nashville, TN: National Center for Performance Incentives, Vanderbilt University.

Buchmueller, Thomas C., Richard W. Johnson, and Anthony T. LoSasso. 2006. "Trends in Retiree Health Insurance, 1997 to 2003." *Health Affairs* 25(6): 1507–16.

Bureau of Labor Statistics. 2007a. "National Compensation Survey: Employee Benefits in Private Industry in the United States, 2005." Bulletin 2589. Washington, DC: U.S. Department of Labor. http://www.bls.gov/ncs/ebs/sp/ebbl0022.pdf.

————. 2007b. "National Compensation Survey: Employee Benefits in Private Industry in the United States, March 2007." Summary 07-05. Washington, DC: U.S. Department of Labor. http://www.bls.gov/ncs/ebs/sp/ebsm0006.pdf.

————. 2008. "National Compensation Survey: Retirement Benefits in State and Local Governments in the United States, 2007." Summary 08-03. Washington, DC: U.S. Department of Labor. http://www.bls.gov/ncs/ebs/sp/ebsm0008.pdf.

————. 2009. "Employer Costs for Employee Compensation." Washington DC: U.S. Department of Labor. http://www.bls.gov/schedule/archives/ecec_nr.htm.

Clark, Robert L. 2004. "Changing Faculty Demographics and the Need for New Policies." Paper presented at TIAA-CREF Institute Conference, New York, April 1–2.

————. 2009. "Retiree Health Plans for Public School Teachers after GASB 43 and 45." Conference Paper 2009-03. Nashville, TN: National Center for Performance Incentives, Vanderbilt University.

Clark, Robert L., and Lee A. Craig. 2009. "Determinants of the Generosity of Pension Plans for Public School Teachers, 1982–2006." Conference Paper 2009-05. Nashville, TN: National Center for Performance Incentives, Vanderbilt University.

Costrell, Robert M., and Joshua McGee. 2009. "Teacher Pension Incentives, Retirement Behavior, and Potential for Reform in Arkansas." Conference Paper 2009-10. Nashville, TN: National Center for Performance Incentives, Vanderbilt University.

Costrell, Robert M., and Michael J. Podgursky. 2007. *Golden Peaks and Perilous Cliffs: Rethinking Ohio's Teacher Pension System.* Washington, DC: Thomas B. Fordham Institute.

————. 2009a. "Distribution of Benefits in Teacher Retirement Systems and Their Implications for Mobility." Conference Paper 2009-04. Nashville, TN: National Center for Performance Incentives, Vanderbilt University.

————. 2009b. "Peaks, Cliffs and Valleys: The Peculiar Incentives in Teacher Retirement Systems and Their Consequences for School Staffing." *Education Finance and Policy* 4(2): 175–211.

————. 2009c. "Teacher Retirement Benefits." *Education Next* 9(2): 58–63. Unabridged version, "Teacher Retirement Benefits: Are Employer Contributions Higher Than for Private-Sector Professionals?" Stanford, CA: Hoover Institution. http://media.hoover.org/documents/ednext_20092_58_unabridged.pdf.

DeArmond, Michael M., and Dan Goldhaber. 2009. "Scrambling the Next Egg: How Well Do Teachers Understand Their Pensions and What Do They Think about Alternative Pension Structures?" Conference Paper 2009-13. Nashville, TN: National Center for Performance Incentives, Vanderbilt University.

Edwards, Chris, and Jagadeesh Gokhale. 2006. "Unfunded State and Local Health Costs: $1.4 Trillion." Washington, DC: Cato Institute.

Friedberg, Leora, and Sarah Turner. 2009. "Labor Market Effects of Pensions and Implications for Teachers." Conference Paper 2009-06. Nashville, TN: National Center for Performance Incentives, Vanderbilt University.

Friedberg, Leora, and Anthony Webb. 2005. "Retirement and the Evolution of Pension Structure." *Journal of Human Resources* 40(2): 281–308.

Furgeson, Joshua, Robert P. Strauss, and William Vogt. 2006. "The Effects of Defined Benefit Pension Incentives and Working Conditions on Teacher Retirement Decisions." *Education Finance and Policy* 1(3): 316–48.

Greenough, William C. 1990. *It's My Retirement Money; Take Good Care of It: The TIAA-CREF Story.* Pension Research Council. Philadelphia: Wharton School, University of Pennsylvania.

Gustman, Alan L., and Thomas L. Steinmeier. 1999. "What People Don't Know about Their Pensions and Social Security: An Analysis Using Linked Data from the Health and Retirement Study." Working Paper 7368. Cambridge, MA: National Bureau of Economic Research.

Hansen, Janet S. 2008. "Teacher Pensions: A Background Paper." Washington, DC: Committee for Economic Development.

———. 2009. "An Introduction to Teacher Retirement Benefits." Conference Paper 2009-01. Nashville, TN: National Center for Performance Incentives, Vanderbilt University.

Hansen, Janet S., Michael J. Podgursky, and Robert M. Costrell. 2009. "Teacher Retirement Systems: Research Findings." Research brief. Nashville, TN: National Center for Performance Incentives, Vanderbilt University.

Hanushek, Eric A. 2003. "The Failure of Input-Based Resource Policies." *The Economic Journal* 113(485): F64–F98.

Hanushek, Eric A., John F. Kain, and Steven G. Rivkin. 2004. "Why Public Schools Lose Teachers." *Journal of Human Resources* 39(2): 326–54.

Harris, Douglas N., and Scott J. Adams. 2007. "Understanding the Level and Causes of Teacher Turnover: A Comparison with Other Professions." *Economics of Education Review* 26:325–37.

Johnson, Richard W. 2007. "What Happens to Health Benefits after Retirement?" *Work Opportunities for Older Americans* Series 7. Chestnut Hill, MA: Center for Retirement Research at Boston College.

Johnson, Richard W., and Cori E. Uccello. 2004. "Cash Balance Plans: What Do They Mean for Retirement Security?" *National Tax Journal* 57(2, Part 1): 315–28.

Kaiser Family Foundation and Health Research and Educational Trust. 2006. *Employer Health Benefits: 2006 Annual Survey.* Washington, DC: Kaiser Family Foundation and Health Research and Educational Trust.

Lumsdaine, Robin L., James H. Stock, and David A. Wise 1997. "Retirement Incentives: The Interaction between Employer-Provided Pensions, Social Security, and Retiree Health Benefits." In *The Economic Effects of Aging in the United States and Japan,* edited by Michael D. Hurd and Naohiro Yashiro (261–93). Chicago: University of Chicago Press.

Munnell, Alicia H., Kelly Haverstick, and Mauricio Soto. 2007. "Why Have Defined Benefit Plans Survived in the Public Sector?" State and Local Pension Plans Brief 2. Chestnut Hill, MA: Center for Retirement Research at Boston College.

Murnane, Richard J., and Randy J. Olsen. 1990. "The Effects of Salaries and Opportunity Costs on Length of Stay in Teaching: Evidence from North Carolina." *Journal of Human Resources* 25(1): 106–24.

National Education Association. 1995. *Understanding Defined Benefit and Defined Contribution Pension Plans.* Washington, DC: National Education Association.

————. 2004. *Characteristics of Large Public Education Pension Plans.* Washington, DC: National Education Association.

NEA. See National Education Association.

Ni, Shawn, Michael J. Podgursky, and Mark W. Ehlert. 2009. "Teacher Pension Incentives and Labor Market Behavior: Evidence from Missouri Administrative Teacher Data." Conference Paper 2009-11. Nashville, TN: National Center for Performance Incentives, Vanderbilt University.

Pension and Welfare Benefits Administration. 2001–2002. *Private Pension Plan Bulletin: Abstract of 1998 Form 5500 Annual Reports.* Washington, DC: U.S. Department of Labor, Pension and Welfare Benefits Administration.

Pew Center on the States. 2008. *Promises with a Price: Public Sector Retirement Benefits.* Philadelphia, PA: The Pew Charitable Trusts.

Podgursky, Michael J., and Mark W. Ehlert. 2007. "Teacher Pensions and Labor Market Behavior: A Descriptive Analysis." Working Paper 4. Washington, DC: Center for Analysis of Longitudinal Data in Education Research, The Urban Institute.

Podgursky, Michael J., Ryan Monroe, and Donald Watson. 2004. "The Academic Quality of Public School Teachers: An Analysis of Entry and Exit Behavior." *Economics of Education Review* 23(5): 507–18.

Rivkin, Steven G., Eric A. Hanushek, and John F. Kain. 2004. "Teachers, Schools, and Academic Achievement." *Econometrica* 73(2): 417–58.

Samwick, Andrew A. 1998. "New Evidence on Pensions, Social Security, and the Timing of Retirement." *Journal of Public Economics* 70(2): 207–36.

Standard and Poor's. 2007. "Public Finance: Los Angeles Unified School District, Los Angeles." New York and San Francisco: Standard and Poor's.

Stinebrickner, Todd. 2001. "A Dynamic Model of Teacher Labor Supply." *Journal of Labor Economics* 19(1): 196–230.

Stock, James H., and David A. Wise. 1990. "Pensions, the Option Value of Work, and Retirement." *Econometrica* 58(5): 1151–80.

Tran, Doannie, and Elsie Huang. 2009. "Early Career Teachers' Perceptions of Traditional Versus Innovative Benefits Packages." Conference Paper 2009-15. Nashville, TN: National Center for Performance Incentives, Vanderbilt University.

Vigdor, Jacob L. 2008. "Scrap the Sacrosanct Salary Schedule." *Education Next* 8(4): 36–42.

11

Investing in Human Capital through Teacher Professional Development

Jennifer King Rice

School success depends on quality educators. In response to the current public education climate of high-stakes accountability systems, policymakers have focused directly on issues of teacher quality as a critical resource for realizing ambitious outcomes standards. Much attention has been devoted to examining teacher preparation and defining what counts as a qualified entry-level teacher. In addition, education leaders throughout the education system have recognized the importance of ongoing professional development as a way to enhance the capacity of the existing teacher workforce. In fact, although there is disagreement about the efficacy of current investments in professional development, researchers and policymakers alike have come to recognize that the goals of standards-based reform are unlikely to be realized without enhancing the capacity of existing school personnel through high-quality in-service training (Birman et al. 2000; Corcoran 1995). Investing in human capital through professional development is an essential component of school improvement efforts.

Professional development activities take a variety of forms. A 1998 National Center for Education Statistics analysis of data from the Schools and Staffing Survey identified five broad categories: (1) district-sponsored workshops or in-service programs; (2) school-sponsored workshops or in-service programs; (3) university extension or adult education programs; (4) college courses in a teacher's subject field; and (5) growth activities sponsored by professional associations. In addition, more contemporary conceptualizations of what counts as professional development include shifts in the use of time (e.g., to provide common planning time for teachers of the same subject) and creation of collaborative structures for teachers to learn from one another (e.g., through teacher networks or mentor programs).

Public school systems are making substantial investments in these various forms of teacher professional development. While most estimates of per-teacher spending on professional development range from $2,000 to $3,500 (Fermanich 2002; Killeen, Monk, and Plecki 2002; Little et al. 1987; Miller, Lord, and Dorney 1994; Stern, Gerritz, and Little 1989), some are as high as $15,000 per teacher (Fermanich 2002). In this chapter I discuss the considerable variation in these estimates; the point here is to recognize that spending on professional development is not trivial. Unfortunately, school system investment decisions are often based on thin, if any, evidence on the return on investments in improved teaching practices and student learning. This is borne out by empirical research that shows uneven and, in many cases, disappointing findings associated with teachers receiving professional development (Rice 2000).

This chapter focuses on professional development as a potentially powerful mechanism for improving human capital in schools and explores why this potential has not been realized. The first section describes investments in professional development, including how much is spent on what kinds of programs and activities, and who pays. The second section describes dominant approaches to teacher professional development and identifies features that characterize effective initiatives. The third section links the findings from the first two sections to consider the productivity of investments in professional development. This section explores the broader institutional arrangements that influence professional development offerings, both the options made available to teachers as well as the choices that teachers make, and discusses factors that undermine the productivity of these investments. The chapter concludes with a set of considerations for researchers and policymakers that could strengthen the impact of professional development on teacher and school performance.

Investing in Professional Development: Expenditures, Costs, and Burden

Almost every education program has some professional development component, and school districts typically sponsor their own efforts in addition to subsidizing training and education opportunities for individuals. Like any intervention, professional development requires resources, such as time and money, and these costs are shouldered by various individuals and organizations. The justification for these expenses is the belief that professional development will promote better teaching, and ultimately improved student outcomes, so these resources are generally thought to be investments in greater productivity.[1]

Although some research documents the costs of teacher professional development in specific states and districts or to particular levels of the educational system (e.g., the district budget), the actual level of resources committed to teacher professional development is largely unknown in a comprehensive sense, in part, because professional development accounting is often buried under program-level expenditures. Even less is known about the comparative costs of alternative approaches to professional development, despite the fact that many are emerging. Such information has the potential to be helpful to policymakers who need to make important consequential decisions about how to invest limited resources.

Throughout this section, it is important to be mindful of the distinction between costs and expenditures. Assessing the total cost of any program, policy, or practice involves identifying and assigning a value to the full array of resources that are required to realize the goals of the initiative. In some cases, like the direct purchase of a good or a service, the cost of a program or initiative can be represented easily by monetary expenditures. However, educational interventions like professional development generally require a variety of hidden and widely dispersed resources that may not translate into additional expenditures. For example, professional development requires substantial time of personnel, sometimes compensated and sometimes not. To the degree that individuals are willing to donate their time, the overall explicit price tag (in accounting terms) of the initiative will decrease. However, this time is still a cost and must be recognized as such for planning and implementation purposes. Likewise, to the degree that the cost burden is distributed in such a way that external sources of support cover substantial portions of the cost, the burden on the school or school system will decrease. While shifting the distribution of the cost burden does not affect the overall cost of the initiative, it could have important consequences (e.g., opportunity costs to teachers, incentive structures, overall price tag to states and districts). For example, providing paid release days for teachers to participate in a particular activity decreases the opportunity costs for teachers, increases the incentive for teachers to choose this activity over others that may not come with release time, and increases the cost to states and districts.

Several frameworks have been developed to help standardize efforts to estimate the cost associated with teacher professional development (Odden et al. 2002; Rice 2003). These frameworks recognize the range of resources associated with professional development activities, including teacher time; trainers and coaches; administration; facilities, materials, and equipment; travel and transportation; tuition and fees; future salary obligations; and research, development, and dissemination.[2]

Caution should be exercised in drawing broad conclusions about the level of investment in professional development given the limited number of studies and the range of methods used to estimate costs. Some studies present estimates in total costs, others present cost per teacher, others present cost per student, and still others present cost as a percentage of the operating budget. A number of studies focus only on expenditures, whereas others include a range of resources, including uncompensated participant time and other opportunity costs. Moreover, there is a healthy academic debate over whether future salary obligations arising from professional development participation (e.g., associated with obtaining a master's degree) should be included as a cost of professional development, and the treatment of these costs varies across studies. Finally, differences in the design and delivery of professional development initiatives result in variations in the study of their costs; some studies examine total district expenditures of professional development, whereas others focus on the costs associated with specific professional development programs and strategies. I categorize the research on the cost of professional development into two sets of studies. One set deals broadly with the expenditures on professional development across selected states, districts, and schools. The second set estimates the costs of specific alternative approaches to professional development.

Spending on Professional Development

Studies of the costs of professional development have provided valuable information about at least three central issues: how much is spent on teacher professional development, how money devoted to teacher professional development is spent, and who pays for teacher professional development.

Several studies provide a sense of *how much* professional development can cost across individual schools and districts. Taken together, these studies show substantial variability in spending. Despite this variability, some general conclusions can be drawn. The majority of these studies have estimated that per-teacher spending ranges from $2,000 to $3,500 (Fermanich 2002; Killeen et al. 2002; Little et al. 1987; Miller et al. 1994; Stern et al. 1989).[3] Presented as a share of district spending, most analyses have estimated that expenditures on professional development tend to account for between 2 and 4 percent of districts' operating expenditures (Education Commission of the States 1997; Elmore 1997; Elmore and Burney 1999; Killeen et al. 2002; Little et al. 1987; Miles et al. 2004; Miller et al. 1994; Moore and Hyde 1981). This range is typical of those found in the research, but some studies have estimated the expenditures on professional development to be as high as $13,959 and $15,233 per teacher (Fermanich 2002; Gallagher 2002) and more than 8 percent of operating expenses (Killeen et al. 2002). Explaining a range of more than $13,000 across a single urban district, Fermanich (2002) argues that higher spending is associated with lower-performing schools, schools with access to more Title I funding,[4] and schools implementing comprehensive school reform models.

Studies also have examined what the professional development dollars purchase—*how the money is spent.* For instance, a study of state and district teacher professional development expenditures in 16 school districts shows that the majority of district professional development dollars is spent on in-service training days (40 percent) and on conferences and workshops (37 percent), whereas the largest share of state spending on professional development goes to university subsidies for graduate programs in education (36 percent), followed by state-administered special programs (26 percent) (Education Commission of the States 1997). Other studies examining expenditures with conventional budgeting categories report that the vast majority of professional development expenditures are associated with spending on personnel time, including teacher participants and trainers and coaches (Archibald and Gallagher 2002; Elmore 1997; Fermanich 2002; Gallagher 2002; Little et al. 1987; Miller et al. 1994; Moore and Hyde 1981). When future salary obligations are included as a cost, they represent the largest taxpayer investment in staff development at 160 percent of the direct costs of professional development (Little et al. 1987; Stern et al. 1989), though controversy surrounds the appropriateness of including this expenditure in the calculation of the total cost of professional development.[5]

The literature also provides a sense of *who pays* for staff development, or how the cost burden is distributed across levels of government and stakeholder groups. Most studies report a shared responsibility across federal, state, and district levels to support professional development (Elmore 1997; Little et al. 1987). Several studies employ the Odden and colleagues' (2002) cost framework to show that schools dedicate significant discretionary funding to professional development activities, accounting for the majority of the spending (Archibald and Gallagher 2002; Fermanich 2002; Gallagher 2002). In addition, research has recognized the considerable investment made by participants themselves (Little et al. 1987; Rice and Hall 2008). Although this time commitment may reflect an investment in the development of knowledge and skills to improve teaching, it could also be a direct response to state and district requirements for employment eligibility.

Costs of Alternative Approaches to Professional Development

A second set of studies examines the costs of specific forms of professional development. Many studies report on overall expenditures associated with specific interventions, but a thorough search of the literature revealed only five studies that present per-participant cost estimates that allow for comparisons across alternative programs (Cohen and Rice 2005).[6] These studies focus on a variety of approaches to teacher professional development, including induction programs, programs associated with comprehensive school reform models, institutes and academies focused on developing specific knowledge and skills, and master's degree programs. Generally speaking, this literature review reveals a scarcity of comparable cost estimates of alternative approaches to teacher professional development.

The few studies that exist suggest that the costs of professional development vary dramatically, ranging from $1,439 per participant for a statewide induction program to $9,833 per participant for an intensive five-week leadership institute (Cohen et al. 2001). Not surprisingly, per-participant costs associated with alternative approaches to teacher professional development are generally lower for programs that are relatively less intense in their duration and time requirements, and for programs that serve large numbers of teachers (Cohen and Rice 2005). However, data on program effectiveness are needed to draw conclusions about the relative cost-effectiveness of the alternatives. It is likely that programs serving large numbers of teachers (e.g., all the teachers in a district) do not adequately tailor learning opportunities to the needs of particular teachers and, consequently, can be less effective than programs targeting more limited numbers of teachers. The point here is that the least costly programs are not necessarily the most desirable alternatives on economic grounds.

One alterative deserving special attention given its historical policy relevance is research on the cost of earning a master's degree. Knapp and colleagues (1990) estimated the cost of obtaining a master's degree to teachers and their prospective employers. They compared the cost of teachers attending a 36–credit hour degree program full time, at night-school, and during the summertime. Their estimates include costs to teachers including tuition, books, travel, and forgone earnings, plus a state subsidy ($5,832 per teacher) defined as "the state expenditure for instructional and administrative programs per FTE [full-time equivalent] minus the tuition the school receives from the student" (1990, 33). The study reports that when teachers pursue their master's degrees on a full-time basis, the degree takes two years to complete, resulting in a total cost of $84,494.[7] However, teachers who attend graduate school during the evenings or summer need to attend for five years, and the total cost would drop to $36,925 and $52,995, respectively. The difference in cost is a result of decreased forgone earnings associated with the evening and summer options. A teacher attending graduate school full time would be losing $34,106 per year that could be earned teaching. The study assumed that a teacher attending graduate school during the summer may lose earnings from summertime employment, but that the forgone earnings for a teacher attending an evening program would be relatively small.[8] The statewide costs, once the program is established, range from $118 million to $285 million annually, depending on the circumstances.

Summary

Two observations follow from this review of the studies that have examined the costs of teacher professional development. First, the research base is insufficient for drawing strong conclusions about the precise aggregate level of investment in professional development. The studies are few in number, and despite efforts to use shared-cost frameworks (Odden et al. 2002; Rice 2003), the studies use a range of methods and reporting conventions. The lack of a clear sense of overall spending on professional development is matched by the limited evidence on the costs associated with alternative forms of professional development.

Second, although there are some central tendencies among the cost estimates generated by these studies, the more apparent finding is that spending on professional development varies considerably across schools, districts, individuals, and initiatives. According to the studies reviewed, spending on teacher professional development ranges from 2 to 8 percent of a district's operating budget. These percentages translate into dollar values in the millions and are comparable to other major line items in district budgets, such as central office administrative costs, student transportation, and instructional materials. Further, future salary obligations, largely related to the premium teachers receive for attaining a master's degree, swamp the other costs of professional development, but some would argue that including these as costs of training artificially inflates the cost estimates. However calculated, the investment of time and money in activities associated with professional growth is not trivial, and its impact on productivity should be scrutinized.

Identifying Effective Professional Development

Professional development activities take a variety of forms, which have evolved over the past decade from traditional to more contemporary approaches (Garet et al. 2001; Rice 2000). Traditionally, professional development has encompassed a range of formal activities that practicing teachers engage in (usually outside the classroom) to further develop their teaching skills, learn new skills or content, and familiarize themselves with new education policies that affect their teaching and classroom practices (e.g., changes to the curriculum, new standards and assessment programs). Common activities have included workshops sponsored by schools and districts, college courses in a teacher's subject field, and seminars and conferences sponsored by professional associations (NCES 1998). These traditional approaches to professional development generally have required after-school time, in-service days, or release time during the school day for teachers to participate, and participation in some form of professional development is generally part of a teacher's contractual agreement (Rice 2000).

More contemporary conceptualizations of what counts as professional development include shifts in schools' organizational structure and use of time to create collaborative arrangements for teachers to learn from one another in the context of the school day (e.g., through teacher networks, mentor programs, and common planning time for teachers of the same subject or grade) (Rice 2000). In general, the evolution from traditional to more contemporary forms of professional development has involved moving from an understanding of professional development as a district-driven process of providing training and information through a menu of alternative activities to an approach that emerges from local needs and interests, is relevant to specific school communities, and is open to a variety of methods (Little 1993; National Foundation for the Improvement of Education 1996; Sparks 1995; Sykes 1996). Garet and colleagues refer to these newer forms as "reform types of professional development." Compared to traditional forms of professional development, reform activities "often take place during the regular school day, . . . may enable activities of longer duration than traditional activities, and . . . may make it easier to encourage the collective participation of groups of teachers from the same school or department" (2001, 921).

There is limited research on the level of investment being made in teacher professional development, and even less is known about the effectiveness of teacher professional development strategies. Researchers have generated lists of the characteristics of "high-quality" professional development. For instance, the National Partnership for Excellence and Accountability in Teaching asserted eight research-based principles to promote high-quality professional development (Hawley and Valli 1998). Professional development should (1) be based on analyses of the differences between actual student performance and student learning goals; (2) involve teachers in the identification of what they need to learn and in the development of the learning experiences in which they will be involved; (3) be primarily school-based and built into the day-to-day work of teaching; (4) be organized around collaborative problem solving; (5) be ongoing and involve follow-up and support for further learning—including support from sources external to the school that can provide necessary resources and new perspectives; (6) incorporate evaluation of multiple sources of information on student outcomes and instruction; (7) provide opportunities to gain an understanding of the theory underlying the knowledge and skills being learned; and (8) be connected to a comprehensive change process focused on improving student learning. While it is difficult to imagine someone disagreeing with these characteristics as important considerations in the design and implementation of professional development, direct evidence linking these components with teacher and student learning outcomes is scarce. Further, the vague nature of these kinds of characteristics seriously undermines their policy relevance. State legislatures and district administrators would be hard pressed to make policy recommendations around these kinds of principles.

One limitation of research analyzing the effectiveness of teacher professional development is specification and measurement of outcomes. Figure 11.1 offers a simple schema for professional development and what it "produces." The immediate measurable outcome is that a teacher has participated in (and sometimes completed) a professional development program, module, or experience. But professional development is not just about participation or "seat time"; rather, these experiences are intended to increase teachers' knowledge, whether in the area of content or pedagogy, to influence changes in teaching practices, and ultimately, to produce more-effective teachers as measured by student learning. Teacher salary schedules commonly reward teachers for participation (e.g., passing approved college courses or completing a graduate degree) with little attention to the impact of these experiences on teachers' knowledge, teaching practices, or effectiveness. In part, this is due to limited research on the impact of teacher professional development on these more meaningful outcomes.

The majority of studies on the effectiveness of teacher professional development focus on self-reported outcomes on improvements in teacher learning and changes in teaching practices. Taken together, these analyses help identify features of professional development to be further tested with externally measured teacher and student outcomes. For instance, a study using a national probability sample to estimate the impact of professional development on teachers' perceptions of increases in knowledge and changes in teaching practices identifies three core features (focus on content, active learning, and coherence with learning activities)

Figure 11.1. Student Learning through Teacher Professional Development

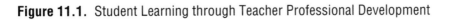

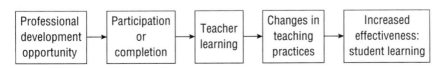

and three structural features (the form of the activity, collective participation, and the duration of the activity) (Garet et al. 2001). Further, a study of 207 teachers in five states used hierarchical linear models to estimate that teachers are more likely to report changed teaching practices if the professional development focuses on specific instructional practices and involves active learning opportunities (Desimone et al. 2002). When asked about the "most meaningful" professional development activities, teachers from four schools identified those that are subject-specific, involve hands-on active learning opportunities, and apply directly to their teaching (Sandholtz 2002).

Until recently, the only form of professional development that had a substantial body of research analyzing its impact on student achievement was the earning of graduate degrees. A number of studies have examined the impact of earning an advanced degree on teacher effectiveness, and the findings vary by level of education. Quasi-experimental studies examining the impact of teacher degree at the secondary level have been plagued by inconclusive findings (e.g., Ehrenberg and Brewer 1994; Harnisch 1987; Monk 1994; and Summers and Wolfe 1975, 1977), but more recent studies that have attended to the subject area in which the advanced degree was earned have been relatively consistent in their findings of a small positive effect of teacher degree on high school student achievement, particularly in mathematics and science (Goldhaber and Brewer 1998, 2000).

A clear picture is beginning to emerge about the effect of high school teachers with master's degrees in these subjects, but the evidence at the elementary level remains mixed and inconclusive. The evidence of a positive effect of teacher degree level on elementary student achievement (Ferguson and Ladd 1996) is overshadowed by the many studies that find either no discernable effect (Croninger et al. 2007; Link and Ratledge 1979; Murnane and Phillips 1981) or even a negative effect (Eberts and Stone 1984; Kiesling 1984; Murnane 1975; Rowan, Correnti, and Miller 2002) of teachers' holding master's degrees on elementary student achievement. Taken together, this evidence demonstrates that a master's degree is not typically predictive of teacher effectiveness. This finding seriously undermines policies that reward (and even require) advanced degrees, particularly when those policies do not specify that the degree be aligned with the teacher's assignment.

A growing body of research is also emerging around induction programs, a particular form of professional development targeted at new teachers. Induction programs range in their design, often including orientation sessions, mentoring opportunities, classroom observation, and other forms of professional development. Theory holds that comprehensive professional development that is intensive, structured, and sequentially delivered to meet the needs of new teachers will help districts to attract, develop, and retain quality teachers (Berry, Hopkins-Thompson, and Hoke 2002). However, research on the impact of induction programs for new teachers has been largely inconclusive (Ingersoll and Kralik 2004). Adding to the existing literature is a recent study with high-quality, rigorous methods, including experimental design, to examine the effects of comprehensive induction services (Glazerman et al. 2008). The treatment group included teachers who received comprehensive induction support, and the control group included teachers who received the "usual set of induction services" (xxii). The analysis found no impact of participation in comprehensive induction on teacher attitudes, teacher practices, student test scores, or teacher retention after one year. However, when the authors examined the specific types and intensity of support received by teachers across treatment and control groups, they found that some components of induction programs may affect outcomes. Specifically, students of teachers who received coaching and feedback on their teaching scored higher than students of teachers who did not receive these services. In addition, teacher retention was higher among teachers who had an assigned mentor, received guidance in content areas (math and literacy), or engaged in content-specific and pedagogical professional development. Since these findings were not generated through experimental methods, the authors caution readers that they "should be used to generate hypotheses rather than to establish causal inferences because any association may confound effects of the induction services themselves with the pre-existing differences between the types of teachers who receive different levels of services" (xxxv). Nonetheless, these findings are important given the growing number of induction programs (Berry et al. 2002) and the substantial costs associated with these initiatives (Alliance for Excellent Education 2004; Villar and Strong 2007).

Toward More Productive Investments in Professional Development

Several key findings follow from the empirical literature presented in the previous sections. First, while the level of investment in professional development is highly variable across schools and districts, the expenditures on teacher professional development are substantial, particularly when future salary obligations are included. Second, despite sophisticated studies examining teachers' perceptions of the impact of professional development, few studies directly measure teacher outcomes by improved learning or changes in teaching practices. Earning a master's degree and participating in induction programs are the only forms of professional development that have a rigorous research base analyzing their impact on student achievement, but the effects are limited in their scope and disappointing in their magnitudes. So it appears to be common practice to invest considerable resources in professional development across levels of the system, with little evidence of a return in student achievement.

This final section proposes several considerations for enhancing the productivity of professional development investments. Arguably, three key factors have undermined the effectiveness of professional development: (1) a limited knowledge base on effective professional development, (2) a problematic incentive structure that rewards participation rather than performance, and (3) a lack of targeted resources for professional development in chronically low-performing schools. I discuss each of these issues.

A Limited Knowledge Base

The thin literature base offers policymakers little guidance in how to construct meaningful and effective professional development opportunities for teachers. Further, many of the findings presented above (Hawley and Valli 1998; Sparks 1995; Sykes 1996) coupled with qualitative evidence from teachers working in difficult-to-staff schools (Rice 2008) recognize that professional development should be tailored to the specific needs of schools and learning communities. For example, teachers in low-performing schools need site-specific professional development to enhance the skills they need to be effective *in those environments.* This may include skills needed to work with large populations of English language learners, students from culturally diverse settings, and students lacking educational resources at home.

Although site-specific professional development is intuitively appealing, we have little evidence to guide such efforts. If we knew what worked, for whom, and under what circumstances, we could mandate and encourage through incentives activities that would lead to increased productivity in particular school settings. Unfortunately, because policymakers don't have this important information, most districts leave considerable discretion to teachers to decide, a situation that is largely affected by the incentive structure that typically rewards teachers for seat time rather than for improved performance.

A Problematic Incentive Structure

In most school districts, professional development is a central component of certification renewal and advancement, and in many cases, compensation. While some professional development activities are determined by school, district, and state policies (e.g., mandatory induction programs for new teachers or required district-sponsored workshops), teachers generally have some discretion over their professional development activities. In fact, school districts' professional development policies increasingly involve professional development programs for individual teachers. Many require teachers to develop and complete individualized professional development plans that include workshops, courses, and other opportunities provided by school districts, universities, and professional associations.

Assuming teachers to be rational decisionmakers, they seek to maximize benefit and minimize cost. Without a doubt, there are teachers who will opt for high-quality, rigorous professional development because they wish to improve their teaching to better help the students they serve. But for many in the teacher workforce, this intrinsic reward of improving job performance may not be the overriding consideration when choosing among professional development options, and the incentive structure in most school systems does not explicitly reward teachers for making choices that promote effectiveness. Given a fixed reward (e.g., certification renewal), a rational decisionmaker would arguably choose the alternative with the lowest opportunity cost for the time, money, and effort required. In the most perverse case, a teacher may choose the professional development alternative that involves the least time and effort to satisfy the district requirement even if that alternative is the least effective for their own learning and, ultimately, that of their students. Given that the reward, in this case certification renewal, is for seat time rather than for actual teacher or student outcomes, this scenario is not surprising.

To the extent that district policymakers know what professional development options are most effective, they could structure incentives in ways that shift the cost burden to reduce the opportunity costs associated with those forms of professional development (e.g., provide release time during the school day for mentoring opportunities). In the absence of such knowledge, however, those incentives simply increase the cost to the school or district without any promise of an increase in effectiveness.

Master's degrees present an even more extreme case. Since most teacher salary schedules include degrees as a step that comes with increased compensation, teachers commonly pursue master's degrees as part of their professional development plans. The cost of state policy that rewards, and sometimes requires, master's degrees can be enormous, especially in future salary obligations. If advanced degrees were strongly associated with large increases in teachers' effectiveness, this might be a wise investment. However, the evidence on the effectiveness of master's degrees suggests otherwise. Even among the more consistent findings of a positive effect for high school math and science degrees, the effects are too small to justify the investment.

Further, Knapp and colleagues raise other potential problems likely to be associated with the requirement of a master's degree for teachers. These include exacerbation of teacher shortages and additional burdens on institutions of higher education. They reason that, "on the basis of policy considerations, empirical data, and cost analysis, . . . a universal master's degree requirement is an inefficient method for improving elementary and secondary education" (1990, 27). Likewise, tuition remission policies and salary schedules that reward teachers for earning advanced degrees regardless of whether they are directly related to their teaching assignments or effectiveness may be a poor use of resources. At the very least, support for courses and rewards for advanced degrees should be contingent on alignment between the degree earned and the teacher's content area.

Taken together, these inefficiencies in the provision of professional development suggest that a different model may be needed. For instance, rather than pay for participation, districts should consider rewarding improvements in teachers' performance (this option is discussed more extensively by Steven Rivkin in chapter 9). Referring back to figure 11.1, policymakers should shift their attention from a focus on the first two boxes and give more attention to the boxes toward the right. In other words, teacher and student outcomes, not seat time, should drive investments in professional development.

Measuring teacher performance in ways that are fair and acceptable to teachers is certainly a challenge. Value-added measures that capture growth in student achievement, controlling for other factors, are one approach. Perhaps a better strategy is to use a broader set of measures (including, for example, principal, peer, and parent evaluations and multiple measures of teachers' knowledge and skills) to capture the many ways that effective teachers have an impact on students. These measurement issues are critical to the success of restructured compensation for teachers and are at the heart of shifting professional development investments from a model of "pay for participation" to one of "pay for performance" or "pay for improvement."

A Need for Targeted Support for Professional Development

A final consideration that has important implications for the productivity of investments in professional development is the distribution of resources to support these efforts. Teachers working in chronically low-performing schools and districts may have special professional development needs that warrant close attention and additional support. In many cases, these schools are characterized by large concentrations of students who come from low-income families, who are English language learners, and who have special needs. Even fully qualified teachers often find themselves ill-prepared to teach the diversity of students in low-performing schools (Rice forthcoming). In particular, many teachers who come to those schools with little experience and limited preparation may need additional support to develop the knowledge and skills that they need to be effective. In these cases, states and districts should consider allocating additional time for professional development activities (e.g., decreased teaching loads, full-time substitutes), again with appropriate incentives so teachers are rewarded for enhancing their knowledge and skills in ways that translate into improved student outcomes. Given the hefty costs associated with these policies, research is needed to understand the effects of these highly targeted investments.

Conclusion

Improving teachers' knowledge and skills through high-quality professional development is potentially one of the most important investments of time and money that local, state, and national leaders make in education. However, in the face of limited information about effective professional development, current practice is inefficient. Studies document a substantial investment being made across schools, districts, and states, with little evidence of a return on that investment. The crux of the problem appears to be an incentive structure that rewards seat time rather than improved performance. Policymakers need to consider better ways to structure incentives so that teachers engage in professional development directly related to their work with the potential to improve their teaching practices and, ultimately, their effectiveness. Further, additional resources should be targeted to chronically low-performing schools in ways that decrease the opportunity costs for those teachers to engage in productive professional development that is directly linked with the work they do and, ultimately, to the performance of their students. However, shifting from a "pay for participation" to a "pay for performance" model requires a broader understanding of teacher effectiveness and multiple measures of teacher performance. Clearly, much work is needed in this area. Without a broader understanding of teacher performance and a more comprehensive set of supports for teachers in chronically low-performing schools, professional development will continue to fall short of its promise to enhance human capital.

NOTES

1. This section is adapted from Rice (2000).

2. Odden et al. (2002) do not include future salary obligations or research, development, and dissemination in their cost framework.

3. All estimates have been converted to 2008 dollars.

4. Title I funding is often used to support initiatives that may involve additional professional development for educators.

5. Scholars have debated the appropriateness of including compensation rewards as part of the overall cost of professional development initiatives. Some have argued that future salary obligations should not factor into estimates of the cost of professional development, but should be considered as a routine personnel cost (rather than a training cost) (see Odden et al. 2002). However, others contend that these financial incentives should be included if they serve as a mechanism used by policymakers to encourage teachers to engage in certain types of professional development, to do this at particular stages of their careers, and to achieve certain levels of performance (see Rice 2000).

6. Cohen and Rice identified nine studies, but four were studies of district-wide expenditures that were included in the previous section.

7. These cost estimates are presented in 2008 dollars.

8. However, evening time is not without value. By focusing on daytime working hours in the calculation of forgone earnings, the Knapp et al. study could underestimate the full cost of the programs. Further, to the extent that the forgone earnings approach

to valuing time neglects to include all the time required for teachers to earn the degree (e.g., writing papers, transportation), the former would result in an underestimation of cost.

REFERENCES

Alliance for Excellent Education. 2004. *Tapping the Potential: Retaining and Developing High-Quality New Teachers.* New York: Carnegie Corporation.

Archibald, Sarah, and H. Alix Gallagher. 2002. "A Case Study of Professional Development Expenditures at a Restructured High School." *Education Policy Analysis Archives* 10(29).

Berry, Barnett, Peggy Hopkins-Thompson, and Mandy Hoke. 2002. *Assessing and Supporting New Teachers: Lessons from the Southeast.* Chapel Hill, NC: Southeast Center for Teaching Quality.

Birman, Beatrice F., Laura M. Desimone, Andrew C. Porter, and Michael S. Garet. 2000. "Designing Professional Development That Works." *Educational Leadership* 57(8): 28–33.

Cohen, Carol E., and Jennifer King Rice. 2005. "National Board Certification as Professional Development: Pathways to Success." Washington, DC: The Finance Project.

Cohen, Carol E., Peter Gerber, Claire Handley, Robert Kronley, and Megan Parry. 2001. *Profiles of Selected Promising Professional Development Initiatives.* Washington, DC: The Finance Project.

Corcoran, Thomas B. 1995. "Helping Teachers Teach Well: Transforming Professional Development." RB-16. New Brunswick, NJ: Consortium for Policy Research in Education, Rutgers University.

Croninger, Robert G., Jennifer King Rice, Amy Rathbun, and Masako Nishio. 2007. "Teacher Qualifications and Early Learning: Effects of Certification, Degree, and Experience on First-Grade Student Achievement." *Economics of Education Review* 26(3): 312–24.

Desimone, Laura M., Andrew C. Porter, Michael S. Garet, Kwang Suk Yoon, and Beatrice F. Birman. 2002. "Effects of Professional Development on Teachers' Instruction: Results from a Three-Year Longitudinal Study." *Educational Evaluation and Policy Analysis* 24:81–112.

Eberts, Randall W., and Joe A. Stone. 1984. *Unions and Public Schools.* Lexington, MA: D.C. Heath and Company.

Education Commission of the States. 1997. *Investment in Teacher Professional Development: A Look at 16 Districts.* Denver, CO: Education Commission of the States.

Ehrenberg, Ronald G., and Dominic J. Brewer. 1994. "Do School and Teacher Characteristics Matter? Evidence from High School and Beyond." *Economics of Education Review* 13(1): 1–17.

Elmore, Richard F. 1997. *Investing in Teacher Learning: Staff Development and Instructional Improvement in Community School District #2, New York City.* Washington, DC: National Commission on Teaching and America's Future, Consortium for Policy Research in Education.

Elmore, Richard F., and Deanna Burney. 1999. "Investing in Teacher Learning: Staff Development and Instructional Improvement." In *Teaching as the Learning Profession: Handbook of Policy and Practice,* edited by Linda Darling-Hammond and Gary Sykes (263–91). San Francisco: Jossey-Bass.

Ferguson, Richard F., and Helen F. Ladd. 1996. "How and Why Money Matters: An Analysis of Alabama Schools." In *Holding Schools Accountable: Performance-Based Reform in Education,* edited by Helen F. Ladd (265–98). Washington, DC: Brookings Institution Press.

Fermanich, Mark L. 2002. "School Spending for Professional Development: A Cross-Case Analysis of Seven Schools in One Urban District." *Elementary School Journal* 103(1): 27–50.

Gallagher, H. Alix. 2002. "Elm Street School: A Case Study of Professional Development Expenditures." *Education Policy Analysis Archives* 10(28).

Garet, Michael S., Andrew C. Porter, Laura M. Desimone, Beatrice F. Birman, and Kwang Suk Yoon. 2001. "What Makes Professional Development Effective? Analysis of a National Sample of Teachers." *American Educational Research Journal* 3(4): 915–45.

Glazerman, Steven, Sarah Dolfin, Martha Bleeker, Amy Johnson, Eric Isenberg, Julieta Lugo-Gil, Mary Grider, and Edward Britton. 2008. *Impacts of Comprehensive Teacher Induction: Results from the First Year of a Randomized Controlled Study.* NCEE 2009-4034. Washington, DC: U.S. Department of Education, Institute of Education Sciences, National Center for Education Evaluation and Regional Assistance.

Goldhaber, Dan, and Dominic J. Brewer. 1998. "When Should We Reward Degrees for Teachers?" *Phi Delta Kappan* 80(2): 134–38.

———. 2000. "Does Teacher Certification Matter? High School Teacher Certification Status and Student Achievement." *Educational Evaluation and Policy Analysis* 22(2): 129–46.

Harnisch, Delwyn L. 1987. "Characteristics Associated with Effective Public High Schools." *Journal of Educational Research* 80:233–41.

Hawley, Willis D., and Linda Valli. 1998. "The Essentials of Effective Professional Development: A New Consensus." In *The Heart of the Matter,* edited by Linda Darling-Hammond (127–50). San Francisco: Jossey-Bass.

Ingersoll, Richard M., and Jeffrey M. Kralik. 2004. *The Impact of Mentoring on Teacher Retention: What the Research Says.* Denver, CO: Education Commission of the States.

Killeen, Kieran M., David H. Monk, and Margaret L. Plecki. 2002. "School District Spending on Professional Development: Insights Available from National Data." *Journal of Education Finance* 28(1): 25–50.

Kiesling, Herbert J. 1984. "Assignment Practices and the Relationship of Instructional Time to the Reading Performance of Elementary School Children." *Economics of Education Review* 3(4): 341–50.

Knapp, John L., Robert F. McNergney, Joanne M. Herbert, and Harold L. York. 1990. "Should a Master's Degree Be Required of All Teachers?" *Journal of Teacher Education* 41(2): 27–37.

Link, Charles R., and Edward C. Ratledge. 1979. "Student Perceptions, I.Q., and Achievement." *Journal of Human Resources* 14:98–111.

Little, Judith Warren. 1993. "Teachers Professional Development in a Climate of Educational Reform." *Educational Evaluation and Policy Analysis* 15(2): 129–51.

Little, Judith Warren, William H. Gerritz, David S. Stern, James W. Guthrie, Michael W. Kirst, and David D. Marsh. 1987. "Staff Development in California: Public and Personal Investments, Program Patterns, and Policy Choices." Policy paper PC87-12-15, CPEC. San Francisco: Policy Analysis for California Education and Far West Laboratory for Educational Research and Development.

Miles, Karen Hawley, Allan Odden, Mark Fermanich, and Sarah Archibald. 2004. "Inside the Black Box of School District Spending on Professional Development: Lessons from Five Urban Districts." *Journal of Education Finance* 30(1): 1–26.

Miller, Barbara, Brian Lord, and Judith Dorney. 1994. *Staff Development for Teachers: A Study of Configurations and Costs in Four Districts.* Newton, MA: Education Development Center.

Monk, David H. 1994. "Subject Area Preparation of Secondary Mathematics and Science Teachers and Student Achievement." *Economics of Education Review* 13(2): 125–45.

Moore, Donald R., and Arthur A. Hyde. 1981. *Making Sense of Staff Development: An Analysis of Staff Development Programs and Their Costs in Three Urban School Districts.* Chicago, IL: Designs for Change.

Murnane, Richard J. 1975. *The Impact of School Resources on the Learning of Inner-City Children.* Cambridge, MA: Ballinger Publishing Company.

Murnane, Richard J., and Barbara R. Phillips. 1981. "Learning by Doing, Vintage, and Selection: Three Pieces of the Puzzle Relating Teaching Experience and Teaching Performance." *Economics of Education Review* 1(4): 453–65.

National Center for Education Statistics. 1998. *Toward Better Teaching: Professional Development in 1993–94.* NCES 98-230. Washington, DC: U.S. Department of Education, Office of Educational Research and Improvement, National Center for Education Statistics.

National Foundation for the Improvement of Education. 1996. *Teachers Take Charge of Their Learning: Transforming Professional Development for Student Success.* Washington, DC: The National Foundation for Improvement of Education.

Odden, Allan, Sarah Archibald, Mark Fermanich, and H. Alix Gallagher. 2002. "A Cost Framework for Professional Development." *Journal of Education Finance* 28:51–74.

Rice, Jennifer King. 2000. "Recent Trends in the Theory and Practice of Teacher Professional Development: Implications for Cost." Manuscript prepared for the National Partnership for Excellence and Accountability in Teaching.

———. 2003. "Investing in Teacher Quality: A Framework of Estimating the Cost of Teacher Professional Development." In *Theory and Research in Educational Administration, Volume 2,* edited by Wayne K. Hoy and Cecil G. Miskel (209–33). Greenwich, CT: Information Age Publishing, Inc.

———. 2008. "From Highly Qualified to High Quality: An Imperative for Policy and Research to Recast the Teacher Mold." *Education Finance and Policy* 3(2): 151–65.

———. Forthcoming. "High-Stakes Accountability and Teacher Quality: Coping with Contradictions." In *Transforming Teacher Education: History, Implementation, and Accountability for the 21st Century,* edited by Chance W. Lewis and V. Hill-Jackson. Greenwich, CT: Information Age Publishing.

Rice, Jennifer King, and L. Jane Hall. 2008. "National Board Certification for Teachers: What Does It Cost and How Does It Compare?" *Education Finance and Policy* 3(3): 339–73.

Rowan, Brian, Richard Correnti, and Robert J. Miller. 2002. "What Large-Scale, Survey Research Tells Us about Teacher Effects on Student Achievement: Insights from the 'Prospects' Study of Elementary Schools." CPRE research report. Philadelphia, PA: Consortium for Policy Research in Education.

Sandholtz, Judith Haymore. 2002. "Inservice Training or Professional Development: Contrasting Opportunities in a School/University Partnership." *Teaching and Teacher Education* 18(7): 815–30.

Sparks, Dennis. 1995. "A Paradigm Shift in Staff Development." *The ERIC Review* 3(3): 3–4.

Stern, David, William H. Gerritz, and Judith Warren Little. 1989. "Making the Most of a School District's Two (or Five) Cents: Accounting for Investment in Teachers' Professional Development." *Journal of Education Finance* 14:368–79.

Summers, Anita A., and Barbara L. Wolfe. 1975. "Equality of Educational Opportunity Quantified: A Production Function Approach." Philadelphia, PA: Federal Reserve Bank of Philadelphia.

———. 1977. "Do Schools Make a Difference?" *American Economic Review* 67:639–52.

Sykes, Gary. 1996. "Reform of and as Professional Development." *Phi Delta Kappan* 77(7): 465–67.

Villar, Anthony, and Michael Strong. 2007. "Is Mentoring Worth the Money? A Benefit-Cost Analysis and Five-Year Rate of Return of a Comprehensive Mentoring Program for Beginning Teachers." *ERS Spectrum* 25(3): 1–17.

PART III
Politics of Education Reform/Prospects for the Teaching Profession

12

Reactions from an Education School Dean

David H. Monk

T he chapters in this collection address numerous important issues surrounding the preparation of teachers in the new century and are highly informative and timely. The richness of the essays makes it difficult to prepare a short commentary, and so I can comment on only a subset of the worthy topics. I have also been asked to respond to two questions: (1) How technically and politically feasible are the proposed reforms? and (2) What can be done to improve the performance of schools of education? I will weave my responses to these questions into each of the topics I address.

On the Teacher Labor Supply

I read these chapters and pondered the points about the loss of highly talented women from the teacher labor supply and the increasingly truncated nature of careers during a recent trip to Romania, where I had the opportunity to visit an elementary school. The school's director greeted me warmly and treated me to a tour during which I experienced firsthand the high degree of pride the director and her colleagues took in the school. I asked what had led the director to enter the field of education. She seemed surprised by the question and said, "I could imagine doing nothing else. Working as a teacher has always been my dream."

In my role as the dean of a school of education, I have the opportunity to ask similar questions of our incoming students, and I am struck by how similar their answers are to the heartfelt response by the school director in Romania. Teaching is a field that *calls* people. Penn State students feel this call, and their passionate desire to teach comes from deep places within their souls.

I have little doubt that career paths in education are changing and that we should be making better use of sojourners who enter the field for some portion of their careers, but it would be a mistake to lose sight of those who have a deep-seated passion to teach. I hasten to concede that not all people with this passion have the capacity to be effective. But imagine choosing between a candidate with this passion who needs some assistance to become highly effective and an already-more-capable candidate who lacks the passion and who is looking to make a choice between alternative lines of work based on perceived returns. Yes, we could spend money to bid the more disinterested candidate away from choosing another field, but this could be expensive given the absence of passion. Or we could spend money to build up the skills and capabilities of the candidate who is genuinely called to the field but who needs some extra help to develop the requisite skills. It is not obvious to me which of these choices is the better option, but passion for teaching needs to be recognized as a real resource that can and should be developed and nurtured.

A complementary strategy would involve changing the nature of the work of teachers so it becomes more attractive to intellectually talented people who might otherwise choose other fields. Some recent accountability-inspired initiatives have arguably moved the field in the opposite direction by becoming more prescriptive about how teachers need to spend their time. If the nature of the work is in fact becoming more off-putting to intellectually talented people, schools will need to spend more on salaries to attract them and to overcome the perceived drawbacks. An important underlying question is whether greater accountability can be achieved without undermining the intellectual appeal of teaching as an endeavor. In my more optimistic moments, I believe it is possible to have both intellectually meaningful work for teachers and reasonable levels of accountability.

On Pay for Performance

Several chapters discuss various aspects of linking compensation more directly to measures of performance. Sean P. Corcoran, for example, questions in chapter 3 whether traditional salary schedules properly reward effective teachers, and he links evenness in the treatment of teachers with the drawbacks of uniformly low levels of performance. For me, the problem is not so much with the evenness of performance but with the degree to which the evenness is at a low level. Is it obvious that a highly differentiated system where there are performance high-flyers and bottom-feeders is a good thing? Why not build a system that fosters uniformly high levels of performance with a cleansing mechanism to root out those teachers who are not salvageable? The problem I see is that we have fallen down on cleansing and that there are too many teachers in place who are not living up to the ideals of their profession (even one is too many). Though the cleansing mechanism may be inadequate, it does exist, and critics sometimes overlook the degree to which poor performers select themselves out or are pushed out of the field.[1] It seems possible to move in the direction of more successfully clearing out problematic teachers, and the authors dealing with pensions, deselection, value-added performance appraisal, and the use of enlightened human resource policies all provide guidance about how this can be accomplished.

Differentiated pay is going to be more palatable if there is an obvious reason for the differences in treatment. For example, if a teacher can handle a larger class size than his or her peers, that could count as a legitimate reason for higher pay. Of course, much will depend on what it means "to handle" the larger class, but here is an area where elements of private choice could be introduced. Suppose parents had more discretion over selecting their child's teacher, with the understanding that class sizes would be allowed to vary. The popular teacher would presumably teach more students (and receive more pay), and parents would have to decide whether they prefer to have their child in the larger class with the more-popular teacher or the smaller class with the less-popular teacher.[2] Similar premiums could be attached to the willingness to teach in schools that have histories of being difficult to staff.

I found several jarring assertions in the chapters dealing with pay for performance, and these warrant comment. For example, in chapter 6, Frederick M. Hess notes that teaching is a less-attractive profession for those who want to be recognized and rewarded on the basis of their accomplishments and hard work. Why presume that teachers do not want to be recognized for their accomplishments? How does it follow that a commitment to a collective endeavor where the goal is to raise group performance is tantamount to being indifferent about there being rewards to accomplishment? Teachers can still be interested in rewards to performance even if the system is not structured to separate teachers.

Eric A. Hanushek makes a similar point in chapter 8 and speculates that a serious effort to deselect teachers will make more risk-averse people shy away from teaching. Current candidates for teaching positions are arguably among the most intensively evaluated people on earth. The criteria in use may not be to Hanushek's liking, but aspiring teachers are scrutinized with stunning frequency during their preparation programs. The feedback is highly personal and can be quite dispiriting. Teaching is an intensely personal act, and it is hard to provide criticism without the comments striking raw nerves. Students in pre-service programs are typically young and unsure of themselves. It takes courage to teach and it takes time to develop teaching skills. Harsh or ill-considered criticism can scar a candidate irreparably, and Hanushek is too quick to slide over the fact that students pursuing teacher preparation programs currently accept considerable risk.

Moreover, exemplary human resource practices can be antithetical to some of the other reforms advocated elsewhere in this volume. Human resource best practice emphasizes due process and the avoidance of legal challenge. This posture can make it devilishly difficult to dismiss people for cause. The deselecting ideas advocated by Hanushek, even if we sweep away the vexing problems associated with making sure the low performers have really been identified, will run into implementation problems if conventional best practice human resource policies are followed.

On Technology

Several authors address the role technology can and should play in the new teaching profession, most notably Paul T. Hill (chapter 7) and Hess. The points they make are compelling, and I agree that technology offers great potential to transform the schools and to gain more cost-effective operations. I also agree that great challenges surround the realization of this potential.

In the business-as-usual world, computing and telecommunication technologies develop in ways that are largely disconnected from the needs of schools. The development is driven by an exploration of what is possible to do electronically, with the focus on applications coming later. Moreover, these technologies tend to be viewed as add-ons to the resources already present in the classrooms. Thus, the computers become tools used by teachers in classrooms to enhance what they are already doing. This is not necessarily a bad result, but it is expensive and fraught with missed opportunities.

In a better world, research and development efforts would be much more closely connected to what is being learned about teaching and learning cognitive processes. In a better world, technology need not take second seat to prevailing practice but instead becomes an engine of reform and improvement.

In a better world, there is a realization that content knowledge can come from many sources and that we need not rely as heavily as we currently do on the proximate classroom teacher as the font of content knowledge. Teachers can rely more heavily on embodied human resources that arrive in the classroom thanks to technology and can thereby work more effectively with larger numbers of pupils.

In a better world, teachers have access to better diagnostic information thanks to modern and largely unobtrusive assessment instruments that are infused into the instructional program due, in part, to technology. And in this better world, teachers have the time they need to make sense of the diagnostic information and can harness technology to better tailor instructional experiences to meet the needs of their students.

In short, the better world makes more effective use of existing as well as future technologies and can actually cut down on costs. Hill is skeptical about the degree to which education schools can help reach the better world. I tend to be more optimistic and note that researchers in education schools are actively exploring what is possible with technology. The larger challenge I see involves stimulating demand in the schools for the more enlightened types and uses of technology.

On the Mistrust of Education Schools

Given my role as an education school dean, I suppose it is not surprising that I am more upbeat about the role education schools can play in building the new teaching profession than some of the authors in this volume. The shriller critics of education schools tend to portray them as shaky academic units that delight in working with weak students for the sake of driving K–12 schools into the ground. My view is different. I see these schools, instead, as academic units that are focused on some of the most intellectually complex and interesting phenomena imaginable. One byproduct of the complexity is a research base for the field that is not nearly well enough developed. And, as a consequence, the education schools are in the unenviable position of having to design programs absent the necessary underlying scientific knowledge. Education schools are not unique in this regard, but in the field of education the gaps between the definitive knowledge base and practice are large. Moreover, education schools have little choice but to work with those who are currently seeking entry into the field of education. Some, but not all, of these students have strong academic records, and the presence of weaker students raises challenging questions about what to do with less-than-ideal candidates who are nevertheless in demand to populate the nation's classrooms as teachers.

Thus, I am sympathetic to what education schools are trying to accomplish. I am also heartened by the progress being made to deepen and extend the knowledge base of the field and by the indicators suggesting that students with stronger and stronger academic credentials are entering the field of education (see Gitomer 2007).

Particularly Promising Policy Options

As I took a final look at the chapters, I was struck by a number of particularly promising policy options that perhaps would not be too difficult to pursue:

- Reducing the prevailing tendency for K–12 school districts, particularly large urban school districts, to hire late in the hiring cycle;
- Moving the pension system in the directions recommended in chapter 10, particularly the greater use of a defined-contribution approach;
- Moving toward differentiated pay by tying extra compensation to readily observable indicators of greater productivity, such as the ability to handle a larger class or the willingness (and ability) to teach in a difficult-to-staff school; and
- Introducing elements of the private market into the existing public governance model by providing more choice to parents about

the teacher for their child even if class sizes began to vary among teachers.

I was tempted to add modifying human resource policies to make it less difficult to dismiss low-performing teachers, but this cannot really be counted as an easy policy to pursue given the high stakes involved. There is a tendency to view this as an all-or-nothing kind of reform (i.e., like abolishing tenure), and perhaps we have reached a level of sophistication and alarm that will permit us to take a few steps in the direction of making dismissals for cause more acceptable while still protecting teachers' rights. Pre-service teacher preparation programs do dismiss people for cause; this typically happens at the student-teaching level when it becomes clear that the aspiring teacher is not going to succeed. Perhaps there are ways for school districts to benefit from what education schools have learned about how to dismiss teacher candidates who are not performing well, particularly during the probationary tenure period when the due process requirements for a dismissal are relatively modest.

Conclusion

What stands out from this volume in terms of policy relevance is that the authors do more than repeat what is already known. Rather, they show that changes are taking place, and this is what policymakers need to know and want to know. For example, Corcoran shows that the tendency for low-income students to have teachers with questionable credentials is growing. If things are getting worse, policymakers need to know, and the focus needs to be on what can be done to reverse the erosion. Something is happening that is making things deteriorate, and steps can and should be taken to make the necessary changes. This focus on dynamics is helpful and well considered. It is one of the defining features of this volume and accounts for what I expect to be the significant positive impact of the collection.

NOTES

1. It is painful to watch a poor performer in front of a class. It must be even more painful to be the poor performer.

2. For more along these lines, see Monk (2007).

REFERENCES

Gitomer, Drew H. 2007. "Teacher Quality in a Changing Policy Landscape: Improvements in the Teacher Pool." Policy information report. Princeton, NJ: Educational Testing Service.

Monk, David H. 2007. "Out of the Box: Fundamental Change in School Funding." Working Paper 12. Seattle: School Finance Redesign Project, Center on Reinventing Public Education, University of Washington.

13

Reactions from an Urban School Superintendent

Joel I. Klein

In education reform, a realm where disagreement is far more common than agreement and universal agreement is almost unheard of, nearly everybody concurs that effective teachers are the most essential school-improvement ingredient. Although there is concurrence that effective teachers are critical to transforming education, we are far from a consensus about how to get more effective teachers through development, recruitment, and in-service training. There's even disagreement about how to measure the effectiveness of a teacher. Welcome to my world!

This volume documents many of the challenges facing urban school districts in thinking through effective teacher policies, especially in high-needs schools. It also chronicles the evolution of the policy, labor, and social forces that have, in recent decades, changed the teaching force in New York City and in other urban districts across America. The authors in this volume agree that the results, particularly for our poorest, highest-needs students, are unacceptable. The views they express are the ones that many school reformers have grappled with for years: though we know that the capabilities of teachers and school leaders are essential to student learning, we have not done nearly enough to act on this knowledge in ways that will create the kinds of learning gains our students need to be successful. It's time for America to fundamentally rethink its approach to preparing, recruiting, developing, assessing, and compensating our educators.

The editors of this book asked me to comment on which ideas presented herein are politically and operationally feasible.

In answer, I will first detail how we have approached talent management in New York City and what we have accomplished. As with all of our Children First school reforms, the key to talent management has not been a single initiative or strategy; it is an insistence on, first, setting clear and common goals and expectations, and then managing the entire talent cycle—from recruitment and development through performance management and compensation—against those goals and expectations. I will describe this cycle in more detail, but to be clear, by "goals and expectations," I mean quantitative measures of student learning that are supplemented by qualitative assessments of the skills teachers and principals need to help students learn. If it's ultimately not about student learning, it's not important.

Second, I will argue that doing merely what is "feasible" is not enough to change schools and improve outcomes for students. If we aim for what is feasible, we're aiming too low. Urban school districts like New York City must balance many competing interests. But this challenge cannot be used as an excuse for accepting the status quo—or marginal increments thereto—as the inevitable. I cannot claim that we have implemented the perfect solution in New York. In many cases, we have had to abide by state policy and union contracts rather than implementing the reforms I would consider ideal. But we have nevertheless tackled some thorny, politically charged issues to good effect for our children.

As policymakers, we must always think critically and reconsider our assumptions (along the lines of what Frederick M. Hess describes in his chapter on the seven anachronistic views of teaching). We must then adopt an aggressive and holistic approach to attract, develop, and retain the most capable people.

New York City's Children First Reforms

In New York City, we called our reform strategy "Children First," and we did that for a reason: I believe every initiative must be focused on the needs and interests of children, not those of the adults, which have generally been the organizing principal in education. To that end, Children First focused on three key areas: leadership, empowerment, and accountability. Why? Because school leaders will meet our high standards if we give them the authority, the tools, and the resources they need to make and execute smart decisions (including hiring the best teachers and, yes, firing those who shouldn't teach).

Since we launched our Children First reforms, we have achieved significant results. Six years ago, roughly half of New York City's 4th graders and one-third of the city's 8th graders were meeting or exceeding state standards in math and reading. Today, seven in ten New York City public school students in grades 3 through 8 are meeting or exceeding state standards in math, and almost six in ten are meeting or exceeding these standards in English language arts. Between 2002 and 2007, our graduation rate increased by more than 10 percentage points after having been stagnant for the preceding decade. In fact, this past year, 11,000 more students graduated as compared to when we started, and many of them are now in college. As a result of significant gains like these, as well as our progress in narrowing the achievement gap separating students of different races and need levels, New York City is receiving national recognition. Last year, the city won America's most prestigious education award, the Broad Prize for Urban Education. I am very proud of how far we have come as a system and all that students, principals, teachers, and other school staff have accomplished.

Developing a Systemic End-to-End Approach to Talent Management

In general, I have found that "programs" and "initiatives" are not capable of fixing schools. True reform requires a comprehensive approach that goes to the heart of the overall systemic culture. When it comes to improving the effectiveness of teachers and school leaders, we must look at every stage of the process and think expansively as we develop solutions. I would caution anybody who attempts to "solve" the problem by focusing on one or two elements of the challenge (such as hiring teachers or training principals). To improve the quality of educators, it is important to think about how to dismiss poor performers, how to address the causes of attrition, and how to effectively compensate educators. School districts must innovate at every stage of talent management—end to end—from teacher preparation, recruitment, and selection to development, performance management, working conditions, and compensation. And the same goes for school leaders, who, after all, are the talent managers of teachers.

If I had to pick one place to start, it would be clearly defining the outcomes expected of teachers and school leaders. In New York City, we define outcomes in terms of student learning and progress toward graduation from high school. Measuring outcomes is not easy and is certainly controversial, but it is imperative to ensuring that all the work that goes into recruiting, developing, and retaining teachers and principals results in coherent progress toward improved results for students.

We have developed multiple measures of student outcomes. We have also assessed teachers and school leaders against a set of skills that, research shows, is needed to advance student learning. These sorts of assessments shed light on what development steps will improve teacher performance and student outcomes.

As our outcome and skills assessment measurements have improved, and as we collect data at every stage of the talent management cycle, we now have a coherent end-to-end system of talent management that can be steadily improved in ways that directly benefit our students. This work never stops.

As chapter 4 describes, the private sector took the lead in creating the discipline of human capital management involving clear outcome measurement and aligned actions at all stages of the talent cycle. School systems will benefit from this work if they implement a comprehensive and structured process to recruit, develop, and retain educators based squarely on student achievement outcomes, with data gathered at every stage to diagnose and improve the process.

Managing Principal Talent in New York City

Under New York City's Children First reform strategy, principals are the key agents of change in our system. We believe change must be directed from schools, where the students are, not be imposed from a central office. Meaningful change may be different in every school, and we have examples of schools in the same building, drawing students from the same communities, with very different reform strategies and equally impressive results for their students.

For our approach to work, each of our 1,500 principals must be an agent of change. To make plain what we expect principals to achieve, we have established clear expectations for our school leaders and created ways to measure the outcomes for which we hold them accountable.

We issue annual school Progress Reports, which measure each school's student achievement in absolute results and each student's growth over time. The reports also show how well schools are meeting the needs of parents, students, and teachers, whose feedback is captured during our annual Learning Environment Survey. Principals are further evaluated during Quality Reviews, on-site evaluations by experienced educators who analyze how well schools are organized to help students achieve.

As we have implemented a robust set of accountability tools, we have also given our principals unprecedented freedom in decisionmaking at their schools. It is now principals, not external administrators, who take the lead in hiring staff, developing curricula, allocating budgets, and creating professional development opportunities for their staff. Our principals now have increased authority to make decisions about the support they receive, the members of their teams, how days are programmed, and how budgets are allocated. Today, for example, principals in New York City can choose from among five public and four private (nonprofit) school support organizations and select the one they think is best equipped to help them do everything from deciding which textbooks to purchase and which enrichment programs are most appropriate, to determining the best ways to leverage community partnerships and communicate with diverse parent populations. These support organizations have to compete for principals' business and only succeed if principals succeed.

All of this means that talent management practices around principals have to ensure we select, develop, and keep the principals who can achieve the outcomes we want through effective exercise of their newfound empowerment. We have moved on every front with leadership empowerment and accountability in mind:

- In 2003, we created the New York City Leadership Academy to prepare aspiring principals to succeed and to coach early-career principals as they put their training into practice. Principal candidates who are not yet certified can earn their certification at the Leadership Academy. But certification alone, as defined by New York State, is not adequate training to be an effective principal. To go beyond certification and prepare for success as a school leader, aspiring principals build their skills and develop their leadership through the Leadership Academy's year-long residency with a proven mentor principal in a high-needs school.

- We have also overhauled our principal selection process to ensure every school is led by a confident, competent leader. We rigorously screen candidates for principal jobs against a defined set of leadership competences that evidence suggests relate to success in driving student outcomes. It's no longer "who you know" but rather "what you know."

- Once hired, principals receive annual performance reviews that are tied directly to the Progress Report and Quality Review described above. They also sign detailed performance agreements in which they set performance goals for their schools and agree to be held accountable for meeting these targets.

- Compensation has been redesigned to attract and keep the best principals. We have increased principal starting salaries by 23 percent since 2002 in recognition of the important and challenging job they hold. In addition, every principal is eligible for annual bonuses of up to $25,000 based on achievement results. We have additional bonus opportunities for "Executive Principals" with outstanding track records who agree to transfer to a school in need of a dramatic turnaround.

- As we hold principals accountable for student learning, we hold much of the rest of the organization accountable for how they serve principals through a biannual Principal Satisfaction Survey. As an organization, we are constantly evolving and adapting to better serve our principals so they can better serve our students.

Our groundbreaking approach to hiring, training, and developing our principals is fundamentally important in attracting the best and brightest to New York City schools. With more than three qualified candidates for every vacant principal position, we can be selective, making sure we hire only the strongest leaders able to be full and constructive participants in our reform efforts. And by empowering principals and treating them as professionals, we are making their position a more desirable and valued one in our city. To ensure that positive trends continue, we measure results at every stage of the process, rewarding school leaders who succeed and removing those who don't.

Significant Progress in Teacher Talent Management

We have also made great strides in ensuring the quality and effectiveness of our teachers. It wasn't long ago that the school year started with many teacher positions unfilled. It wasn't long ago when teachers didn't receive their first paychecks until October. In those days, teachers hired with minimal screening under "emergency certification" provisions filled many jobs, especially in schools with the highest rates of poverty and students with disabilities and in hard-to-staff subject areas such as math, science, and special education. Teachers who remained on the job for three years earned tenure virtually automatically, and few teachers were ever removed for poor performance.

As with principals, no one teacher-quality initiative could have corrected these problems. A number of meaningful changes were needed to produce real results. Our common objective, raising student achievement, guided the design and implementation of our new initiatives.

To bring the best teachers to our system, we now provide financial incentives for teachers to accept positions in subject areas with shortages and in hard-to-staff neighborhoods. We make aggressive use of alternative certification programs, including our own Teaching Fellows program and Teach For America, to hire teachers who will teach in shortage subject areas such as math, science, and special education and take jobs in our highest-needs schools. We have increased starting salaries by 43 percent since 2002. These steps have made becoming a teacher in New York City an attractive and rewarding career choice. As a result, we now have seven applicants for every new hire.

With this large pool of applicants, principals have many choices as they select teachers for their schools and classrooms. With data from extensive research on teacher effectiveness with student learning, we now screen every applicant for traits and skills that best predict their future success. Principals have new online tools to help them make the best choices among candidates. Principals are free to make those choices now that we have worked with the teachers' union to make contract changes eliminating forced placements of teachers in open positions and "bumping" of less-experienced teachers by more senior transferees. And, if a teacher discovers that his or her school is not an appropriate match, we have made it possible for teachers to transition smoothly into new assignments. More than 2,000 teachers transfer within our system every year, and both teachers and principals report that they see the benefit from having mutual choice around transfers.

No matter how vast our candidate pool or how rigorous our screening, we cannot stop at teacher recruitment and selection to ensure the effectiveness of our teaching force. In our schools, we work hard to support our teachers to develop the skills that evidence suggests give them the best chance to help their students learn. All new teachers are mentored by more-experienced teachers in their schools and receive professional development opportunities selected by their principals. Professional development used to be "one size fits all." Today, it is school driven and tailored to the needs of individual teachers. Chapter 11 describes a contemporary conceptualization of professional development as a more collaborative enterprise among teachers engaged in improving instruction together.

We are empowering teachers to take more ownership of student learning and their own development at the same time. Teachers now have new and unprecedented technology tools to collect and analyze data about their students, and every school has several inquiry teams that allow teachers to collaborate to solve instructional problems at their schools. Teachers are taking charge of their own support and development needs through new online knowledge management and social networking programs that facilitate the sharing of successful strategies and materials.

If teachers are able to develop their skills and contribute to student learning, they deserve reward and recognition. If they don't develop and contribute, our performance management systems have to make sure they don't continue to teach. Because teacher tenure brings with it significant job protections for life, our principals are now more active in the teacher tenure decision process, and we have fostered a culture that supports them in being more selective when granting lifetime job protection. We have also provided new legal and supervisory resources to principals to remove the least effective tenured teachers, making sure that a burdensome process is not a roadblock in removing teachers who have not demonstrated their effectiveness in the classroom. Historically, only 10 in 55,000 tenured teachers have been removed for incompetence, and in a city with nearly 80,000 teachers, we know that more than 0.01 percent of tenured teachers are failing our students.

Rewards for excellent performance should include compensation. This is an area of reform in which we must work with the United Federation of Teachers to implement changes. Together, we have developed three key initiatives dealing with compensation. First, our Lead Teacher Program allows teachers selected on the basis of their performance, not their seniority, to earn an extra $10,000 a year to move to or remain in a high-needs school and do professional development half-time while teaching half-time. Second, we recruit talented and experienced math, science, and special education teachers from other jurisdictions by paying them a three-year signing bonus of $15,000 if they teach in our high-needs schools. And in the 2007–08 school year, we created a schoolwide bonus program for 200 high-needs schools that provides a school with a bonus pool of up to $3,000 per teacher if the school meets its student achievement goals. A school committee (with representatives for teachers and the principal) decides how to allocate the bonus.

As teachers develop into effective educators, we need them to remain committed to their profession and to our students. Working conditions matter here, and teachers are justified in expecting to be treated as professionals, just like in any other line of work. When I came into this system, teachers had to wait months to be paid for the first time and had great difficulty getting the answers to basic human resources (HR) questions about benefits and employment. This was unacceptable. We overhauled our system of supports, creating HR Connect, a call center that now answers more than 1,000 calls a day from teachers and other staff members. We also gave teachers a voice through our annual Learning Environment Survey. In recent years, we created a new web site and e-newsletter devoted exclusively to serving teachers by providing helpful instructional resources and the answers to many HR questions.

By innovating at all stages of the teacher talent management cycle, we are seeing more teachers coming to and staying in New York City. With seven applicants for every teaching job, almost no schools open with teacher vacancies. Teacher attrition rates have dropped since 2002, with the overall attrition rate falling by nearly 3 percentage points and the first-year attrition rate declining by nearly 6 percentage points. Research (see Boyd et al. 2008) has documented a narrowing in the teacher qualification gap between high- and low-poverty schools and has also shown a narrowing in the achievement gap in these schools, credited directly to our teacher recruitment and selection practices.

We expect our results will continue to improve as we collect additional data on applicants, new hires, and seasoned teachers so we can pick out trends in teacher development, retention, and effectiveness. We use data to find what works. Once we identify these qualities and strategies, we act on this information to target our weaknesses and replicate our strengths, always looking for continuous improvement in our human capital management cycle.

Moving Forward

We have focused intently on improving the effectiveness of our teachers and school leaders since 2002—and we have made significant progress. The changes we have made represent hard work, courage, and perseverance on the part of many: our partners at the teachers' and principals' unions, district staff, nonprofit partner organizations, private foundations that have supported research and development in key reform areas, and school principals and teachers who have stepped up to the challenges in a fast-changing environment. Today, leaders in New York, the nation, and even other countries are pointing to our example when they discuss strategies for improving the quality and effectiveness of public education.

Although it is heartening to receive recognition for the value of our reforms, it is also important that we—and our colleagues who are committed to meaningful school reform—acknowledge that the changes we have fought for and implemented here in New York City have not gone nearly far enough. We cannot afford to be remotely satisfied with what we've accomplished.

Going forward, we must do at least the following:

1. Ensure we have fair and rigorous ways to measure teacher impact on student learning for all teachers.
2. Rethink teacher certification requirements to better match supply with demand for effective teachers.
3. Fundamentally overhaul our systems of teacher compensation and benefits.
4. Exploit the promise technology holds for improving both the education of our students and the working environment for educators.

Ensure We Have Fair and Rigorous Ways to Measure Teacher Impact on Student Learning for All Teachers

New York City has a multifaceted and robust system to assess school and principal contributions to student learning, but our measures of teachers' impacts are less developed. Just recently, in December 2008, we provided all schools and teachers in grades 4 through 8 reading and math with Teacher Data Reports showing the value-added contribution of teachers to student learning. Today, the information in these reports may be used for developmental purposes only and not for evaluations. I believe these kinds of measurements need to become part of a comprehensive approach to teacher talent management, not as a single determinant of performance, but definitely as one way to determine development needs, assess performance, and reward effectiveness.

I am unapologetic about using test-based measures such as our school Progress Reports and the Teacher Data Reports as one way to gauge the effectiveness of our schools and educators. Although the tests behind the metrics can and should be improved, far too many of our students have failed to master the critical basic skills these tests measure, and research shows that if they do not master these skills, they will have greatly diminished chances for positive life outcomes beyond school. We also know that teachers vary tremendously in their impact on student learning as measured by tests. We must use the insight we get from these kinds of measures to improve instruction. We must use it as one input at every stage of the talent-management cycle to ground our actions in the reality of the impact we are having on student learning.

And, as we proceed, we also must extend our ability to quantify teacher impact to other grades and subjects. Similarly, we must develop ways to measure teacher impact on the development of the critical thinking and creativity skills called for in chapter 2, but not at the expense of ensuring student mastery of the basics.

We also need to innovate on classroom observation tools and performance measurement of teacher skills and competencies to find robust but implementable approaches, validated empirically as being related to student achievement, which can be combined with quantitative measures for a rich picture of teacher strengths and development needs. A combination of validated skills measurements, schoolwide achievement, and teacher value-added measures could be combined into a fair and balanced performance management process. For all the controversy, some of which is discussed in chapter 9, around the validity of test-based teacher value-added measures, it amazes me that we continue to rely on subjective teacher performance management systems that proclaim 99 percent of the adults in our schools to be doing a satisfactory job while so many of our students are plainly failing.

This reluctance to hold teachers accountable is particularly remarkable because for decades, reformers have talked about the need to look at how well teachers are actually teaching.

The iconic teachers' union leader Al Shanker long ago observed, "The key is that unless there is accountability, we will never get the right system. As long as there are no consequences if kids or adults don't perform, as long as the discussion is not about education and student outcomes, then we're playing a game as to who has the power."

Nevertheless, we continue to avoid focusing on the most important thing: how to measure the quality of classroom teaching and its impact on student learning. As Mike Schmoker recently wrote, when it comes to teaching, we have had a "crippling, if unintended, tradition of averting our eyes from what actually goes on in the classroom for the sake of harmony." As a result, he concluded, "we were kept from seeing evidence that some teachers were vastly more effective than others" (2006, 14, 27).

Rethink Teacher Certification Requirements

America's stubborn resistance to measure teachers based on their effect on student learning has led urban school systems to try to regulate inputs in ways that can actually inhibit outcomes. One powerful example is the regulation around teacher certification. We have created barriers that discourage noncertified people from working in our schools—even if they could be committed, effective teachers. These regulations push teachers to gather up credit hours and credentials, even though research shows consistently that credentials are not correlated with student learning. We leave teacher preparation to education schools that are producing a vast oversupply of teachers in areas like elementary education while producing far too few in math, science, and secondary special education. Certification rules and our union contracts force us to divert resources to fund master's degrees for our Teaching Fellows as a way of attracting shortage subject-area teachers when we would prefer to use those funds for direct compensation or performance bonuses. We are disregarding research and practice in deference to a theory (that certification makes teachers more effective) that has been disproven.

Not focusing on student outcomes thus bars effective teachers from classrooms and entrenches inside the classroom teachers who are not effective. It also allows people who demonstrate that they are not good at the job to remain in classrooms, teaching students.

Performance management systems that declare all teachers equally "highly qualified" don't make sense—especially when we know that most urban school districts are failing students.

Some states see the merit in this argument and have allowed in their urban districts more competition in the preparation of teachers. The programs that have emerged are sharply focused on ensuring their graduates have positive impacts on student learning. Boston and Chicago have small but promising "teacher residency" experiments in which new teachers can earn certification while spending a year as co-teachers in classrooms. Formal coursework is limited and carefully designed around what new teachers need. Louisiana permits the New Teacher Project to run a certification program that is separate from education schools and publicly produces measurements of the student learning outcomes of graduates of all its teacher preparation programs. Private funding has enabled three charter school organizations to attract Hunter College to work with them to start Teacher You, which will go beyond New York State's certification requirements and set up graduation standards that ensure the positive impact of its graduates on student learning.

Fundamentally Overhaul Our Systems of Teacher Compensation and Benefits

We cannot expect that if we maintain the same rigid, undifferentiated, seniority-based pay system with the highest reward coming at the end of a career in both pay and pensions, we will be able to attract and retain the kinds of teachers that our students need and deserve.

In almost every industry, people are paid what they are worth in the marketplace. In education, however, people are paid what everybody else—with the same seniority and credentials—is paid, no matter how well they do, no matter what they teach, no matter what special skills or knowledge they bring to the job.

In New York City, we've created some special bonus programs that pay principals or teachers extra for strong performance. But these are limited programs and don't fundamentally change the way our educators are compensated.

We must start looking hard at the way we compensate our educators. And we must ask hard questions that most people do not want to ask. Does it make sense, for example, to use 10-month pay rates? Does it make sense to give out raises that do not correspond to improvements in productivity? Does it make sense to maintain a traditional defined-benefit pension system that, as chapter 11 points out, is illogical for the needs of today's workforce?

I would argue that districts and their unions must come to grips with issues of shortage-area pay, variable compensation based on team and individual performance, and the end of lockstep raises and back-loaded pension systems. Our school systems could always use more money, but given the constraints of the real world, I believe we must use the funds in our combined compensation and benefit systems very differently if we are to attract and retain the caliber of teachers across all subject areas that we need and to reward those who contribute to the challenges of educating our students.

Technology Holds Promise for Improving the Quality of Education and the Working Environment for Educators

As Paul T. Hill describes in chapter 7, technology is changing the way students learn and has much underexploited potential for our schools to help students learn. He also describes at length how greater adoption of instructional technology in schools will force change to pre-service teacher education, certification rules, and the nature of the daily work of teaching and school leadership.

What I see from the early work we have done in New York City is that technology has potential to dramatically improve student learning and empower educators as individuals and teams to direct effective instruction in schools in professionally fulfilling ways. In New York, we now provide schools with rich data about the achievement and learning needs of every student and give all teachers powerful online tools to find teacher-support resources they need and to collaborate with colleagues. We believe that school-based inquiry teams, enabled by technology tools, can help us to improve educational outcomes for students. They may also eventually replace traditional professional development as the main way to build teacher skills and competencies. I can foresee even more dramatic uses of technology to enable teachers to more effectively reach the varied learning needs of each student in the class while making learning more relevant and engaging to today's youth. And if the job of educating our students becomes more doable, it will also become more desirable to those contemplating entering the profession. Perhaps more than anything else, teachers want to succeed and feel valued for their work, and we must do everything in our power to help them make that happen. I think technology provides a largely untapped opportunity in this regard and, while we are still in the early phases of exploring these kinds of technology-driven instructional approaches, I am confident they merit significant attention and investment.

REFERENCES

Boyd, Donald J., Hamilton Lankford, Susanna Loeb, Jonah E. Rockoff, and James H. Wyckoff. 2008. "The Narrowing Gap in New York City Teacher Qualifications and Its Implications for Student Achievement in High-Poverty Schools." Working Paper 14021. Cambridge, MA: National Bureau of Economic Research.

Schmoker, Mike. 2006. *Results Now: How We Can Achieve Unprecedented Improvements in Teaching and Learning.* Alexandria, VA: Association for Supervision and Curriculum Development.

14

Reactions from a Teachers' Union Leader

Randi Weingarten

I n this chapter, I respond to some of the ideas and strategies for improving the quality of teachers and teaching in the United States suggested in this volume.

Creating a New Teaching Profession offers a number of ideas that could potentially improve the teaching profession, and I appreciate the opportunity to review it. I have been asked to do so with an eye to what is politically and technically viable. As the elected leader of 1.4 million practitioners, including many who teach in schools every day, I will attempt to provide some insight to both what is viable and what has been tried and has been successful in improving teaching and learning in our nation's schools.

A central part of the American Federation of Teachers' (AFT's) mission is to strengthen the institutions where our members work. To do that for our public schools, we need to ensure that all children have teachers who know their content and how to teach it. We also need to ensure that schools are safe, respectful, and nurturing environments for all students and staff. Repeatedly we have talked about the four C's—rich curriculum, the capacity to build the profession, the collaboration that is necessary for schools to work well, and bringing in the community and auxiliary services, because schools cannot do it all.

Teacher Recruitment and Retention

As is noted repeatedly throughout this volume, teacher quality is the most important school-related variable affecting student achievement. AFT members will vouch for that and would agree with the thrust of this book, that schools with children with the greatest needs must not be staffed by teachers with the least experience.

This volume offers several innovative ideas to attract and retain teachers in needy schools. I am intimately familiar with this challenge through my work in New York City. To attract and retain teachers in New York's schools, the mayor and I negotiated a total 43 percent salary increase between 2002 and 2008, which made us competitive with surrounding districts. As opposed to bonuses, these raises increased teachers' standard of living because they were ongoing and predictable.

Professional Development

Money was part of but not the entire solution. We also focused our attention on ensuring that each school was safe and orderly and had the necessary teaching materials and facilities. The district and union also provided relevant professional development tailored to the needs of the teachers in each school—much of which was done through on-site union-operated Teacher Centers. The result of the combination of these three efforts has been an increase in the number of experienced teachers in the district, and a more even distribution of teacher experience across schools regardless of poverty levels. Now, New York City schools with more than 80 percent poverty levels have the same proportion of experienced teachers as all other schools in the city.

Eric A. Hanushek and Jennifer King Rice, the authors of chapters 8 and 11, respectively, agree that the ideal way to improve teaching and learning in America's schools is through high-quality professional development. However, both authors fail to see measurable results in higher student achievement, so they have sought alternative methods. In Hanushek's case, the solution is to identify ineffective teachers and fire them; Rice wants to pay teachers for results instead of credentials.

Rice argues that, given the limited return on investment districts receive for paying teachers more for advanced degrees or additional credits, districts should abandon this policy and simply pay teachers based on their students' test results. A better solution would be to ensure that every teacher teaches only the subject areas for which he or she is prepared and, second, to improve the quality and relevance of the pre- and post-service training provided to teachers and future teachers. Although the research is mixed on the effects on teacher effectiveness of earning an advanced degree, we do know that in some subject areas, advanced degrees make a difference in student test scores. For example, teachers with master's degrees in math and in science produce students who outperform students of teachers without advanced degrees in those subjects (Goldhaber and Brewer 1997).

Of course, the quality of professional development varies widely. High-quality professional development is classroom-based, focused on instruction, embedded in the school day and in the work of teachers, collegial, and collaborative. It includes induction, mentoring, and ongoing support. Low-quality professional development is brief, episodic, and disconnected from what is happening in classrooms. Unfortunately, it happens all too often in America's schools. It is no wonder that it does not yield a return on investment.

Rice mentions in passing that reworking schools' organizational structures and use of time to allow for teacher collaboration and mentoring programs is one of the more promising developments in the professional development arena. The AFT strongly supports both high-quality mentoring and induction programs and innovative uses of time, including dedicated time during the school day for teachers to problem solve and share successful strategies to strengthen student learning.

The solution is to figure out what are the critical components of professional development that spur student achievement. It is highly unlikely that this will translate into professional development that is the same for all teachers, with all sorts of learning styles and at all grade levels, and for all groups of students. So, I concur with King that we should prioritize professional development that will help teachers in chronically low-performing schools be effective. This will require a significant amount of research and an investment by the federal government and philanthropic organizations, and will also require willing participation by state and local school systems and their teachers.

In many ways this is what the new AFT Innovation Fund seeks to address. Announced in fall 2008, the AFT Innovation Fund is intended to support local union-led efforts to improve public schools across the country. The fund will award grants to local and state labor management partnerships that advance programs with a successful track record or that encourage the implementation of promising new programs.

Performance Pay

On the idea forwarded about differentiated pay, I can share my experiences in New York City. After increasing salaries across the board, Mayor Bloomberg and I reached agreement on a schoolwide performance-pay system in more than 200 high-needs schools. These schools, through a vote by staff, elected to participate and then decided on the distribution of the bonus, provided that everyone in the school could share in a portion of it. This was essentially an experiment to see if collaboration, strong professional support, and additional money could spur student achievement. The result in this first year of implementation is that in 128 schools, staffs are receiving bonuses. Even more promising, all but two of the participating schools have elected to participate again this year. I believe that this success speaks for itself and provides an essential lesson for those who want to experiment with differentiated compensation: If innovation is collaborative and fair, and if a support system is in place, teachers will embrace innovation and it will succeed.

Sort and Fire

These positive approaches will yield better results than "teacher deselection," discussed in chapter 8 in this volume, which forwards the proposition that school systems should systematically identify and remove poorly performing teachers. Hanushek does not specify how teachers are to be "deselected." We know that the current models for measuring teacher effectiveness (and ineffectiveness) are wrought with problems, and I discuss these problems in detail below.

Setting aside for now the problem that even if we wanted to, we could not properly identify which teachers to deselect, Hanushek's foundation—that academically struggling schools are the result of concentrations of bad teachers—ignores the fact that appropriate supports for both students and their teachers are often lacking in academically struggling schools.

Even Hanushek concedes that a better alternative to deselecting some teachers would be to improve the current pool of teachers through induction, mentoring, and other professional development programs. He argues that although improving the current pool is ideal, past efforts have been unsuccessful at large-scale implementation. Yet this was not the outcome in one of the most highly touted success stories in recent years— the Benwood Initiative—which focused on the lowest-performing schools in Chattanooga, Tennessee. In 2000, education leaders in Chattanooga recognized that, in the city's nine schools with concentrated student poverty, high teacher turnover was the primary cause of low student achievement. The district invested heavily in attracting teachers through housing and salary incentives, as well as through comprehensive professional development that included training in reading instruction, coaches for all new teachers, and assistance to principals to guide and evaluate instruction. The result has been a dramatic drop in teacher turnover rates and an increase in the number of applicants for every job opening in the Benwood schools.

Peer Assistance and Review

Teacher unions are often accused of preventing incompetent teachers from ever being fired, and though we certainly object to the term "deselection," we are not in the business of giving bad teachers a job for life. As I recently said, with the exception of vouchers, no issue should be off the table, provided it is good for students and fair to teachers.

One fair way of addressing teacher quality is peer assistance and review (PAR), which the AFT has supported and promoted to our local affiliates for many years. Peer assistance and review provides new teachers the professional development and support they need from experienced, expert teachers, and it establishes and enforces a system by which only capable, well-prepared teachers who meet high entry standards are offered permanent positions.

Peer assistance and review, done correctly, is fair both to those receiving the assistance and review and to those providing it. Details matter, and they must be devised collaboratively by the district and the union. Several AFT affiliates, notably Cincinnati and Toledo in Ohio and Rochester, New York, have pioneered PAR and have identified the components necessary to make it viable and sustainable. Peer assistance and review initiatives must begin with hiring and orientation of teachers and continue through a final review that determines whether each aspiring novice meets high standards of practice. In addition, AFT affiliates' experience with PAR tells us that these programs must include the following characteristics:

- intensive professional development, support, and mentoring;
- high-quality teachers, selected through a fair and quality-conscious process, who are responsible for mentoring and assisting new teachers, preferably on a full-time basis;
- district-provided training, time, resources, and responsibility for expert teachers to mentor new teachers through at least their probationary period;
- expert teachers who are responsible for making wise, tough, evidence-based recommendations to decisionmakers about whether a new teacher merits continuing employment;
- recommendations based on agreed-upon, transparent, evidence-based professional standards; and
- adequate and sustained budget support guaranteed through the regular district budget.

No successful reform can be achieved without the input of teachers. No matter the reform, and no matter how controversial, from improving teaching and learning conditions to improving professional development, from differentiated pay to incentives for teachers to go to and stay in hard-to-staff schools, from induction programs to peer assistance and review, successful implementation hinges on teacher support.

Teacher Evaluation

As a teacher and union leader, I am gratified to see that, after years of being undervalued, good teaching is finally receiving the recognition it deserves as a critical factor in children's learning. Obviously, the relative importance of an individual teacher among the many other influences on student performance—including demographic, family, peer, school, and environmental effects—will be discussed well into the future. Regardless of how much influence a teacher has, we owe it to both our students and our teachers to find ways to ensure that every year every child has the best teachers we can provide.

That mission leads us to several important strategies, many of which are laid out in this book. It will take a multifaceted approach to ensure the highest teacher quality, both in conjunction with and separate from ongoing compensation strategies. It will have to include upgrading the schools and programs that prepare our teachers; attracting and recruiting the most highly qualified candidates; providing new teachers lots of support through excellent induction and mentoring efforts; identifying teachers' strengths and weaknesses and tailoring ongoing, relevant, job-embedded professional development to their needs; and retaining the best teachers and making sure that those who don't measure up are helped through intensive intervention or, failing that, are removed from the profession.

Accountability

Now let me be perfectly clear. Teachers do not fear being held accountable for student achievement. In fact, we embrace it, if the measures of our performance are fair, accurate, and transparent.

What we seek and need is *genuine* accountability:

- Accountability that is meant to fix schools, not to fix blame.
- Accountability that recognizes that student, teacher, and school success mean much more than producing high scores on two tests a year.
- Accountability that takes into account the conditions that are beyond the teacher's or school's control.
- Accountability that holds everyone, including school and district leaders, responsible for doing their share.

The first of these is, of course, a matter more of attitude than method. If teachers believe that those proposing a system of accountability are motivated by a "Gotcha!" mentality, they will be understandably wary. But if a method is developed collaboratively *with* teachers and not *to* them, if it includes the concept of shared responsibility, if teachers are given the time and training to access data and use it to improve their instruction, and if there is a sincere, shared desire to make it good for kids and fair to teachers (which is my personal litmus test), I believe it will receive an open-minded reception.

The last of the criteria listed above for a good accountability system—mutual or 360-degree accountability—is largely beyond the scope of this chapter, but it means that you can't hold people accountable for results if you don't give them the tools they need to do the job. You cannot expect an artist to paint in a poorly lit room without paints and a canvas. Even the most skilled instructors find it hard to help their students excel in schools that suffer from inadequate leadership, physical facilities, supplies and materials, student support services, and safety, to name a few of the necessary tools and conditions.

The second and third criteria listed above—using a broad range of measures and creating a level playing field for evaluating each teacher's contribution—will be the focus of the rest of this commentary. In particular, I will address the use of new statistical methods to measure the amount of value added to a student's learning by an individual teacher. The question I ask is, does using value added as an accountability tool help meet these criteria and make the resulting teacher evaluation more fair, accurate, and transparent?

Both criteria address the issues of fairness and accuracy. A result that accounts for a teacher's performance on only one or two goals out of several she aims for would be neither fair nor accurate. And a result that accounts for only a few of the many influences on student achievement that are beyond a teacher's control would be an equally inaccurate and unfair measure of her true effectiveness.

Let's first address the issue of goals.

Test scores as success. Clearly, the purpose of education is multifaceted and complex and therefore so are the goals of most teachers. They may aim to give kids basic skills, to prepare them for productive work, to equip them to be responsible family and community members, to be active citizens, and so on. Yet the designers of value added—perhaps taking a cue from the No Child Left Behind Act—have reduced the education process to a single target: a high score on a standardized test (or two or three standardized tests).

Now, if standardized tests actually measured student proficiency on a comprehensive, representative sample of skills and knowledge across the formal and informal curriculum, then the question of how to measure student and teacher performance would be simple. (By formal I mean the usual academic subject matter courses of study. By informal I mean the multitude of life skills that teachers have always been charged with imparting—from social skills such as courtesy, honesty, and respect to habits of mind like curiosity, perseverance, and creativity, to a desire to strive for social goals like justice, tolerance, and understanding.)

But by their very nature, standardized tests cannot measure most of these elements of the informal curriculum; few paper-and-pencil tests could, and if they tried, they surely could not be graded quickly, cheaply, and objectively—key necessities for standardized tests. Nevertheless, we can't settle for this narrow definition of what we want to hold teachers accountable for.

Sadly, judging teachers by their students' performance on such limited tests can easily mean the "deselection" (Hanushek's term, not mine) of the most imaginative and inspiring teachers, the ones we all remember as having led us to new insights or to lifelong pursuits and thus changed our lives. Can schools dominated by the "drill and kill" test prep approach ever attract the best and brightest candidates from the tops of their graduating classes, as some "reformers" hope to do? And if they come, will they stay?

Further, as Alan S. Blinder so convincingly demonstrates in chapter 2, if our schools produce only employees who can deliver products and services that computers or overseas workers can do just as well, our schools will have failed in their most basic mission—enabling their students to earn a living. The labor market of this generation of kindergartners will require "creativity, inventiveness, spontaneity, flexibility, interpersonal relations, and so on—not rote memorization," Blinder says, and I agree with him.

To ensure quality, the criteria for judging a teacher's performance should be rigorous and multifaceted. It should include multiple measures of student learning and instructional practices associated with exemplary teaching, such as knowledge of subject matter, the ability to tailor instruction to the needs of their students, and engagement with parents and the greater school community. Broader and more qualitative teacher evaluations could include direct observations and videotapes, teachers setting and meeting individual goals, portfolios of classroom work, surveys of parents and even students, and assessment of classroom management skills and student engagement by outside evaluators. In combination, such diverse measures, especially over at least three years, will yield the fairest and most accurate assessments.

In addition, using test scores to measure teacher effectiveness fosters a tendency to focus not on learning, but on improving test scores. Hours and hours of instructional time are devoted to strategies for improving the odds of guessing right on multiple-choice questions. More hours are spent taking practice exams. And teachers scour past tests to determine what topics are most likely to be covered so they can further restrict their instruction to those topics.

Finally, there are the many measurement issues that impair the validity of test results, especially comparing the results of different tests, year to year. Education measurement experts have detailed these issues (e.g., the eye-opening Koretz 2008). Even the test makers themselves, in a warning that is widely ignored, say that individual test results should not be used for making high-stakes decisions, as the tests were not designed for those purposes.

Exacerbating the danger, small databases are much more prone to yielding skewed results. That is one reason the AFT favors measuring performance schoolwide rather than holding each individual teacher responsible for the performance of her own students. And partly for that reason, the New York City Department of Education and the United Federation of Teachers in New York, which I also head, agreed that any pay-for-performance plan would be schoolwide. Among hundreds of test takers, a few outliers will not have as much statistical effect on the outcome.

More important, schoolwide rewards, in which every staff member participates, foster the kind of collaboration that makes a school successful. Teaching is not by nature a competitive activity, and individual rewards discourage the sharing of successful strategies that help to improve instruction.

All that having been said, however, let me be clear: there is a role for standardized tests in both compensation and evaluation models. In the recent debate in the New York state legislature over the use of test scores in tenure decisions, the United Federation of Teachers supported a provision that allows teachers to be evaluated on how they use student performance data to shape their lessons.

Test data can tell teachers a great deal about what and how well their students are learning. Teachers can use test results as a starting point to reflect on their practices and how they can improve their instruction. However, as a way to gauge the effectiveness of a beginning teacher, such data are fatally flawed. The research, plus common sense, clearly demonstrates that teachers improve their skills over the course of their first few years. Therefore, the test results a teacher's students achieve in her first two or three years of teaching—the usual time when tenure is decided—are not a reliable measure of the teacher's future performance.

A recent study by Dan Goldhaber (2006) that looked at how well value-added assessments of students' test scores for pre-tenure teachers predict their post-tenure performance addresses that very issue. The answer is, not very well. Almost 30 percent of North Carolina 5th-grade teachers would have been denied tenure based on value added (for ranking in the bottom 20 percent in either math or reading over the four-year probationary period), but these same teachers were among the top 40 percent in reading in post-tenure years, and 25 percent were in the top 40 percent in math during post-tenure years.

We should be wary of deselection decisions that are based on blind reliance on data alone. In 2008 a well-regarded Dallas teacher was released because of a low classroom effectiveness index (the district's measure of test score growth). When the teacher appealed, the state commissioner of education reinstated her, in large part because the index did not account for all the factors, such as administrative competence and support, that influence student performance.

That misuse of test scores is an excellent example of what Frederick M. Hess (2008) has termed the "New Stupid." In an article in the December 2008 issue of *Educational Leadership,* he astutely warns of the many errors in judgment that educators can and have made when they rely on a few simple metrics instead of more complex and nuanced information on which to base their conclusions.

In New York, after the tenure debate, the state legislature decided to establish a commission to study the potential of teacher value-added models. New York State United Teachers has urged the state to follow through on this legislation, and all of us should be interested in the study's results.

Leveling the field. So far I have focused on the test scores that underlie value-added teacher accountability, not the value-added method itself.

Teachers have long objected to using test scores as a measure of their value because they, more than most, recognize that children's performance has as much to do with what the children bring to the classroom as what the teacher brings. The teachers I know are more than willing to work with children however they arrive in the classroom, but they are tired of taking the rap for things they can't control. And principals' observations are too often subject to personal bias. So a value-added evaluation system that accurately and fully isolates the teacher's contribution and factors out all the other influences on children's learning would truly be welcomed.

Unfortunately, value added, at least in its current state of the art, simply cannot fulfill that promise. And when the inherent statistical flaws in the value-added methodology are compounded on top of the inherent measurement errors in standardized tests, the results are often far from accurate or fair.

Steven Rivkin makes this perfectly clear in his chapter on teacher value added. He lays out the trade-offs made every time the weaknesses of one approach are "fixed" with another approach. And while some carefully constructed models will work for most teachers in a district, they will inevitably overlook important considerations for a substantial number of others.

Of course, there are many value-added models and great variations in the amount and type of data that districts have collected. Therefore, it is difficult to draw universally applicable conclusions on what value added can and cannot do. But in talking to teacher-union leaders across the country, some of whom have great hopes for value added to contribute to fairer measures of teacher performance in the future, I have yet to encounter one who believes that the method is well developed enough to be a valid, reliable, or dispositive evaluation measure for individual teachers right now.

This skepticism presents a huge obstacle. The calculations are complex, and few teachers will be able to fully understand them, let alone replicate them to see if their "score" is correct. Trust will have to play a big role in acceptance. And in too many instances, trust between frontline educators and district administrators may be lacking.

In New York, a new data-based "report card" is being issued for each teacher, and the union has conducted information sessions for its members to learn how to use them. Even with all the efforts the statisticians made to ensure that all the influences beyond the teacher's control have been factored out, teachers in those training sessions point out important considerations that are not accounted for, usually because they are not quantifiable or the data are not available. Poverty measures, for example, are inadequate because older students and immigrant children frequently do not apply for free or subsidized lunches. Parents' education level is unreported. Family crises are unrecognized. And even for those factors that are included, teachers barrage the trainers with questions about how much weight is given to each one and how that is determined.

Further, even if the technocrats could somehow manage to plug all these factors into their multiple regressions, the results would be hard to attribute to an individual teacher rather than the teamwork of a group of teachers (including teachers of other subjects), guidance counselors, tutors, teacher aides, and other adults. The New York standardized test scores illustrate this perfectly. Since the tests are given midway through the school year, the results represent the combined contributions of at least two teachers—the previous teacher (from spring of the last academic year) and the current teacher (from fall of the current academic year)—and it is virtually impossible to measure them separately.

This attribution problem is another argument for schoolwide measures rather than individual evaluations. Schoolwide measures avoid many of the statistical conundrums of school and leadership effects, nonrandom student–teacher matching, and small amounts of data that occur in individual teacher ratings. The schoolwide data also help support the teachers and administrators in collaborative school-improvement efforts.

Unfortunately, the first exposure most teachers have to value-added assessments is in connection with high-stakes consequences. It would be better if teachers could get some years of experience with it, to iron out the glitches, to build confidence in its validity, before linking it to the "sort-and-fire" staffing systems some are advocating.

Many advocates of value-added models for teacher evaluation, recognizing its imprecision, argue that it should be used as only one piece of the total evaluation picture—and I would certainly agree. But let's be real. School principals have tremendous responsibilities—and workloads to match. Thorough teacher evaluations are difficult and time-consuming. New teachers in particular usually must be observed in their classrooms several times a year for two, three, or four years, and be graded in more than 20 categories. The demands of the process often lead to so-called drive-by observations and checklist evaluations, which are inadequate and unfair. The certainty and simplicity of a data-based numerical rating is alluring to overburdened administrators. And inexperienced principals may even doubt their own judgment, faced with a contradictory result from what seems like a very scientific study. What started out as an adjunct to a rigorous evaluation process may end up driving it.

Value added can be a promising way to assist in the evaluation of teachers, but it is still in an embryonic stage. In its present state, it is applicable to too-few teachers and assesses only a narrow range of teacher contributions to students' learning. At best, it should be used in a schoolwide context or only to validate broader and more qualitative methods.

For wide teacher buy-in, design and implementation must be collectively bargained. Implementation should be gradual, with a few years of no-consequence and low-consequence uses until its validity is firmly established and accepted. This time will not be wasted. Teachers will become familiar with value-added systems and learn to use the data to drive instructional improvements. Value added–based evaluations and performance-pay programs that are schoolwide are more consistent with the cooperation and collaboration necessary for school improvement.

Conclusion

All the reforms discussed here, and many others proposed in this volume and elsewhere, have promise. Their success hinges on whether teachers feel they are fair and help them to educate children. I agree with what President Obama said throughout his campaign: that reform must be done *with* teachers, not *to* them. With the confidence that policymakers and supervisors share their goals, teachers will always be eager to support innovative ideas for improving the education of their students.

REFERENCES

Goldhaber, Dan. 2006. "Everyone's Doing It, but What Does Teacher Testing Tell Us about Teacher Effectiveness?" Working Paper 2006-1. Seattle: Center on Reinventing Public Education, University of Washington.

Goldhaber, Dan, and Dominic J. Brewer. 1997. "Evaluating the Effect of Teacher Degree Level on Educational Performance." In *Developments in School Finance 1996*, edited by William J. Fowler, Jr. (197–210). Washington, DC: U.S. Department of Education, Office of Educational Research and Improvement, National Center for Educational Statistics.

Hess, Frederick M. 2008. "The New Stupid." *Educational Leadership* 66(4): 12–17.

Koretz, Daniel. 2008. *Measuring Up*. Cambridge, MA: Harvard University Press.

15

Reactions from an Education Policy Wonk

Andrew J. Rotherham

American public education faces a human capital crisis stemming from inattention to the vital importance of focusing on the quality and effectiveness of personnel in a labor-intensive field such as education. Researchers differ about how much and how teachers matter, but there is little disagreement that teacher effectiveness matters more to student learning than any other within-school factor. Yet despite this, American public education is still organized, at least implicitly, around the idea that teachers do not matter all that much. Methods for recruiting, training, and deselecting teachers pay scant attention to measures of quality or effectiveness; induction and support remains sporadic and weak; and all teachers are largely treated the same regardless of differences in the scarcity of skills and knowledge they possess, differences in the assignments they take on, or evidence of their effectiveness. These practices must be substantially reformed if the nation is serious about creating a school system that is substantially more equitable than it is today and that can help address the long-term economic competitiveness challenges the nation faces over the next several decades.

The chapters in this volume describe different challenges that American public education faces on human capital and ideas for improving policy and practice. Three primary themes can be drawn from them. Most notably, it is clear that American public education has an outmoded approach to human capital that must be retooled for today's educational and labor market challenges. Given the changes in American society and the world, standing still amounts to sliding backward. Second, in thinking about these challenges the field remains too parochial and fails to sufficiently engage a broader range of ideas from other fields and sectors or engage with seemingly radical ideas like focusing on deselecting teachers after a trial period rather than trying to train everyone to do the work. Finally, to a significant extent, politics, institutional arrangements, and capacity constraints heavily influence the parameters of the debate about education human capital today and create challenges for the kind of ideas in this volume.

This chapter considers the question of improving human capital in education from the perspective of public policy, the governing arrangements of American public education, and the attendant politics. In particular, it focuses on two questions: From a policy standpoint, what are the salience, viability, and applicability of the ideas discussed in this volume and, second, from the standpoint of the decentralization of the American public education system, and in particular the lack of coordination and institutional obstacles, what are the prospects of these ideas and reform more generally?

The Need and the Challenge

The need to improve education's approach to human capital is clear. Qualitatively and quantitatively, we know that as a nation we have a teaching problem. We do not treat teaching as professional work, and the labor force and policymakers respond accordingly. In fact, it's not an overstatement to say that in few regards does the daily work routine of teachers or their longer-term career trajectories have the hallmarks of what is generally considered professional work. The data show that top students are less likely to go into teaching—and to stay in teaching—than other students, and quality has declined overall during the past several decades. Attention to these problems should not denigrate the hard work of millions of teachers or the many outstanding teachers who labor tirelessly in our schools with too little recognition or remuneration. But we ignore aggregate data and trends at great risk to currently underserved students and the long-term challenges facing the nation.

Today's human capital problems are in part a byproduct of other social policy successes. For a long time American public schools did not have to hunt hard for talent because talent had few places to go. For women and racial and religious minorities, teaching was one of the few professional career paths open to them, and public schools grew accustomed to a captive labor market and inattentive to human capital management. This supply of talent made the profession inattentive to the nuts and bolts of human capital management or the need to become more talent sensitive as the labor market and demands on schools changed. Thankfully, these employment barriers have been largely knocked down. Unfortunately, public schools have not adapted to a more competitive labor market and still approach human capital much as they did a generation ago. Meanwhile, the demands on public schools, especially pressure for dramatically better performance, have increased substantially in the past two decades.

In many fields the quality of talent matters to the overall level of performance. We would be surprised to learn, for instance, that airlines paid little attention to the quality of their pilots, or that newspapers worried little about the abilities of reporters. But in education, insufficient attention has been paid to teachers, the key link in the education chain. The result is the quality problems we see today as well as the inequitable distribution of teachers for low-income and minority students. These students are less likely to have the most effective or qualified teachers relative to other students. These problems are not isolated but are trends across the field. One might argue that teaching, with its millions of teachers, is not comparable to aviation or journalism, but as the chapters in this volume indicate, we can do more to focus on effectiveness and quality, even at the scale of American public education. From recruitment through compensation and retirement, there is scant attention through practice and policy to measures of effectiveness or quality. In fact, the two primary benchmarks used today—years of service and various earned degrees—have scant relation to classroom effectiveness.

The challenges to improving the system are substantial. For starters, there is still a great deal of debate about exactly what the problem is, and getting to the empirical issues in the public arena is often difficult. Too often discussion of the human capital problem is greeted with cries of "teacher basher" and other strident responses intended to stifle rather than foster debate. And these are not easy issues for educators, policymakers, and politicians to discuss. Education is a mass profession and almost everyone knows dedicated, hardworking, and effective teachers getting results, often under difficult circumstances. At the same time, even among those who acknowledge real problems there is a debate about the best way to improve things: Should reformers call attention to problems, in an effort to fix them, or is putting the best face on things the best way to maintain or grow public support?

The problem is more than rhetorical as there are also serious institutional barriers to reform. America's public education system is decentralized across states and local communities. The revenue for public schools comes from diffuse and often inequitable sources. Most school districts have their own taxing authority, states contribute varying percentages of funding, and the federal government contributes about 9 percent of school districts' funding. Absent a unitary appropriations source, policymakers at all levels encounter trouble creating integrated or seamless approaches to issues such as human capital, as coordination between different levels of government is a challenge. In addition, because there are so many intergovernmental choke points on reform, it becomes difficult to implement policies with fidelity.

Consider an education law passed by Congress. It is implemented, with accompanying regulations, by the Department of Education. It then devolves the authority to states, which add regulations and implementation interpretations and instructions. The policy then further devolves to local school districts, of which there are about 13,000. Although not as complicated in terms of intergovernmental relationships, state-to-local policy implementation also presents the same dynamics. Obviously, the opportunities to thwart, shave the sharp edges off, or simply subvert a policy are numerous.

At the same time, in most states there are interlocking governance arrangements, further complicating efforts to develop coordinated reform strategies. Governors and legislatures have authority, but so do elected or appointed state boards of education. And there are often ancillary boards and commissions, with varying degrees of authority, that advise state boards of education or promulgate policy and regulations themselves. In the case of human capital, these boards are often populated by the very institutions—for instance, teacher preparation organizations or unions and associations—that public officials are ostensibly supposed to be regulating. Meanwhile, state boards themselves are often heavily influenced by interest groups. Overall, this regulatory capture stifles dissenting views and substantially complicates reform efforts today.

These institutional barriers also make blocking reform easier for various interests opposed to changes because there are multiple points at which they can stop policies they perceive as adverse. In addition, frequently at the state level they help create an "iron triangle"-like arrangement where reform-averse legislators, interest groups, and public officials can work together to oppose ideas they do not like. Again, overall in public policy, the more places where implementation decisions have to be made, the more opportunities there are for those opposed to a policy to continue the fight in a different venue. In education, the implementation decision points, which often function as choke points, are numerous.

Human capital reforms are even more acutely susceptible to these challenges because of the labor-intensive nature of public education. Reforms have consequences. Interest groups representing education's labor force, teachers, principals, superintendents, aides and paraprofessionals, and various specialized personnel are organized, vocal, and able to work their will on the political and policy process to oppose policies and consequences they perceive as adverse to their memberships. Though the national debates generally capture headlines, as a rule, the influence of interest groups becomes stronger and more acute the further one travels from Washington, D.C. At the federal level there are a variety of dynamics acting on policymakers that influence their decisions. Generally, interest group pressure becomes more intense at the state and local levels because of more concentrated electoral and political dynamics.

One additional and not insignificant complication affects policymaking around human capital: a lack of knowledge about exactly what works in this area. Outside of a few obvious, albeit still contentious, policy remedies such as differentiating teacher pay to reflect shortage areas and hard-to-fill assignments, there is more innovation and experimentation needed than there are policy solutions with ample evidence behind them. This also makes opposing reform politically easier, because those seeking to stop reforms can evoke the specter of unforeseen risks or perverse consequences associated with new ideas. Not surprisingly, against the backdrop of these institutional and political dynamics, coupled with the conservative nature of the public's attitudes toward public education, a "devil you know" strategy has real traction. But against the backdrop of today's problems and the ineffectiveness of today's remedies, the demonstrable need for policymakers to embrace responsible innovation is clear.

Ideas in This Volume

So how applicable and salient are the ideas in this volume, and what do the structural and political dynamics mean for these ideas? For starters, Paul T. Hill's skepticism about the power of technology to fundamentally change the basic policy and political dynamics undergirding education human capital is broadly illustrative and worth heeding—especially with the current enthusiasm for the transformative potential of technology in education. So far the record of classroom technology is mixed. And the system has thus far shown an ability to absorb disruptive innovations while mitigating their more dynamic effects. For instance, state-run virtual education programs continue to thrive while charter school–run or independent virtual programs face intense opposition. Because public education will remain a politically controlled marketplace for the foreseeable future, comparisons of technological change on the basis of other sectors' experiences generally overlook key factors of the education marketplace.

At the same time, there is reason to question the broad appeal of truly virtual education programs in the first place. Among their other, nonacademic functions, public schools play a custodial role for children. As the experience with homeschooling demonstrates, it is questionable how many parents will want to give that role up, taking on the added time commitments themselves, and rapid percentage growth at the margin should not be mistaken for rapidly increasing market share. Consequently, it is more likely that virtual and technology-driven educational options will still expand in a context of intense labor needs for public schools.

More generally, these dynamics mean that rather than trying to outflank education's labor-intensive nature, policymakers must find strategies to work within the substantive and political constraints. That is why Frederick M. Hess's discussion about different ways of thinking about the profession is so important. As he notes, if we continue to narrow the definition of professionalism to fields like law and medicine, we will impose unnecessary constraints on education in training, credentialing, and professional growth and movement. Since the 1950s the teacher professionalism movement has sought credibility by seeking to link teaching to fields such as law and medicine. Yet millions of Americans earn their living working as professionals outside of medicine or law. Management, finance, consulting, journalism, public relations, and policy analysis are just a few examples of respected professional work that lacks the hallmarks of medicine and law. And, as Hess has pointed out elsewhere, if various credentials and certifications were themselves the path to professional respect, we would see many professions such as dog grooming and massage therapy among the most highly regarded. The point here is that educators and most education interest groups representing them ignore the larger context of professional work in America at the expense of more effective training regimens and professional structures within the education field.

Likewise, if we continue to think about teaching as a lifelong vocation, then the ensuing policies and incentives will continue to be misaligned with a labor market that is increasingly fluid, especially for younger teachers. One obvious example here is retirement benefits. The back-loading of benefits so that the biggest savings for retirement come in the later years of a teacher's career disadvantages younger teachers and, in an environment of scarce resources, works at cross-purposes with efforts to recruit and retain teachers earlier in their careers. In the same way, a salary system based overwhelmingly on degrees and years of service can work at cross-purposes with the reality of today's teaching profession and is at odds with efforts to improve equity around the distribution of teachers.

The labor market realities also bear on Eric A. Hanushek's discussion of deselecting of teachers after some period, an idea with great salience in the policy community but much less traction in school districts today. There are several reasons for this besides a basic cultural aversion in education to hard decisions around personnel questions. First, there is disagreement about measures and teacher accountability more generally. Some of this is just a continuation of the ongoing debate about whether schools can be expected to substantially improve student learning and outcomes, especially for disadvantaged students. But there are also legitimate technical and capacity issues, as the Hanushek and Steven Rivkin chapters show. For instance, administrators are too infrequently trained to conduct quality evaluations that will ensure fidelity to established standards, and even in subjects such as math and reading that are regularly assessed, the quality of data on student achievement varies widely among states and school districts.

Second, analysts should not underestimate the old adage that "there is never a teacher shortage on the first day of school." Rather than make tough decisions about class size, teacher distribution, or other productivity-enhancing reforms, school districts will put someone—even an unqualified or emergency-credentialed person—in front of a classroom. In other words, on deselection the policy community thinks about quality and teacher effectiveness, whereas school districts think about labor market realities and the parental expectation that every class has a teacher, or at least some adult passing for one, in front of it.

The labor market problem is one reason; despite the existence of qualitative and quantitative evidence about teacher effectiveness, the data are infrequently acted on, as Hanushek notes. The implication for policy is that, given the constraints that school districts operate under, simply making data available is insufficient as a policy lever. Rather, it is important to design systems that force responsible decisionmaking and action. This is more common in other industries. Not only do line managers have the authority to make decisions, they also have accountability for doing so and a support system in place to facilitate their decisionmaking. Today in education there is generally either authority without support or insufficient agency around making key decisions. Although analysts can make a strong case for deselection on the empirical merits and the probabilities around teacher effectiveness, such a strategy must be coupled with aggressive support for recruitment of replacement teachers or alternative delivery systems that are acceptable to parents and other measures to ensure effective decisionmaking.

Some, though far from all, of today's constraints and obstacles to deselection obviously stem from teachers' contracts or similar provisions that exist in many state laws and policies, and any discussion of human capital obviously involves teachers' unions. There are three primary schools of thought about how to address the unions: work with them, work around them, and work against them. Reasonable people can, of course, disagree, but given the political context of education and the positive things the unions can accomplish, a strategy of trying to work with them wherever possible has much to recommend it. Working with the unions does not mean dodging the thorny issues where there are serious disagreements—for instance, around forced transfers of teachers; equity in teacher distribution; and how to accurately account for teacher salaries in local, state, and national policy decisions—but it means that where there is common ground, the unions can bring a great deal to the table.

One promising strategy is to involve the teachers' unions more in human resource management, which can be a core strength for them as institutions and, as this volume shows, a substantial problem. Unions could, for instance, help screen teaching candidates, serving as job banks for teachers and schools in open-market hiring systems. Similarly, unions could take on more of a role in professional development, as some do today. Helping teachers' unions adopt new and value-adding roles in human capital management has several advantages. First, in many cities the unions are a more stable and long-term presence than the school district leadership. Although overall there is not a crisis of leadership turnover in school districts, among the larger cities there is frequent turnover and a lack of leadership stability. The high-profile and longer tenures of New York City's Joel Klein, Boston's Tom Payzant, or Chicago's Arne Duncan should not obscure the reality of frequent turnovers in the nation's larger school districts. The Council of the Great City Schools estimates that the average tenure is just 3.5 years in the nation's largest cities (an increase from 2.3 years in 1999).

Strategies to help teachers' unions take on new roles can also help change the reform debate from a zero-sum one where the unions are constantly in the position of saying no to one where they can shift into more productive roles and consequently move their memberships toward reform. At the same time, innovation at the bottom can have a trickle-up effect on national union policy. After the Denver teachers' union approved a differentiated and pay-for-performance scheme, their national umbrella union, the National Education Association, was forced to modify its stance on the issue.

Reformers should also be cognizant of the context in which teachers' unions operate. Their internal dynamics mean that the needs of current members take precedence over what might be good for future members (i.e., those that do not yet vote in union elections). That means strategies to "hold harmless" current teachers and phase-ins of reform ideas are more promising strategies. In Denver, for instance, the school district differentiated teacher pay for new teachers and teachers who elected to opt into the new plan, but pledged to keep the standard "steps and lanes" salary scale until the last teacher using it either left the district or retired. That approach helped ease the adoption of the new plan.

Finally, although it is important to look at the experience of other countries, we should be mindful of the importance of context. Policies and practices cannot just be grafted from one country onto another absent underlying commonalities. Similarly, we should be careful not to confuse correlation with causation for the results in other countries, because so many different factors bear on educational performance.

It is also important to look at human capital in the context of the entire system, not only teachers. If, for example, we fail to make more schools places where teachers want to work, then a strategy of focusing on people will fail. This points to issues like induction and support, well-defined and -articulated curricula, opportunities for quality professional growth, and learning for teachers. In particular, there is too little innovation with different ways to staff schools and use teachers' time in order to provide a more professional work environment for teachers. These other issues should not serve as an excuse to duck the hard human capital challenges this volume discusses and the field faces, but they should be a constant reminder that these issues must be addressed comprehensively. The wide-ranging needs also point to the culpability that school districts have in these problems and is why it is important to view the role that the teachers' unions play in an accurate context.

Going Forward

So what can national policymakers do to most constructively foster reform? First, they can keep the pressure on for educational improvement more generally. Accountability systems by themselves do not lead to good decisionmaking, but coupled with other strategies they help create an environment where a focus on results becomes an important gravitational tug on all decisionmaking. Because the politics of reforming human capital systems are so treacherous, local and state policymakers are generally less likely to take them on (absent strong external incentives), and a focus on accountability helps create those incentives. Today's successful examples of reform should not distract from the scale of the challenge facing American public education and the need for a systemic emphasis on improved performance.

Second, national policymakers can foster innovation. The human capital discussion in education is still in its infancy. We know more about what does not work than we do about what works. It is, of course, a perverse political riddle that many of those who work politically to thwart innovation then cite the lack of evidence as a reason for not proceeding with reform. Nonetheless, at this point seed money for various innovations is the most valuable resource national policymakers can bring to the table. We know that today's methods for teacher recruitment, training, evaluation, and compensation are woefully insufficient, so there is a compelling case for fostering new ideas in these areas, rigorously evaluating them, and subsequently changing policies and practices accordingly. Likewise, although technology may not transform teaching and learning, there certainly are plenty of ways where instruction less bounded by time and place (for instance, virtual and online alternatives) can help address aspects of education's human capital problems.

Demonstrations, pilots, and grassroots initiatives offer a dual promise. First, they offer ways to innovate with new strategies to address today's challenges. At the same time, they offer strategies and pressure for bottom-up change that—although insufficient to leverage broader change to human capital policy by itself—can complement and support other efforts. As this volume indicates, we should not only look within education for these ideas but to other sectors and abroad as well. Public education is not the only industry with labor needs at scale and dispersed, context-specific, and sometimes hard-to-measure work, and there is much the field can learn from elsewhere.

Policymakers, especially state and local policymakers, must be willing to engage with the evidence and reform policies accordingly. Right now, billions of dollars are steered in ineffective directions because of state and local policies with no grounding in research around teacher compensation, professional development, and other components of teachers' work. Again, we may not know exactly what works, but there is empirical evidence about much of what does not, and we must be willing to repurpose dollars toward more promising ends in order to finance reform.

Finally, leaders at all levels of government must clearly communicate the stakes, the scale of the challenge, and the promise of potential solutions. For too many Americans, especially those with access to excellent public or private schooling options, the debate about human capital and school reform is a solution in search of a problem. Without a clear, jargon-free understanding of the issues, the political support for reform will fail to match today's institutional and political obstacles.

This last point is not a small issue. Unless coupled with aggressive political engagement and advocacy, volumes such as this are destined to cause more debate and disruption in the halls of think tanks and graduate seminars than they are in the corridors of power. There are no shortcuts to reforming labor practices in a publicly controlled and labor-intensive industry. Very often it's very much about the politics.

16
Conclusion

Dan Goldhaber and Jane Hannaway

This volume began with a simple observation: education is a labor-intensive industry, and schooling is fundamentally a human capital enterprise. Empirical work bolsters the argument for framing education in terms of human capital: research shows both that teachers are the most important schooling factor affecting student learning and that they vary tremendously in their effectiveness.

The findings buttressing the commonsense conclusion that teachers matter are relatively new, emerging over the past decade from rigorous research enabled by new datasets that connect teachers to their individual students. We now know definitively that the difference between having a strong versus a weak teacher can be profound, in some cases representing more than a full year's learning growth. This difference is enough to close much of the average achievement gap we observe between racial and ethnic groups and to offset the academic weakness we often see among economically disadvantaged students.

Taken together, these facts point toward the conclusion that improving the quality of the teacher workforce is key to improving the educational outcomes of America's students. With this in mind, this book outlines provocative ideas for improving the teaching profession.

Our focus on human capital is timely. The nation's schools are under tremendous performance pressure. The achievement gaps across student groups in the United States are persistent, and relative to other industrialized countries, our students perform poorly. The situation is untenable, threatening individual opportunity and our collective prosperity. Finding ways to improve the performance of the teacher workforce is a moral and economic imperative.

But it will not be easy. For many years analysts argued that a student's background largely determined learning outcomes; they claimed that schools made little difference (Coleman et al. 1966; Jencks 1972). While there is no doubt that what goes on in the home is vital, we now know that, beyond home life, good teachers matter a lot. But in many ways, the current infrastructure supporting the teaching profession works against the goal of ensuring that every student has a good teacher. As Toch and Rothman (2008) point out, even though we know the importance of teachers, teacher evaluation procedures vary tremendously in scope, and more often than not, they lack rigor. A recent report by the New Teacher Project, *The Widget Effect,* shows that nearly all teachers receive "good" or "excellent" evaluations. Unfortunately, the Lake Wobegon effect is a mirage: universally good evaluations do not reflect the underlying views of principals (Tucker 1997) or teachers (Keeling et al. 2009). Instead, the fact that most teachers are "above average" reflects political and institutional constraints that discourage honest assessments of teacher performance (see Miller and Chait 2008). The result is a system where differences between teachers are rarely addressed through policy or practice.

With this as a starting point, it is no surprise that the human capital systems that govern the teacher workforce largely treat teachers as if they are interchangeable. It is almost universally true that entry into teaching is regulated by a licensure system that ignores relevant individual teacher differences; the compensation of teachers is determined by generic credentials and experience groupings that are, at best, weakly related to their effectiveness; and the professional development offerings most teachers receive are not tailored to their individual needs or the needs of their students. All these practices fly in the face of research on teacher effectiveness and the notion that "everyone knows who the good teachers are" in any given school.

The task we set for this volume was to assess various dimensions of the human capital system in education and examine ways they might better promote student learning. We enlisted leading scholars to help us examine evidence, think through pertinent issues, and promote various educational reform ideas. We do not necessarily agree with each and every assertion made by the contributing authors, but on the whole we believe their assessments hit close to the mark. The ideas presented here represent fundamental shifts in thinking about teacher policy, not just tinkering around the edges.

Taken together, the chapters identify four critical areas of policy that shape the teaching profession and suggest ways to intervene to improve them.

Drawing Talent into the Profession

Sean P. Corcoran documents that something is amiss in the recruitment and selection of teachers in the United States. Just as the demand for higher cognitive skills among workers has risen, the overall academic quality of teachers has declined. The decline among teachers at the top of the distribution is particularly marked. Increased opportunities for women, especially talented women, in higher-prestige and higher-paying fields are no doubt part of the explanation for the decline in a profession that has always been female dominated.[1] As Andrew J. Rotherham notes in chapter 15,

> for a long time American public schools did not have to hunt hard for talent because talent had few places to go. For women and racial and religious minorities, teaching was one of the few professional career paths open to them, and public schools grew accustomed to a captive labor market and inattentive to human capital management. This supply of talent made the profession inattentive to the nuts and bolts of human capital management or the need to become more talent sensitive as the labor market and demands on schools changed.

Labor market opportunities surely explain some of the decline in the talent pool, as does the structure of compensation in teaching relative to the broader labor market (discussed below). It is also interesting, however, that the U.S. teacher development system looks very different from that of many of its international competitors. The success of other countries in enticing their top talent into teaching is a point to which scholars and policymakers are beginning to pay close attention.

Dan Goldhaber, in chapter 5, describes how a number of high-performing countries do things. One difference among countries is teacher salaries. On teacher salaries relative to national GDP, American teachers' salaries rank 24th out of 29 countries, suggesting that teachers in the United States are relatively worse off than their colleagues in many other countries. But comparisons of teacher salary and student performance across countries show no clear relationship, suggesting that salary changes alone are insufficient for improving the system. Surely compensation policies are important, but other factors, such as working conditions and professional recognition, no doubt also come into play.

Mechanisms for selection into the profession vary across countries. In the United States, entry into a teacher training program (the dominant route into the profession) tends to be nonselective, and the student largely pays his or her own way. In Korea and Singapore, however, the government heavily subsidizes the cost of training, and the number of slots is limited, making this initial entry into the profession competitive and prestigious. In addition, the heterogeneity in training in the United States is larger than in other countries because the number of authorized teacher training providers is far greater in the United States than in other countries, which typically have more centralized systems. On balance, system-level controls over the quality of entrants and the quality of training they receive in the United States appear weak relative to other countries.

There is evidence that we could be doing better to draw talent into teaching. For example, the recruitment strategy of groups like Teach For America has had astounding success in attracting academically proficient college graduates into teaching. In 2009, 11 percent of seniors at Ivy League colleges applied to be part of Teach For America.[2] If the talents of new academically proficient entrants could be paired with supervisors who are highly effective teachers or with technological support, the capacity of the system might be vastly improved.

The general system of teacher preparation in the United States is, by comparison, incoherent. Most of the responsibility for education, including teacher training and licensure, rests at the state level. States authorize multiple and diverse training providers, and different states require different qualifications for prospective teachers. Thus, some talented but mobile professionals will turn away from teaching, knowing that a credential obtained in one state may not be accepted in another. In fact, we have no idea how many teachers who leave the profession early in their careers are lost to the system simply because they move to a different state and opt not to jump through the hoops necessary to obtain a license in that state.

Perhaps more important, the decentralized structure of the training and credentialing system in the United States makes it unlikely that we can simply adopt national-level teacher recruitment reforms, consistent with countries like Singapore and Finland. Those systems rely on centralized control over selectivity at the front end of the recruitment process, while the U.S. system has relatively little front-end narrowing of the teacher pipeline. To be sure, individual states could provide attractive student aid programs for prospective teachers and exercise more quality control over training programs, both in who enters them and in their content. But a coordinated cross-state effort would be required to make it worthwhile since prospective teacher labor is not captive.

Rethinking the Shape of a Teaching Career

A particular notion of a teaching career dominates the human capital systems in public education. This view comes through most clearly in Frederick M. Hess's chapter, which challenges the conventional conception that teachers enter teaching young and remain for their entire career in a profession that is flat and largely undifferentiated by skill or specialization. On day one, most first-year teachers assume the same professional responsibilities as a twenty-year veteran, and highly skilled and effective teachers are treated the same as poor performers. With low entry requirements and little subsequent differentiation, Hess argues, there is in fact little reason to believe that the modal teacher is likely to be any more successful than a lateral entrant into the profession who might bring valuable life experiences to the classroom.

Rethinking the structure of the teaching career requires examining the pros and cons of differentiated teacher roles. Differentiated roles might allow for far greater specialization—for example, a specialization in teaching math at the elementary level—or for more of a career hierarchy so highly effective teachers supervise or mentor less-effective teachers or new recruits.

Restructuring the teaching career might also involve more effective use of technology. This possibility is one that Paul T. Hill considers in chapter 7. Education is one of the few fields that has not reaped the productivity payoffs of substituting technology for labor. Staffing the nation's classrooms with 3.5 to 4 million highly talented teachers is a huge challenge. Hill's chapter opens the door to the idea that we could use technology to spread specialized teaching skills across more students, especially disadvantaged students (or those in remote schools) who typically do not have access to the most talented teachers. All teachers do not have to be the masters of all the skills and knowledge that promote student learning; technology might substitute and, perhaps in some areas, be more effective and reliable. As Hill notes, it is also clear that "fully integrated instructional systems would bring major changes in teacher human resource use and would likely require a rethinking of the traditional teacher role in a school." It is not difficult to imagine such new roles, such as materials developers, online tutors, managers of individualized programs of instruction for students, and creators and managers of online teacher communities in specialized subjects.

The thinking presented in this volume about teaching career structure is in sync with the marked shift away from a single occupation commitment witnessed in the U.S. labor market over the past three decades. Making a lifelong career commitment may be unattractive to new entrants into the labor market, especially when it involves a heavy up-front investment in training to be eligible for employment. Allowing greater flows in and out of teaching, perhaps in different roles, may be an important means of drawing in new talent as well as retaining the best and most committed individuals in the profession.

A potentially important inhibitor to the free flow of teachers is the system of retirement benefits public schools use. Virtually all school systems provide retirement benefits for teachers, structured in the form of defined benefits (and thus not generally portable). As Robert M. Costrell, Richard W. Johnson, and Michael J. Podgursky explain, this system differs fundamentally from the system that has come to predominate in the broader labor market—the defined-contribution system—in that retirement benefits for teachers are not portable across professions or even state lines. Further, the system of retirement benefits used in schools back-loads benefits since only those who become vested in the system will ever receive the benefits.

The back-loading and nonportability of retirement benefits are likely to make teaching a relatively undesirable profession to individuals who are not sure they will remain in teaching for their entire careers. And the system clearly makes the cost of leaving relatively high after teachers become vested. This may be beneficial, by keeping effective teachers in the profession for some time, but the strong retirement incentives associated with defined-benefit systems also encourage these effective teachers to leave the profession at age 55 (or thereabouts). This encouragement occurs even if, benefits aside, they would opt to continue working. The flip side of vesting is that the cost of leaving the profession is also higher for ineffective teachers who are vested. As we describe in more detail below, this is problematic when there are very few workforce management tools that can encourage ineffective teachers to leave the profession.

Drawing talent into teaching is certainly one way to upgrade the profession, and changes to our conception of what a teaching career ought to look like might open doors for thinking about alternatives. But the truth, borne out by empirical work, is that some people with the most stellar academic credentials don't make good teachers; other people, who do not come across on paper as good teacher candidates, turn out to be enormously effective in the classroom. The bottom line is that teachers differ in ways that are hard to detect without seeing their impacts on students, which underscores the importance of workforce policies informed by actual teacher performance.

Managing Performance in the Classroom

A primary mechanism for developing teacher talent is professional development. Investments in professional development have a certain degree of face validity, so it is hardly surprising that school districts invest heavily in this area. Unfortunately, Jennifer King Rice's chapter, which reviews what we know about the efficacy of this investment, suggests this strategy of talent development fails to live up to its promise.

Typically, school districts spend professional development funds on in-service training days, conferences, and workshops for teachers; they also provide subsidies for graduate studies. Expenditure levels are difficult to come by, but Rice estimates that they are probably similar to amounts spent on district administrative costs; in short, professional development expenditures are nontrivial amounts.

Solid information on the effectiveness of professional development, or what works, is even scarcer than information on expenditures, and the evidence that is available is largely inconclusive. As a result, school districts have little guidance in developing professional development offerings, and teachers largely rely on personal preferences when deciding about participating in various activities. Perhaps, then, it is no surprise that convenience plays a role in teachers' decisions and that we observe no systematic links between participation in professional development and teacher effectiveness. As Rice notes, even if teachers knew the performance merits of different activities, how that information would shape their behavior is unclear. Teachers are largely rewarded for "seat time" in professional development activities; if they were rewarded for student performance, their choices might be different. Indeed, we might expect that their experiences and demands as interested consumers of professional development might improve the offerings and the system as a whole.

The idea of using performance incentives for teachers is well grounded in labor economics, but there are some compelling reasons for caution when it comes to applying this idea to teaching. New data and statistical methods have renewed interest amongst policymakers in the notion of linking teacher pay to measures of their value added to student achievement. Steven G. Rivkin's chapter, however, raises cautions about using value-added measures in a simple, mechanical way to evaluate teacher effectiveness, a position echoed by AFT leader Randi Weingarten.

It cannot be denied that measures of teacher value added bring new information to bear in education. There are ways to use this information carefully to help restructure the teaching profession in more productive ways. Eric A. Hanushek, for example, argues that appropriately constructed performance measures that use these data are fairly good indicators, at least, of the weakest teachers, and such measures tend to be corroborated with other performance assessments such as principal ratings and, perhaps, ratings of colleagues. Despite all these complications and controversy, both Rivkin and Rice suggest that linking pay and performance is an option that should be on the table.

Staying and Leaving

In theory, teacher tenure policies are designed to protect teachers from arbitrary treatment by administrators. In practice, the vast majority of teachers who enter the profession receive tenure effective for life. Once tenured, intricate and time-consuming procedures must be followed to dismiss teachers, even for low performance; in practice, a minuscule number of teachers are ever let go. Michael M. DeArmond, Kathryn L. Shaw, and Patrick M. Wright report in chapter 4 that only a little more than 1 percent of public school teachers are ever dismissed, a rate significantly lower than in charter and private schools that are less bound by institutional and political constraints. Moreover, because tenure decisions are made early in a teacher's career—in some jurisdictions, after only two years on the job—there is almost no time for administrators to gather and process information about teachers that can inform the tenure decision.

Hanushek indirectly argues for tenure reform by making the explicit case for a hard-edged mechanism of teacher selection, or "deselection" as he calls it, linked directly to performance. He argues that developing policies that systematically trim off the least effective teachers (i.e., simply culling the bottom of the teacher distribution) would result over time in dramatic improvements in student learning. This in turn would lead to marked increases in national economic growth.

One of the reasons that deselection—an all-or-nothing proposition—has emerged as a hotly contested reform notion is that policymakers lack other tools to provide teachers with meaningful cues about their value. This is most obvious in the case of the single-salary teacher pay system, which inherently constrains human resource management. Under this system, a teacher's salary is determined solely by years of service and advanced degrees. So teachers with the same level of experience and degree status earn the same salary, regardless of how well they perform.

In most other organizations, however, employee performance is reviewed annually, and employees who perform well are generally rewarded with higher salaries (or promotion) than employees who do not perform well. The salary sends a clear signal to employees about the value of their performance to the organization. Employees whose salaries are stagnant are thereby encouraged to improve their skills, expend greater effort, or move on to a different job or different organization. In effect, they are told that their contribution is not highly valued. Conversely, employees who receive steady salary increases receive a clear signal that their contributions are highly valued and are thereby encouraged to continue contributing. In education, no such mechanism exists.

In short, a number of policies and practices affect the entry and exit of teachers into and out of the profession over the course of a career, but these rules are mechanical and are not linked to teacher performance.

Putting It All Together

If we have learned anything from the decades of research on public schools, it is that there are no silver bullets when it comes to educating students. Thus, an important idea that readers ought to take away from this volume is that human capital systems have to do multiple things right to have much impact on the educational system. As DeArmond, Shaw, and Wright point out, best practices in the private sector suggest that packages of complementary reforms make a difference in the successful management of human resources.

There are certainly compelling arguments for reforms such as dese-lection or performance pay, but these type of changes to the employment bargain make teaching a more risky occupation from an employee's standpoint. In isolation, then, we might expect these reforms to have a deleterious impact on the talent in the profession. If, however, they are paired with a combination of better feedback on teacher performance, higher salaries and differentiated teacher roles, or career paths that allow for greater specialization and a less-flat hierarchy, they may be more suc-cessful. And although we have focused exclusively on teachers, many of the reforms advocated in this volume entail changes in the roles and responsibilities of other key actors in the education system as well, from district superintendents all the way down to school principals. At a min-imum, human resource departments—often treated as a backwater in school systems—would have to become more flexible and innovative, moving from a compliance role to a far more active and prominent posi-tion within the system.

Unfortunately, the policymaking process that surrounds schools makes major policy changes difficult. It is rare to observe more than changes at the margin in a legislative session or at the collective bargaining table as interests group struggle for influence. But if what we suggest about the importance of aligned reforms is right, this approach to reform is not likely to yield many rewards.

The reforms advocated by some authors in this volume would clearly stimulate significant, pitched, political battles. Those reading between the lines in the chapters by the "reactors" may hear the distant echoes of past debates. And while we are not sure which of the reforms described in this volume would be effective, the bottom line is that we cannot begin to know what works without trying various alternatives. For this reason, we argue for tolerating and even fostering disruption in the predominant systems of human capital management that govern the teaching profes-sion. We advance this idea believing the authors in this volume have made a good case that the teaching profession appears in many ways to be stuck in the past, ruled by policies and practices that largely ignore sig-nificant changes in the broader labor market.

To those who believe the strategies espoused here are too risky, we ask whether the standard for change is being set far higher than the standard for the status quo. We believe the answer is yes, and that our calculation of risk must reverse before the quality of the nation's teacher workforce can be meaningfully affected. As we articulate at the beginning of this book, the status quo is such that too many needy students are not provided with the highly effective teachers they need to help them succeed in an increasingly global market for human capital.

If we had the opportunity to create the teacher human capital system from scratch, would we end up with a system that looks like the one we have today? Our answer is a resounding no. We agree with Andrew J. Rotherham that "it is clear that American public education has an outmoded approach to human capital that must be retooled for today's educational and labor market challenges. Given the changes in American society and the world, standing still amounts to sliding backward." As Randi Weingarten states, we believe that "no issue should be off the table, provided it is good for students and fair to teachers."

NOTES

1. The gap between earnings in teaching and in other professions has increased, though fewer working hours and generous benefits offset some of the earning differential.

2. Teach For America, "Teach For America Adds Largest Number of New Teachers and Regions in 20-Year History," press release, May 28, 2009, http://www.teachfor america.org/newsroom/documents/20090528_Teach_For_America_Adds_Largest_ Number_of_Teachers_in_History.htm.

REFERENCES

Coleman, James S., Ernest Q. Campbell, Carol J. Hobson, James McPartland, Alexander M. Mood, Frederic D. Weinfeld, and Robert L. York. 1966. *Equality of Educational Opportunity.* Washington, DC: U.S. Government Printing Office.

Jencks, Christopher. 1972. *Inequality: A Reassessment of the Effect of Family and Schooling in America.* New York: Harper Colophon Press.

Keeling, David, Jennifer Mulhern, Susan Sexton, and Daniel Weisberg. 2009. *The Widget Effect: Our National Failure to Acknowledge and Act on Differences in Teacher Effectiveness.* New York: The New Teacher Project.

Miller, Raegen, and Robin Chait. 2008. *Teacher Turnover, Tenure Policies, and the Distribution of Teacher Quality: Can High-Poverty Schools Catch a Break?* Washington, DC: Center for American Progress.

Toch, Thomas, and Robert Rothman. 2008. *Rush to Judgment: Teacher Evaluation in Public Education.* Washington, DC: Education Sector.

Tucker, Pamela D. 1997. "Lake Wobegon: Where All the Teachers Are Competent (Or, Have We Come to Terms with the Problem of Incompetent Teachers?)." *Journal of Personnel Evaluation in Education* 11(2): 103–26.

About the Editors

Dan Goldhaber is professor in Interdisciplinary Arts and Sciences at the University of Washington, Bothell; an affiliated scholar at the Urban Institute; and an editor of *Education Finance and Policy*. He previously served as an elected member of the Alexandria City (Va.) School Board from 1997 to 2002. His work focuses on educational productivity and reform at the K–12 level and addresses the role that teacher pay structure plays in teacher recruitment and retention; the influence of human resource practices on teacher turnover and quality; and the role of community colleges in higher education. Dr. Goldhaber's work has been published in leading journals and has appeared in major media outlets such as National Public Radio, *Education Week, Washington Post,* and *USA Today.*

Jane Hannaway is a senior fellow and founding director of the Education Policy Center at the Urban Institute, where she oversees the work of the Center and is a member of the Institute's senior management team. Dr. Hannaway is also the director and overall principal investigator of the National Center for Analysis of Longitudinal Data in Education Research (CALDER). An organizational sociologist, her work focuses on the effects of education reforms on student outcomes as well as on school policies and practices. Her recent research is heavily focused on the effects of various accountability policies and issues associated with teacher labor markets. She has written or edited seven books and numerous articles in education and management journals. Dr. Hannaway previously served on the faculty of Columbia, Princeton, and Stanford universities. She has held several national positions and currently serves on the National Academy Committee on Value-Added Methodology for Instructional Improvement, Program Evaluation and Accountability.

About the Contributors

Alan S. Blinder is the Gordon S. Rentschler Memorial Professor of Economics and Public Affairs at Princeton University and co-director of Princeton's Center for Economic Policy Studies, which he founded in 1990. He is a member of the board of the Council on Foreign Relations, the Bretton Woods Committee, and a former governor of the American Stock Exchange. Blinder has had an extensive role in governmental policy. He served as vice chairman of the Board of Governors of the Federal Reserve System from 1994 to 1996 and as a member of President Clinton's Council of Economic Advisers from 1993 to 1994, where he was in charge of the administration's macroeconomic forecasting and worked on pressing budget, international trade, and health care issues. Blinder is a columnist for *The New York Times* Sunday business section and appears frequently on PBS, CNBC, CNN, and Bloomberg TV.

Sean P. Corcoran is assistant professor of Educational Economics at New York University's Steinhardt School of Culture, Education, and Human Development and is an affiliated faculty of the Robert F. Wagner Graduate School of Public Service. His research focuses on the economics of school funding, the political economy of school choice, and the labor market for elementary and secondary school teachers. Corcoran is a research associate at the Economic Policy Institute in Washington, DC, and was a visiting scholar at the Russell Sage Foundation from 2005 to

2006. His recent publications have appeared in the *Journal of Policy Analysis and Management, Journal of Urban Economics,* and *American Economic Review.*

Robert M. Costrell is professor of Education Reform and Economics and holds the Endowed Chair in Education Accountability at the University of Arkansas. His academic career has featured seminal publications on the economic theory of educational standards and teacher pensions, as well as publications on school finance litigation. Costrell has an extensive background in policymaking. From 1999 to 2006, he served in major policy roles for three governors of Massachusetts, including policy research director, chief economist, and education advisor to Governor Mitt Romney. He represented the administration on the Public Employee Retirement Administration Commission from 2001 to 2003. He also serves on the National Technical Advisory Council for No Child Left Behind, appointed by Secretary Spellings.

Michael M. DeArmond is a researcher at the Center on Reinventing Public Education at the University of Washington, Bothell, and a doctoral student in educational leadership and policy studies at the University of Washington. His research interests include teacher labor markets and the reform of district-level operations. His recent work has focused on teacher pensions and the reform of school district human resource practices. DeArmond is a former middle-school history teacher.

Eric A. Hanushek is the Paul and Jean Hanna Senior Fellow at the Hoover Institution of Stanford University. He has been a leader in the development of economic analysis of educational issues, and his work on efficiency, resource use, and economic outcomes of schools has frequently entered into the design of both national and international educational policy. His analysis measuring teacher quality through student achievement forms the basis for current research into the value added of teachers and schools. His most recent book, *Schoolhouses, Courthouses, and Statehouses,* describes how improved school finance policies can be used to meet our achievement goals. He has produced 15 books along with numerous widely cited articles in professional journals. He served as deputy director of the Congressional Budget Office.

Frederick M. Hess is director of Education Policy Studies at the American Enterprise Institute and an educator, political scientist, and author. His influential books include *Spinning Wheels, Revolution at the Margins,* and *Common Sense School Reform.* His work has appeared in scholarly journals, including the *Harvard Educational Review, Teachers College Record,* and *Urban Affairs Review,* and major media outlets such as the *Washington Post, U.S. News and World Report, Forbes,* and *National Review.* A former high school social studies teacher, he has taught education and policy at universities including Georgetown, Harvard, and the University of Pennsylvania. He serves as executive editor of *Education Next,* a faculty associate with Harvard's Program on Education Policy and Governance, and on the board of directors for the National Association of Charter School Authorizers and the review board for the Broad Prize in Urban Education.

Paul T. Hill is the John and Marguerite Corbally Professor at the University of Washington, Bothell. He directs the Center on Re-Inventing Public Education, which studies alternative governance, financing, human resource, and accountability systems for public elementary and secondary education. He is also a nonresident senior fellow in the Brookings Institution's Governmental Studies Program and a senior fellow of the Hoover Institution. Hill's recent work has focused on reform of public elementary and secondary education, reform of school finance, and school choice. He chaired Brookings' National Working Commission on Choice in K–12 Education and wrote its report, *School Choice: Doing It the Right Way Makes a Difference.* Among his books are *It Takes a City: Getting Serious about Urban School Reform* and *Fixing Urban Schools,* both written as resources for mayors and community leaders facing the need to transform failing big-city school systems.

Richard W. Johnson, senior fellow at the Urban Institute, is an economist specializing in health and income security at older ages. Much of his research centers on older Americans' employment and retirement decisions. His recent studies include analyses of the recession's impact on older workers, occupational change at older ages, changes over time in job demands, and work disincentives created by the tax and transfer system. He has also written extensively about retirement preparedness, including studies of the financial and health risks people face as they approach retirement and the costs of acute and long-term care. He is currently completing a book on older workers for the Urban Institute Press.

Joel I. Klein has served as chancellor of New York City schools since 2002, overseeing more than 1,500 schools with 1.1 million students. Previously, he was chairman and chief executive officer of Bertelsmann, Inc. From 1997 to 2001, Klein was assistant attorney general in charge of the U.S. Department of Justice's antitrust division. His appointment to the U.S. Justice Department came after he served as deputy counsel to President Clinton from 1993 to 1995. Klein has had a long-standing interest in educational issues: he studied at New York University's School of Education and later taught mathematics to 6th-graders at a public school in Queens. He has served as a visiting and adjunct professor at the Georgetown University Law Center and has published several articles in leading scholarly and popular journals.

David H. Monk is professor of educational administration and dean of the College of Education at Pennsylvania State University. Before this, he was a member of the Cornell University faculty for 20 years. He was the inaugural coeditor of *Education Finance and Policy,* the journal of the American Education Finance Association, and serves on its editorial board along with those of the *Journal of Education Finance, Educational Policy,* and *Journal of Research in Rural Education.* Monk specializes in education finance, educational productivity, and the organizational structuring of schools and school districts. He wrote *Educational Finance: An Economic Approach* and *Raising Money for Education: A Guide to the Property Tax* (with Brian O. Brent) and has published numerous articles in leading scholarly journals including *Education Finance and Policy, Journal of Education Finance, Economics of Education Review,* and *Education and Urban Society.*

Michael J. Podgursky is professor of economics at the University of Missouri, Columbia, where he served as department chair from 1995 to 2005. His research focuses on the economics of education. He has published many articles in the area, with a primary focus on teacher labor markets and teacher compensation. He serves on the board of editors for *Education Finance and Policy* and the *Peabody Journal of Education* and on the advisory boards of various statistical agencies and research institutes. He is co-investigator at the National Center for Analysis of Longitudinal Data in Education Research at the Urban Institute and the National Center for Performance Incentives at Vanderbilt University, two national research centers funded by the Institute on Education Sciences of the U.S. Department of Education.

Jennifer King Rice is a professor in the Department of Education Policy and Leadership at the University of Maryland. Her research focuses on education productivity, cost analysis in education, and educational reform for at-risk students. Her current work focuses on teachers as a critical resource in education and addresses the costs of enhancing teacher quality through effective recruitment, retention, and professional development strategies, particularly in difficult-to-staff schools. Rice's work has appeared in leading journals including *Educational Evaluation and Policy Analysis, Economics of Education Review,* and *Journal of Education Finance* as well as in multiple edited volumes. She wrote *Fiscal Policy in Urban Education* and *High Stakes Accountability: Implications for Resources and Capacity.* As a national expert in education finance and policy, Dr. Rice regularly consults with policy research organizations, including The Economic Policy Institute and The Finance Project, and with state and federal organizations.

Steven G. Rivkin is professor of economics and chair of the Department of Economics at Amherst College, associate director of Research with the Texas Schools Project at the University of Texas at Dallas, and a fellow at the National Bureau of Economic Research. He is a member of the Town of Amherst (MA) School Committee. His research centers on the economics and sociology of education. Rivkin has written extensively on teacher quality, teacher labor markets, class size effects, school spending, and school desegregation and has written studies on the effectiveness of charter schools and parental responsiveness to charter school quality, special education, student mobility, peer influences, and the effects of air pollution on absenteeism.

Andrew J. Rotherham is co-founder and publisher of Education Sector, a national education policy think tank. He also writes the blog Eduwonk.com, which an *Education Week* study cited as among the most influential information sources in education today, as well as a regular column for *U.S. News and World Report.* Rotherham previously served at The White House as special assistant to the president for Domestic

Policy during the Clinton administration and is a former member of the Virginia Board of Education. He is the author of more than 100 articles, book chapters, papers, and op-eds about education policy and politics and is the author or editor of four books on educational policy. Rotherham is a senior fellow at the Democratic Leadership Council and serves on advisory boards and committees for various organizations, including The Broad Foundation, Harvard University, and the National Governors Association.

Kathryn L. Shaw is the Ernest C. Arbuckle Professor of Economics in the Graduate School of Business at Stanford University. She served as a member of President Clinton's Council of Economic Advisers from 1999 to 2001 and is a previous editor of the *Journal of Labor Economics*. Shaw's recent research focuses on managing talent in high-performance organizations. She studies how firms attract and build star talent in a range of knowledge-intensive industries and how companies can achieve measurable rates of return from investing in effective human resource management practices. She is a codeveloper of "insider econometrics," in which researchers use internal company data to study the performance gains from such practices as teamwork and incentive pay. Her work has been published in leading journals including the *American Economic Review*, *Management Science*, *Journal of Economic Perspectives*, the *Rand Journal of Economics*, and *Journal of Political Economy*.

Randi Weingarten is president of the more than 1.4-million-member American Federation of Teachers, AFL-CIO. She was elected following 11 years of service as an AFT vice president. In September 2008, Weingarten led the development of the AFT Innovation Fund, an initiative to support sustainable, innovative, and collaborative reform projects developed by members and their local unions to strengthen public schools. She is the former president of the United Federation of Teachers, AFT Local 2, representing approximately 228,000 nonsupervisory educators in the New York City public school system. Weingarten is currently cochair of New York City's Municipal Labor Committee, an umbrella organization for the city's 100-plus public-sector unions, including those representing higher education and other public service employees.

Patrick M. Wright is the William J. Conaty GE Professor of Strategic Human Resources in the School of Industrial and Labor Relations at

Cornell University. He teaches and conducts research in strategic human resource management, with a particular focus on how human resource practices, the human resource function, and human resource leaders can affect firm performance. A prolific author, he has written more than 60 publications and has contributed to more than 15 books and volumes. Wright has served on the board of directors for Human Resource Planning Society, World at Work, and the Society for Human Resource Foundation. He has served as a distinguished academic visitor for the Ministry of Manpower in Singapore, as a senior research fellow in Taiwan, and currently holds a secondary position at Tilburg University in the Netherlands as a senior research fellow.

Index

pay for performance. *See* Pay for
performance
professional development, reward for,
236, 240–42, 243*n*5
quality of teachers and, 5–6, 35, 37, 38,
39–41, 85, 176, 303–304
ratio of primary-schoolteacher salaries
to GDP, 83, 84
as reason for academically proficient
college graduates not choosing
career in teaching, 5, 98, 252
reform of, 5–6, 41–42
to attract more qualified teachers,
39–41, 45
criticisms of, 40–41, 99–100,
107*n*31
incentive programs, 103–104,
105*n*12, 130
in New York City, 271–72
performance measures, use of.
See Pay for performance
structural change in, 41–42
retirement benefits. *See* Retirement
benefit systems
salary vs. math/science achievement
experienced salary, 85, 87
starting salary, 85, 86
as share of school expenditure, 3
value added determinant of, 181–93.
See also Value-added analysis
Conditions of teacher employment, 44
Continuing education. *See* Professional
development for teachers
Corcoran, Sean P., 4, 5–6, 11, 29, 33,
47*n*7, 47*n*13, 98, 118, 252, 257, 303
Costrell, Robert M., 10–11, 195, 218,
306
Council of the Great City Schools, 297
Creativity, 5, 22, 120
Credentialing. *See also* Licensure
requirements for teachers
making teaching more desirable
profession, 102–103
NYC principals, 263–64
professional development and, 240

quality of teachers and, 44
regulation of teacher certification,
270–71
types of tests for, 106*n*25
Cross-national teacher development
systems, 7, 81–111
compensation, 83–88
entry into workforce, 94–95, 303
lessons for U.S. teacher development
system, 7, 98–104
public expenditures on education, 99
selection of teachers into training
programs, 88–91
training of teachers, 91–94
U.S. teacher development system,
95–98
Curriki, 140
Custodial schools using technology,
142–44
human resources in, 147–53
leaders in, 150–53
policy barriers to technology in,
156–62
teachers in, 147–50
Cyber schools, 8, 137, 140–41
costs of, 147, 157
funding, use of, 159
human resources in, 145–47
in-person schooling with, 138
leaders in, 146–47
Czech Republic, teacher compensation
in, 88

Daly, Tim, 53–54
Danielson's Framework, 65, 66
DeArmond, Michael M., 6–7, 53, 217,
308, 309
Defined-benefit (DB) retirement plans.
See Retirement benefit systems
Defined-contribution (DC) retirement
plans, 196, 199, 214–15
in higher education, 211–12, 221
Demonstration projects, 299
Denver teachers' union, 297

Human capital (*continued*)
    quality of teachers. *See* Quality of
       teacher workforce
Human resource management, 6, 53–74
    connection to district central offices, 71
    deselection process. *See* Deselection of
       teachers
    feedback, improvement of, 70–71
    flexibility in, 67–69
    hiring timelines, 55, 61, 256
    identifying practices which should be
       "loose" or "tight," 70
    importance of, 54–56, 69
    interviewing, 55, 60, 62–63
    New York City approach, 261–62,
       265–68
    private sector and. *See* Private sector's
       human resource management
    quality of teachers and, 55, 72*n*5
    recruitment practices. *See* Recruitment
       practices
    reform of, 6, 69–72, 310
    research, role of, 63–64, 70
    selection and hiring, 6, 59–63, 74*n*20,
       254
    strategic, 64–69, 74*n*22
    teacher–school "fit," 55, 72*n*6
    technology's implications for, 144–53
    understanding impact on schools, 70
    union role in, 296–97
Hungary, teacher compensation in, 85
Hunter College, 123, 271

Ichniowski, Casey, 66
Incentive programs
    for principals, 264, 271–72
    for teachers, 42, 73*n*9, 103–104,
       105*n*12, 130, 265, 267, 271–72,
       278. *See also* Pay for performance;
       Retirement benefit systems
Induction programs, 237–38
Industrial revolution
    of 19th century, 17–18
    of 20th century, 18
    of 21st century. *See* Preparation of
       workforce of tomorrow

Ineffective teachers, removal of.
    See Deselection of teachers
Information Age, 18, 26
Innovation in educational reform, 298–99
In-service training, 227. *See also* Profes-
    sional development for teachers
    cross-national comparison of, 105*n*3
    technology-based instructional systems
       as part of, 150
Instructional technology, 8–9, 137–63,
    254–55
    assessment of, 155
    barriers to spread of, 138–39, 154,
       156–60
       removal of barriers, 161–62
    benefits of, 133–34, 294, 305–306
    costs of, 147, 150–51, 154
    custodial schools and. *See* Custodial
       schools using technology
    cyber schools. *See* Cyber schools
    fully integrated instructional systems,
       143–44, 148, 150, 151, 305–306
    funding for, 161–62
    human resource implications of,
       144–53
       resolution of unknowns, 153–55
    investment in use and development of,
       155
    leaders' role in adoption of, 139
    in New York City, 272–73
    performance specifications for, 155
    role of, 139–44
    scholarship program to support
       teacher training in, 155
    training providers for, 155
International comparison of teacher
    development systems. *See* Cross-
       national teacher development systems
Inventiveness, 5, 22

Japan
    public expenditure on students in, 99
    student performance in, 81
    teacher compensation in, 85, 96, 105*n*9
    teacher training in, 92
Job conditions of teacher employment, 44